Swinging for the Fences

Swinging for

Black Baseball in Minnesota

Edited by

Steven R. Hoffbeck

Minnesota Historical Society Press

the Fences

Partial funding for this project has been provided by a Faculty Research Grant from Minnesota State University Moorhead, a Works in Progress Grant from the Minnesota Humanities Commission, and a Research Grant from the Minnesota Historical Society.

www.mnhs.org/mhspress

The Minnesota Historical Society Press is a member of the Association of American University Presses.

Manufactured in the United States of America

10 9 8 7 6 5 4 3 2 1

♾ The paper used in this publication meets the minimum requirements of the American National Standard for Information Sciences—Permanence for Printed Library Materials, ANSI Z39.48-1992.

International Standard Book Number 0-87351-517-X (cloth)

Library of Congress Cataloging-in-Publication Data

Swinging for the fences : Black baseball in Minnesota / [edited by] Steven R. Hoffbeck.
    p. cm.
  Includes bibliographical references and index.
  ISBN 0-87351-517-X (hardcover : alk. paper)
  1. African American baseball players—Minnesota—History. 2. Baseball teams—
Minnesota—History. 3. Racism in sports—Minnesota—History. I. Hoffbeck, Steven R.
  GV863.M6S95 2005
  796.357'64'08996073—dc22

                                                                    2004021866

Title page photograph: Two young boys practice their baseball skills at the Phyllis Wheatley Settlement House in Minneapolis, about 1925.

To the memory of my father, Raymond Peter Hoffbeck (1918–1968), who loved Minnesota Twins baseball. When I was a boy, my Dad and I listened to WCCO Radio broadcasts of Twins games on the barn radio as we did the chores together on our family farm.

Contents

Preface: The Brotherhood of Baseball

A timeless photograph reveals the nature of black baseball. The man, a pitcher, might be white or he might be black—his identity is unclear. His throwing arm appears to be slicing through the fog in a ghostly stadium. His square face registers no emotion, but his eyes are wide open. His garb reveals no team logo. The year is unclear, as is the time of day. It might be summer, because leaves are still on the distant trees. The stands are empty; the game is either over or has not yet begun. The words on the outfield fences are unreadable. The hurler is not even on a pitcher's mound. Who is this man?

He was Walter Ball from St. Paul, Minnesota, one of the best pitchers in all of black baseball in the early years of the last century. The image was a publicity photo from 1909, when Ball played for the Chicago Leland Giants. We know this from methodical research in old newspapers and the records of the Chicago Historical Society.

Beyond those simple facts, Walter Ball's life is shrouded in unknowns. We do not know if he was a cheerful, happy-go-lucky man or a bitter and complaining sort. We know only the basic outlines of his family life. He left no scrapbook filled with newspaper clippings or box full of personal notes and letters.

But we do know that he was a masterful pitcher, a man of summer, playing the National Game. His story and those of many others are the subjects of this book.

Most Minnesota readers know of Kirby Puckett, Dave Winfield, Willie Mays, and Roy Campanella. All played in Minnesota. And so did Bud Fowler and John Donaldson and Maceo Breedlove, athletes of an earlier era whose colorful careers deserve some attention. Each of these athletes would be worthy of watching by today's baseball fans. They held within themselves power, grace, speed, skill. The public came to ball diamonds to see them play because their exploits were bigger than life. Even the names of some became emblematic of the game—Walter Ball and Earl Battey.

We will never know all the stories about black baseball in Minnesota because so many sources of information are missing. The subject is the most difficult research problem I have faced in writing history—and I have written about some really obscure topics, such as the history of brick street pavements in Minnesota. But it has been a pleasure to dig out this story because it relates to my love of baseball and to my own recollections of race and sports.

One of my earliest baseball memories may be the strongest. In 1963, when I was ten years old, Pastor Ray Jensen allowed me to go to a Minnesota Twins game with our church's Luther League youth group, even though I was too little to be a member. I had never been to the Twin Cities before. Our farm was five miles outside of Morgan and 120 miles from Metropolitan Stadium in Bloomington, where the Twins played. I thought that the great curveball pitcher Camilo Pascual pitched for the Twins that day, and I recall hoping that slugger Harmon Killebrew would smash out a home run. I saw my first black man, and he was on the field; it was Earl Battey, the catcher.

I don't remember much else about that day, including the name of the opposing team and whether the Twins won. But I kept the rain check portion of my ticket, and I looked up the results of the game. It was August 17, 1963, and our church youth group was seated in the upper deck reserved seat section. We played the Washington Senators, and the Twins lost, 10–0. Killebrew did not get a hit.

I became interested in the history of African American baseball players in Minnesota when I stumbled across a team photograph of the St. Paul Colored Gophers while I was researching the story of Charles Scrutchin, a black lawyer who worked in Bemidji from 1898 until his death in 1930. When I tried to find out more about the Colored Gophers, I found a big and surprising blank.

I began to research. I spent five years getting to know Bobby Marshall, the first baseman for the Colored Gophers. I talked to his son and his daughter, read his scrapbook, saw his handwriting. I can imagine his personality by looking at his face in photographs. His eyes witnessed a multitude of baseball games during his high school, college, and professional career. Those eyes watched his teammates win and lose, and they carried visions of playing on the national stage. He saw discrimination, and he could see the dark baseball of 1909 pitched over the plate, and he could hit the ball and hit it well. But I don't know how much Bobby Marshall was bruised inwardly by insults and jeers or if he felt tormented by his lot in life.

Racial prejudice is poison. Real life for black American ballplayers was a haphazard maze of discrimination against their best efforts, of denials of rights and denials of opportunities, of narrow-mindedness at best and unreasoning hatred at worst. The white establishment was dead set against black men. These players tried to triumph over the prejudiced attitudes of many Minnesotans. The leaders of the small black community in the state hoped for heroes to bring equal opportunity in baseball and all areas of endeavor.

Had I tried to write this book by myself, it would have taken the rest of my life. In order to tell these stories of struggle and triumph properly, I assembled a team of writers. We have focused on the stories of a single player from each era, avoiding both the haze of endless names and statistics and the temptation to follow the threads of all those other players' careers: some played here for a while and then moved on to greener outfields. But be aware that this history is not like the history of major-league baseball, where the statistics are plentiful and complete. Local newspapers are the best source of information about the teams and players, but the news stories did not always bother to list the first names of the African American ballplayers in Minnesota. We could not find all of the box scores from the games these men played. Sometimes we don't have the line score of the games, and sometimes we only have the final score. At times the local writer left out even that. It took years to puzzle out the names of the 1909 St. Paul Colored Gophers team, photographed in Hibbing (see page 63). I can identify only seven of the eleven players by name and face. I doubt that I will ever be able to match the other four names with the right faces.

Most of the men described in these pages came to Minnesota from other states and found that they had at least two things in common: a love for the game of baseball and a desire to prove they could master the national pastime. Some of the men found a lifelong home in Minnesota with ties of friendship to their baseball teammates to help them through their days after their playing careers were over.

The authors of this volume address three themes: manhood, brotherhood, and fatherhood. Each of the players tried to fulfill his manhood, to prove that he could play baseball as well as any other man. The players held onto their personal dignity in the face of indifferent or hostile racial attitudes. By honing his ballfield skills, a man could gain self-respect and earn the regard of the opposing team. This was a part of the concept of "black achievement" — one could prove he was a man by taking up the bat against white pitchers.

The camaraderie of the ball diamond created a brotherhood of athletes. The men stood beside each other on the playing field and traveled together to the games. They withstood discrimination of one kind or another and felt a bond by winning—or by competing for the victory. Nine men on a level playing field could accomplish together what an individual could not. There were several sets of brothers who played in Minnesota: the Taylor brothers, Candy Jim and Steel Arm Johnny, from South Carolina; Sherman and Eugene Barton, both outfielders; and Steve and Dave Winfield on the Attucks-Brooks

American Legion team in the 1960s. Others became like brothers as they developed friendships and held common experiences of a depth not often found in other fields of human enterprise.

The book also touches on the idea of fatherhood. In 1907, the founder and owner of the St. Paul Colored Gophers ballclub was Phil Reid, known as Daddy Reid by his players. He provided them with an opportunity to play ball, and he was a big man who could give some measure of protection to his players from ragging crowds and corrupt umpires. As for the real fathers of the outfielders, infielders, catchers, and pitchers on these teams, we know very little. We know that some worked as janitors, as barbers, as railroad conductors, or as common laborers, in order to give their sons a chance to play the game of baseball. Their sacrifices are unrecorded in history except in the sense that their children gained opportunities they had been denied. These fathers helped make present-day America possible by working however they could for equal opportunity, whether by buying a baseball for a son or playing catch with him in the park. Some had strong leadership from their fathers, others sought a father figure, perhaps an older player who became a mentor in life and in the game.

These are not simple stories of joyful triumph over adversities. These players were plagued by troubles and doubts as they gained only partial redemption of their hopes on the ballfield; in baseball as in life, perfection remains unattainable. They suffered from human weaknesses, their own and those of others. There is much of the American Dream in these pages—and plenty of the American Tragedy as well. Perhaps Jackie Robinson said it best when he spoke to an audience in Moorhead, Minnesota, in May 1964: "We don't want to be given anything, but rather, we want the equal opportunity to compete."

Swinging for the Fences

They Didn't Want to Play with Fisher

William D. Green

*I*n 1875, W. W. Fisher was the flash point for all kinds of tales. The people in Winona said that although the ballplayer had come from Chicago, he had a regular job in town that made him eligible to play for the Winona Clippers ballclub. Jealous folks in nearby towns called him an interloper from out of state. There were rumors that he might be a professional player on what was supposed to be an amateur team. It was said that he had played for the Chicago Uniques, a black team; therefore, the St. Paul team did not want to play against the Clippers if Fisher was on the field. The St. Paulites were attempting to draw the color line on Fisher.

By the conclusion of the Clippers' season, the townspeople called Fisher a "state champion" as a pitcher and second baseman. Sadly more tales were then told about Fisher, and he was run out of town as a "traitor" who had allegedly "fixed" a game and betrayed his town and team.[1]

This is the story of W. W. Fisher, the first prominent black baseball player in Minnesota, a tale set in the time just ten years after the Civil War had ended. It is a tale obscured by the passing of time and by the fact that the man was referred to only as "Fisher" in published game reports; we do not know his whole given name, only his initials—"W. W."

Winona, a Mississippi River town, was one of the prominent cities in Minnesota in 1875, being the third largest after St. Paul and Minneapolis. It had a population of 10,737, of whom seventy-eight were black.[2] Known as a transport point for shipping wheat down the mighty Mississippi, it was also a destination for steamboats coming upriver from St. Louis. Farmers from all over southeastern Minnesota brought their wheat crops to Winona to the flourishing flour mills there.

Winona's amateur baseball team had not yet matched the city's prominence, but the Clippers were having a good season, winning seven games and losing only three from June 3 until August 13. They had clobbered the Firemen's team 61 to 14, smoked the St. Charles Suckers by a count of 46 to 20, and chewed up the Beaver and Plainview ballclub 36 to 2. But the team had lost to the Silver Stars of Northfield, one of the earliest teams organized in Minnesota and known as one of the best ballclubs around. Most of all, the

Winona management wanted to beat Northfield, and a second game versus Northfield brought a better result, with Winona winning 24 to 22. Another great challenge came from across the border in Wisconsin in the form of the Janesville Mutuals, a professional team and champions of Wisconsin. After losing an August ballgame to the Mutuals by a score of 21 to 14, the Clippers procured the services of W. W. Fisher as their pitcher for a rematch on August 14.[3]

Winona riverfront showing steamboat dock and railroad station at the foot of Winona Street, about 1870

In the game against the Janesville Mutuals, Fisher's performance was note-worthy. "Fisher's pitching won admiration from all sides," wrote a newsman, "his balls were hard to bat and hardly any of them got outside the diamond." The Clippers had been "strengthened by putting Fisher in at pitcher," and in his first game with the team, Winona won 13 to 7.[4]

The Clippers' defeat of the Northfield and Janesville teams gave Winona the best record in Minnesota and thus the state championship. Their success attracted the attention of the well-established St. Paul Red Caps baseball team. In the tradition of the time, the Red Caps sent an invitation to the Clippers to play against them in St. Paul at the Minnesota State Fair, laying out the terms of the contest. The teams were to compete for a $100 prize for the "winning club and $10 badges for best catcher, thrower, general player, and base runner." Winona was invited to play *but without the colored player.*[5]

Observers accused the St. Paul Red Caps of "running the tournament to suit themselves." The Winona players rejected the invitation and refused to play without their teammate. Commending them, the editor of their home-town newspaper wrote, "As Mr. Fisher, the colored person referred to, has been playing with the Clippers for some time past, and is not only an expert player, but a gentleman in his deportment, the [Clipper] boys, with com-mendable pluck and principle, proposed to stand by him."[6]

Winona's management then drafted a letter to the officials of the State Fair Association stating that, while the Clippers wanted to play in St. Paul, they nonetheless needed to know if the rules, in fact, banned colored players from the tournament. Officials responded by declaring that no such rule existed and that only the competing clubs could determine whether or not Fisher played. Because the Red Caps did not want to play against Fisher, then Fisher's whole team would not attend the tournament. A newspaperman from Chatfield put the matter in crude terms: "The Clippers boys became indignant and refused to go, declaring their intentions to stand by their n——."[7]

It appeared to many that the St. Paul ballclub was using racism as an excuse to avoid playing the state champion Clippers. A writer for the *Winona Daily Republican* observed, "As regards the position which the Red Caps has taken, it is shrewdly regarded as an evidence that they are afraid to play the Clippers, and resort to this method [of discrimination] to escape the doughty club that now carries the highest honors and the best record in the State."[8]

As the date of the Clippers–Red Caps game grew near, tournament offi-cials came to realize that racism was bad for business. The prospect of a showdown between Minnesota's top teams—Winona and St. Paul—would be a natural gate attraction. The controversy over the use of a black player might add to the number of baseball fans attending the contest; in fact, some onlookers might be interested in seeing if Fisher's pitching was noteworthy at all. The betting was bound to be prolific in a game that matched St. Paul as the "Northern metropolis against the Southern Metropolis [Winona] of the state" to see if the Winonans could prove to be "worthy of their bats."[9]

Fortunately good sense prevailed. "Certain parties of St. Paul" contacted the Clippers "to see if anything could be done to alter the decision" to stay away from the tournament. The club responded by expressing two conditions that needed to be satisfied before they would play—the winning team would get a $100 prize and W. W. Fisher must be allowed to participate.[10]

The conflict was soon resolved when a telegram arrived from St. Paul with words of agreement on the prize money totals and a brief line that informed the Clippers that they could "play Fisher if they wished."[11] The party deemed responsible for this harmony was F. K. Merrill, a board member for the Red Caps and a well-remembered former resident of Winona. Indeed it was Merrill who succeeded in explaining away the insult to Fisher, the Clippers, and, therefore, the city of Winona itself:

Their opposition to Mr. Fisher [was] not being made on account of his being a colored man, but because they had understood that he was a professional player and had been set up in business in Winona for the purpose of playing with the Clippers. When satisfied that this view of the case was entirely erroneous they withdrew their opposition.

To clear the air further, the St. Paulites backtracked on "the statement which appeared in the *Pioneer Press,* namely that 'Red Caps object to the colored player, Fisher of Winona,' was premature and not authorized by the Board of Managers."[12]

Fisher had found justice and prepared to play with his team in St. Paul; however, he faced insults from other directions in the meantime. Northfield played against Winona twice in early September 1875, and this marked Fisher's first appearance on Winona's home diamond against Northfield. It was "well understood" that Winona "proposed to play the colored member, Fisher," and most of the Northfield team engaged in contemptuous behavior that violated the hospitable and gentlemanly character of previous games. "As an insult to the club and to Mr. Fisher, the members of the [Northfield] Silver Stars—with the honorable exception, be it said, of [shortstop] Swerdfiger and the Bullis boys [the catcher Ed and the second baseman]—went to a crockery store" to buy a "number of little" Negro "babies" figures. The players then pinned the babies "to their badges" and then "marched through the public streets" of Winona prior to the start of the first game.[13]

The initial game proved to be "disastrous" for Fisher's team when William H. Garlock, Winona's catcher, suffered an injury when struck on his left arm, "just above the elbow," as the opposing "batsman reached back" to swing his bat. It was a "hard blow, and disabled Garlock . . . from further playing." Fisher was moved from pitcher to catcher because his team "had no competent catcher to fill the position." He tried his best, but because catching was done barehanded, his hands quickly became so sore that "he couldn't stand it," and Fisher went back to pitching. Frank L. Smith and Frank Lalor each tried catching, but they could not handle Fisher's pitches. Northfield got an "easy victory" over Winona by a score of 14 to 5.[14]

In the second game, the playing by both sides "was exceedingly skillful and brilliant," and "every man of the Clippers played his position with skill and credit." In what was lauded as "the best amateur game in the Northwest," Winona emerged victorious in an 8–1 contest, evening the season series between the two clubs at two games apiece. Northfield's team admitted that Winona's pitcher, Frank L. Smith, and catcher (noted only as Mr. Doe) were "hard to beat," but asserted that the incompetent umpire was even harder to beat.[15]

What really galled the Northfield players was that Frank L. Smith and Mr. Doe were imported players from the Janesville, Wisconsin, team. The Northfield newspaper contended that Fisher had also been brought in to Winona specifically for these games from the Chicago Uniques. The newspaperman admitted that while the "Negro babies" that the Northfield players wore on their badges were in "bad taste, they wanted to make a statement that "this colored man," Fisher, "did not [properly] belong to the club under the rules" of that time and should not have been in the two games at all.[16]

Fisher, Smith, and Doe were all on the Winona roster for the big state fair tournament game against St. Paul on September 17. The injured man, Garlock, had recovered from his earlier mishap and was ready to play. The game was noted as the "prime attraction" at the state fair, and it was "hotly contested on both sides." At first the St. Paul Red Caps held a "decided advantage" over Winona's Clippers, but in the ninth inning, Winona tied the game at 17–all. In the tenth inning, St. Paul went to bat and "made five runs, and this, it was thought, could not be beaten." But the Winona team rallied and "managed to get seven runs, and so came in two ahead!" The final score stood at Winona 24, St. Paul 22. The Clippers took home the $100 prize and showed the rest of the state that they had "fairly won their honors" because they possessed "the skill and the pluck" to defeat their more-established rivals.[17]

The state fair triumph ended the regular season for the Winona Clippers, and it was a year "marked with brilliant success" and a state championship.

The record of the Clippers for 1875 was twelve wins and only four losses, and the players had made "great improvement" in their ball playing. The very best game of the season was said to be the 8 to 1 victory over the Northfield Silver Stars, and with it came bragging rights for the following season. The team disbanded for the year in mid-October, not having practiced since September 30.[18]

If the story had ended there, it would have been a great and memorable season. But it did not. The St. Paul team issued a challenge to Winona for another game, and Frank L. Smith gathered the players together for one more matchup, this time on Winona's home field. The winning team would gain a prize of $100 and some bragging rights to carry over into the next year's baseball season.[19]

The game was set to begin on Saturday afternoon, October 16, but the weather was uncooperative, with the temperatures described as being of a "chilly character." Despite the cold, a "large assemblage" of fans came to witness the second and final game between the Red Caps of St. Paul and the Winona Clippers. Local "interest in the game was intense," and numerous bets were wagered that day.

Frank L. Smith, who was managing the Winona nine and was to be the starting pitcher, became a focal point for controversy on the morning of the big game. An unknown source had circulated the rumor that Smith "had sold the game," and the report created a "decided sensation" in the downtown area. The whispers became a buzz, and Smith responded by insisting "that certain bets must be withdrawn or he would not go into the field." The bettors withdrew those key bets, and the game was on.[20]

All went well for Winona in the early innings, with Winona leading five to zero at the end of the fourth. St. Paul inched back into the game, getting a run in the fifth and three in the sixth, while Winona scored single runs in the seventh and eighth. The score stood at 7 to 6 in favor of Winona until the fateful top half of the ninth inning. St. Paul scored two runs to pull into the lead 8 to 7, and, when Winona could not muster a run in the bottom of the ninth, St. Paul took the game and the $100 prize.[21]

The St. Paul Red Caps celebrated the triumph, enlisting the aid of a touring band of Georgia minstrels, in blackface, to play for them in festive joy for several hours thereafter. It had been a "mighty victory," and the St. Paulites long remembered the celebratory march and laughed about how they had "joined forces with the minstrel band and let everybody in town know that they had won."[22]

All was not joy in Winona, however. The "general talk" in town was that the hometown Clippers had "played well," but it was "freely admitted on all sides—that it was a 'thrown' game." The loss did not hurt so badly as the "conviction that there was treachery in their own camp." The general feeling grew that pitcher "Frank Smith [was] a partner and accomplice in the business" of throwing the game and pocketing some serious cash. It was plain to see that "Frank Smith's pitching for the first half of the game was capital," wrote a newsman, "but he made some bad errors in throwing to first and in the last part of the game pitched wild balls."

Suspicion arose among the public that there "was something rotten" in Winona, and the consensus was that second baseman W. W. Fisher was "a partner and accomplice" in the sellout of the game. Fisher had "played second well" in the game but committed "one or two errors in not stopping balls" hit his way.[23]

Winona was buzzing with indignation over Smith's betrayal and Fisher's treachery in the week following the scandalous game. People in town heard allegations from many sources and came to a firm conclusion "that the game was manipulated in the interest of a lot of gamblers." Frank L. Smith responded to the flurry of accusations by cornering Fisher and inducing Fisher, after a day-long session of persuasion and intimidation, to write and sign an affidavit of guilt. Smith then accompanied Fisher to a notary public, who witnessed the sworn confession and notarized the document. Fisher reportedly made the affidavit "reluctantly."

Smith kept the official paperwork and made sure that Fisher left Winona. It was theorized that Fisher, "fearing that he would be mobbed" by some of the townspeople of Winona, took the "midnight train for Chicago." Smith waited a day and then released Fisher's confession to the newspapers. In the sworn statement, Fisher confessed all. It was he who agreed to "sell the game of ball" for $250 in cash. He stated that he was asked to enlist Frank Smith in the dirty business, but Smith "persistently refused so to do."

Not only had Fisher given the October 16 game to the St. Paul Red Caps, he admitted that he had also tried to lose the earlier game against the Red Caps on September 17 at the state fair. In return, he was to have been paid "$50 and one-half of whatsoever money might be won on bets." Fisher "did his best to 'give' [the] said game of ball to the Red Cap club" until the seventh inning. At that juncture, Frank Smith accused Fisher of "selling" the game, and at the insistence of Smith, Fisher then played the remainder of the game "to the best of his skill and ability" and "his efforts were instrumental in winning" that game.[24]

Fisher was painted as the villain and Smith as the hero. But the townspeople and local press did not buy the heavy-handed fingering only of Fisher. A cloud of suspicion still lingered over Smith due to his not reporting the corrupt actions of Fisher to anyone until long after the game was over.

As for W. W. Fisher, he disappeared from the baseball history of Minnesota, a scapegoat for the sins of Frank L. Smith. He left Winona "quietly," probably going to "one of the Southern cities," but no one really knew where he went. Fisher never returned, but other black ballplayers would soon venture into Minnesota.[25]

"The Song of the Smoke,"
by
W. E. B. DuBois
1907

I am the Smoke King,
I am black!
I am swinging in the sky,
I am wringing worlds awry;
I am the thought of the throbbing mills;
I am the soul of the soul-toil kills,
Wraith of the ripple of trading rills;
Up I'm curling from the sod;
I am whirling home to God.
I am the Smoke King
I am black.

Prince Honeycutt and the Fergus Falls Musculars

The first recorded instance of an African American baseball player in Minnesota was in Fergus Falls, in the lake country of Otter Tail County. A man by the name of Prince Honeycutt helped organize the North Star Ball Club in 1873, the year after his arrival in the community. Born in Tennessee in 1852, Honeycutt attached himself to the unit of Captain James Compton of the Union army during the Civil War. The youngster hoped to become a drummer boy but served with Compton's outfit as a mess boy through the remainder of the war, participating in Sherman's March to the Sea and the march through the Carolinas. He worked for Compton's family in Illinois after the war and accompanied Compton to Fergus Falls when he moved there in 1872.[1]

Prince Honeycutt was the first African American man in Fergus Falls. He may have learned to play baseball with the Union soldiers during the war or perhaps in Illinois afterward.[2] Honeycutt, a wage-earning laborer during the day, became the leader of the North Star team in several games in 1873. The North Stars defeated the Big Fellers' ballclub in a June game in a high-scoring affair, 60 to 54. The box score revealed that Honeycutt scored eight of his team's runs. The teams played again on the Fourth of July, and the Big Fellers won 18 to 14.[3]

In the 1875 season, Honeycutt played left field for the Fergus Falls ballclub, now known as the Musculars. The team journeyed by wagon to Perham for a game in June. The trip took a day and a half

Prince Honeycutt stood in front of his barbershop in Fergus Falls, about 1880.

and apparently wore out Prince and his Fergus Falls mates; they fell to the Perham Norwesters 64 to 43.[4] The teams met again, this time in Fergus Falls, as a part of the Fourth of July festivities, and this time the Musculars prevailed by a score of 23 to 21. Honeycutt, batting second in the order, got six hits, including a triple, and scored three runs.[5]

Honeycutt created some controversy in Fergus Falls in 1878 when he married a white woman, Lena Marsden. A Methodist minister conducted the ceremony in James Compton's house in Fergus Falls. The couple had a baby boy named Albert in 1879. Sadly, Lena died while giving birth to their second child, a daughter named May, in 1882. Honeycutt later married Anna Brown, an African American woman who had been born in Pennsylvania, in about 1884, and they had two children.[6]

Prince Honeycutt worked as a barber for a number of years and, for a time, operated a sauna business in the back of his barber shop in Fergus Falls before becoming a porter. In the 1890s he ran for mayor of the city and finished a distant third in the balloting; apparently his candidacy brought a large voter turnout that year.[7]

Honeycutt lived in Fergus Falls until his death in 1924. His obituary did not refer to his baseball career but mentioned that he had been a barber in town and that he was "always decent and kindly and a law abiding person" and had become "one of the historical personages and land marks" of the community. No doubt he was distinctive partly because of his name as well as for his heritage as a former slave.[8]

The first African American baseball teams in Minnesota organized in 1876, just after Honeycutt took the field for Fergus Falls. The Blue Stars of St. Paul and the Unions of Minneapolis played each other twice that year. In the first game, the Minneapolis Unions won 37 to 28.[9] The next game brought a shutout of the Minneapolis team, which quit playing after just three innings with the score favoring the St. Paul Blue Stars 27 to 0. The Minneapolis ballclub believed that the St. Paul team had unfairly imported three of the best Chicago players. The enthusiasm for "colored base ball" in the Twin Cities was said to have "cooled" after the shutout.[10]

The lineup of the 1876 clubs was as follows:

Minneapolis Unions	St. Paul Blue Stars		Minneapolis Unions	St. Paul Blue Stars
G. Williams	Johnson		T. Williams	W. M. Johnson
Jackson	Allen		Dick Jackson	Wm. B. Perkins
Mason	Edwards		Geo. Todd	W. F. Johnson
Gardner	Murray		Lewis Mason	W. Gill
Cunningham	Bally		D. Williams	C. Allen
Cheatum	F. Gill		James Cunningham	F. Gill
Johnson	W. Gill		E. H. Hamilton	T. Combs
Myrick	W. Perkins		Wm. Berry	W. Barnes
D. Williams	T. Combs		Abe Myrick	J. Combs

[from "Yesterday's Game Between the Colored B.B. Clubs of the Dual City," *Minneapolis Tribune*, August 31, 1876.]

[from "Bad Ball Playing," *Minneapolis Tribune*, September 21, 1876.]

Bud Fowler and the Stillwater Nine, 1884

Dan Cagley

aseball reflected life in America in many ways during the latter half of the nineteenth century. A relatively young United States was becoming an economic and political world power, and the sport of baseball was quickly emerging as the national pastime. As industries expanded and recorded unprecedented profits after the Civil War, there were also the Panics of 1873 and 1893 that shook capitalism and the democracy of this country to its very core. At the same time, baseball grew from being a game played mostly in the North on the East Coast to the point where professional leagues and grass-roots competition flourished in every region of the country by 1887.

The Civil War and Reconstruction did not accomplish so much long-term change as leading Radical Republican leaders had hoped, but the country was permanently altered. Although Jim Crow laws and segregation prevailed in many parts of the country, there had been glimpses of radical social change. While it would take the civil rights movement of the 1960s to assure black people basic rights of citizenship, for a brief time in the late 1800s, many blacks voted in local and national elections.

Areas of the North saw change as well. Most northerners were socially conservative in dealing with issues like abolition and suffrage until the events of the 1850s and the Civil War changed many northern regions into Republican strongholds seeking positive change. The events of that time and the reaction of the citizenry turned northern states like Iowa and Minnesota into some of the leading postwar proponents of black suffrage and additional equal rights under the law. After all, more than 200,000 black men had fought to save the Union: how could they not be given the rights of citizenship?

During this time, blacks had some opportunities to be part of white professional baseball leagues. Long before Jackie Robinson and Branch Rickey re-integrated baseball in 1946, there were at least seventy blacks who played one or more games of organized minor league baseball from 1877, the start of the minor leagues, to 1898. About one-half of the men in the minors played only on all-black teams. Of those on white teams, most played only a few years before leaving the game or joining black independent teams.

John W. Jackson, known in baseball as Bud Fowler, was the first to play in the white leagues and also lasted the longest, ten seasons. His career provides great insight into the racism and instability of baseball and American society.

Fowler's second year in professional baseball was in Stillwater, Minnesota, in the Northwestern League in 1884. Not only was that season one of the biggest in his career because of the high level of talent in the Northwestern League, but his performance helped to provide a limited opportunity for other black players over the next decade.

Bud Fowler was born in Fort Plain, New York, on March 16, 1858. Ironically, by 1860 his family lived in Cooperstown, New York, the current home of the Baseball Hall of Fame and Museum. His father, who was also named John, was a barber and worked in the Cooperstown area for many years. Bud later earned money as a barber during baseball's off-season.[1]

No information is available on when Bud began playing baseball or when he took the name Fowler. It is known that the nickname "Bud" resulted from his inclination to call others by that name. An 1895 article on Fowler indicated that he played professional baseball with the Washington Mutuals in 1869 and with a team in Newcastle, Pennsylvania, in 1872.[2] However, there are no records showing that he was a member of those teams, and he would have been only eleven and fourteen years old when he supposedly played for the respective teams.

The first documented mention of Fowler as a player was on April 24, 1878, when he pitched an exhibition game for the Chelsea, Massachusetts, team, beating the Boston National League franchise, comprised of standouts like George Wright and James O'Rourke, 2–1. When the Live Oaks of Lynn, Massachusetts, from the International Association temporarily lost their ace pitcher to illness, they acquired Fowler from Chelsea. The *Boston Globe* reported on May 18 that "Fowler, the young colored pitcher of the Chelseas," held the Tecumsehs of London, Ontario, to only two hits and was leading 3–0 in the eighth inning when the Canadians became irked over an umpire's decision and left the field.[3] As a result, Fowler won his first official game by forfeit. He pitched in only two more games that month, losing both. Although he was released when the lead pitcher returned to active play, he had broken the color barrier in organized professional baseball.

From 1878 to 1884, Fowler was a pitcher on various semiprofessional teams, mostly in the Northeast and Canada.[4] However, being listed as a pitcher on a roster at that time was much different from today's game. Many leagues formed with around twelve players per team, and each roster would have a few pitchers who would play other positions when they were not pitching. Fowler, by all accounts, had good foot speed and a strong arm, so he was able to see extended time at catcher, pitcher, second base, and all of the outfield positions. His frame of five foot seven, 155 pounds, did not make him a large enough throwing target to play a position like first base on a regular basis.

Bud got another chance to move back into organized professional ball when the Northwestern League expanded to twelve teams in 1884. This league was considered one of the top organizations at the time and had been among the first actually to use a balanced schedule to determine a true league champion. There were many professional "leagues" that were comprised of teams that played wherever and whomever they felt could warrant the biggest payday or cost the least in traveling expenses. The Northwestern League also expanded the schedule from 84 games in 1883 to 110 games for each team. Milwaukee was the biggest city in the group, while Stillwater was the smallest.

A keen interest in baseball in Stillwater is shown by this group of young players in a park on South Broadway, about 1900.

The Northwestern League was also considered one of the top leagues in professional baseball because of its association with the majors. During that era, players from teams often jumped to other teams or leagues, even during the middle of the season. In March 1883, the three most successful leagues, the National League, the American Association, and the Northwestern League, signed a tripartite agreement in which they agreed to honor contracts, establish territories, and create an arbitration committee for disputes. They established minimum salaries, which were guaranteed by a bond filed by the league with the newly created National Agreement organization. Because the National League and the American Association had higher salary limits than the Northwestern League, a working definition of major and minor league was created. The Interstate League joined the next season, and the first structure for organized baseball came into existence. The National Agreement stayed in place until 1901 when the newly formed American League withdrew from the agreement because it did not want to respect territorial rights or the reserve clause of other leagues.

The first season in organized baseball for a team from Stillwater was in 1884, and although the town wanted a professional team, the organizers were not sure that joining the Northwestern League was in their best interests.[5] Eight of the teams already had experience putting together a top professional roster from the 1883 league season, and other newcomers like St. Paul and Minneapolis were bigger markets with more local players to draw from. In addition, as part of the balanced league schedule with each team playing the others ten times each, Stillwater would have to finance traveling for fifty-five road games. Trips by railway to play rivals Minneapolis and St. Paul would be inexpensive, but traveling to places like Grand Rapids, Michigan; Terre Haute, Indiana; and Peoria, Illinois, would be economically draining.

Putting together a competitive team roster from scratch for a top minor league proved to be difficult for Stillwater. Although baseball is presently portrayed as a historically rural game, many of the top teams and players in the 1880s were from big cities like Washington, Cincinnati, Boston, and especially New York. The Midwest had pockets of talent that already had or would eventually make the majors, but many of these players were already on other rosters. Only Joe Visner of Minneapolis was convinced to leave the Twin Cities to join the Stillwater club. In addition, the average player salary of the Stillwater club was only about $1,000. That figure was reported at the time to be as low as any club in the Northwestern League.[6]

As a result, the Stillwater roster was built in large part from Chicago-area players unable to catch on with teams closer to home or who had been released from other Northwestern League teams. Of the thirteen players signed before practice started on April 15, four were sent home before the season began on May 2, and four more were dismissed or left the team during the season, forcing management to pick up other teams' rejects or reserves. Overall, twenty-seven players were a part of the team roster over the course of the season.

A new team desperate for talent, Stillwater was the prototypical example of how black players could be signed by white clubs. If an area lacked good players, a new team could find and sign quality players from a relatively untapped national pool of black talent. However, few stable teams at that time were willing or bold enough to take the social and financial risks to judge someone by his playing skill first and skin color second. The club board of directors hired Fowler out of extreme need, but they still deserve credit for having the courage to sign him. Of the thirteen original members of the Stillwater roster, Fowler was the most successful.

In addition to playing for Stillwater, Fowler cut hair professionally at Hadley's Barber Shop, 113 South Main Street, and boarded at the Live and Let Live in town that summer.[7] Although barbering was a consistent source of income for many black men at that time, it was unpredictable during the season for a traveling professional ballplayer. While Fowler could have always used the extra money to prepare for life after baseball, his salary in 1884 went a long way since he was a single man without a family to support.

The Stillwater team schedule was comprised of unusually long road trips in May and August, while the team would be home during almost all of June and September. In fact, the playing field was not even ready at the start of the regular season since the first home regular season game was not until June 9. The field was located on Sixth Avenue in Stillwater (the present site is currently used for baseball and other sports and is called Old Athletic Field) and was an enclosed field with a large wooden grandstand. Newspapers gave the dimensions of the grounds as 450 by 400 feet and listed the outfield fence as 350 feet away from home plate down the lines.[8]

After playing a five-game exhibition season, the Stillwater Nine started the regular season on a sixteen-game losing streak that dampened fan interest and civic pride in the team. Amazingly, many of the games were not even close. In the opener, Peoria won 15–0 as Stillwater committed seventeen errors. Despite the lopsided score, starting pitcher Harry Yarnell went the distance for Stillwater. The next day the team was more competitive as the offense came to life in a 12–8 loss. Center fielder Fowler, first basemen Joe Pickett, and pitcher Joe Visner combined for seven hits. Peoria also found a way to win in the series finale as Fowler hit into a triple play in a 1–0 loss. Yarnell pitched his best game of the season in limiting Peoria to two hits and one run. Improved defense might have helped Yarnell in his effort as the *Peoria Transcript* cited the play of Fowler: "Fowler, the colored player, is a good one. His two catches in left field were good plays."[9]

Stillwater was next swept in a three-game series against Quincy, Illinois, 7–3, 3–2, and 16–0. The team managed only eleven hits and thought they might have lost Fowler to serious injury in the third game. The *Stillwater Daily Sun* reported, "Fowler, the colored bonanza, broke the bone of one of his toes and will be unable to play for four weeks." However, a more detailed version of the injury and a different diagnosis appeared in the *St. Paul Daily Globe*, which stated that "Fowler, the lightning colored catcher for the Stillwaters, had his foot spiked by a base runner at the home plate, breaking the bone of his big toe. The surgeon says it will be several days before he can play again, but Fowler asserts positively that he will be behind the bat again on Saturday."[10]

An injury to a big toe could ruin a player's career because so much in athletics is dependent on the ability to cut and move with quickness and balance. Fowler did return on Saturday, May 10, and played second base. Even though Milwaukee pounded Stillwater, 11–1, Fowler showed that the toe injury was not going to inhibit his play as he stole two bases.[11] That was about the only high point; the pitching staff gave up 93 runs over the next nine games, all losses.

Bad pitching, awful defense, and inconsistent hitting all contributed to the 0–16 start to the season, but the pitching was the key. Good pitching can hide shortcomings in the other two phases of the game, but it is hard to overcome bad pitching. Yarnell, Peter Fries, and M. J. Bradley had done most of the pitching during that stretch, but Fowler was not used on the mound until two weeks into the season. The team's start was so abysmal that field manager Joel May, a former railroad superintendent, was released so he could accept a position with the Northern Pacific. Joe Miller of White Bear Lake, a former major leaguer from the National Association days, took over and made Fowler his weapon to start winning games.[12]

Fowler finally put Stillwater in the win column on May 26 when he beat Fort Wayne, 7–5. The *Fort Wayne Daily Journal* was impressed with his stuff and felt his fastball "was speedy." For his effort, the team presented him with a then-handsome bonus of ten dollars and a suit of new clothes, a small token of gratitude for breaking one of the worst team starts in professional history.[13]

The Stillwater Nine responded surprisingly by winning five in a row, with particular thanks to Fowler. He started and won four of the games, one of which took only one hour and twenty-five minutes. He also had eight hits in twenty at-bats, and six of his hits were for doubles. He was so impressive during this stretch that fans from the opposing team cheered for him. "Fowler, the colored player who twirled the sphere for the visitors, pitched a fine game and batted well," reported the *Terre Haute Evening Gazette* after an 11–8 win in Terre Haute. "The crowd showed their appreciation of his work by applauding him every time he went to bat." The other victim during the stretch was Fort Wayne. Nevertheless, the *Stillwater Daily Sun* still was unimpressed with the local team. According to the paper, the turnaround had less to do with pitching Fowler for thirty-six quality innings over five days and had more to do with the opposition. "If the Stillwaters could only stay and play at Terre Haute for a month, how happy we might be."[14]

Fort Wayne eventually finished the season 22–43 while Terre Haute was 15–50, so the *Daily Sun* had a valid point.[15] However, without the pitching of Fowler, it is doubtful that Stillwater would have won five in a row with its roster at that point in the season. He was hardly dominant in giving up twenty-two runs in the four starts, but by keeping his team in the game and not asking his offense to get into a slug fest, the team was able to win two of the games in the late innings.

The winning streak ended in a 6–3 loss to Muskegon, Wisconsin, on June 2. The game was tied at 3–3 in the bottom of the seventh, but Muskegon pushed across three runners to go ahead to stay. Even in the loss, the *Muskegon Daily Chronicle* was impressed: "Fowler, the phenomenal pitcher, is a good one."[16] The loss marked the beginning of a stretch of games in which he played other positions, as his right arm must have been fatigued from so much work in such a short span. He still pitched in relief of James McCue the next day, but McCue became the workhorse in throwing three complete games in four days. Although field manager Miller threw his pitchers in bunches that would make modern pitchers cringe and perhaps hurt the long-term stability of the pitching staff, he had finally found a couple of pitchers who gave his team a chance to win.

How could these pitchers log so many innings in a short period of time? No one knows what pitching motion Fowler and other pitchers in the league were using, as the rules had changed significantly in a short period of time. Before the 1883 season, pitchers had to deliver the ball in an underhand angle similar to the motion used by modern softball players. Also the distance between the pitching line and home plate was fifty feet, well short of the modern baseball distance of sixty feet, six inches. If a pitcher like Fowler used an underhand motion, he could pitch more innings without taxing the arm in a way that pitching overhand does.

The first season that sidearm pitching was officially sanctioned was 1883.[17] Although not radically different from the underhand motion in appearance, it made hitting more difficult for the batter. Not only is it harder to throw, but the ball breaks easier and can deceive the hitter. The rule change also made it difficult for umpires to determine what was an illegal pitching motion and what was not; they debated during some games whether a three-quarters delivery was an illegal overhand or a sidearm motion.

As a result of having problems interpreting the 1883 rule changes, many leagues made overhand pitching legal in 1884.[18] For most players, it is easier to throw with velocity in an overhand motion, but as this delivery is severely taxing for the arm, there must have been many injuries as grown men made the switch. Some may never have changed, but many managed to do so within a few years. It is difficult to know just how many switched in the Northwestern League in 1884, as newspapers were much more likely to note if a pitcher was left-handed than whether he had an overhand motion.

It must have been a difficult adjustment for managers who broke into coaching with pitchers who could log numerous innings with an underhand motion. In managing the game the way they themselves had played or watched being played, they might not have known how to handle overhand pitchers and the accompanying potential career-threatening arm injuries and rest issues. Many managers continued to rely on two regular pitchers. Stillwater had problems finding two pitchers who were productive at the same time, let alone three, so overuse of a hot pitcher proved to be an ongoing challenge.

Fowler not only stopped pitching for a time in the 1884 season, but following the loss to Muskegon, he missed three games after being hit by a pitch in the ribs on June 3. According to the *Muskegon Daily Chronicle,* "He was unconscious for some time. It was feared that one of his ribs was broken, but the Stillwater manager informs us that he will be able to play again at the last of the week." The *Stillwater Gazette* disclosed that he had two broken ribs and praised his toughness, and Fowler once again recovered faster than most expected.[19] An injury to the ribs is one of the worst a hitter can sustain. The twisting motion of the swing demands that a hitter have a healthy torso; sometimes hitters have been inactive for weeks while recovering from such an injury.

Fowler missed only three games. Stillwater lost two of the three but finally climbed out of the cellar during the stretch as St. Paul fell to last. Bud returned to the pitching mound with success on June 9 but lost a 3–2 decision to Minneapolis. Two days later, while he did not pitch as effectively, he received more offensive support in a 10–6 win in the series finale over Minneapolis. The victory raised Stillwater's record to 7–23, and Fowler had been the winning pitcher in five games.

Fowler was on the mound again two days later against St. Paul, and signs of overuse became apparent. Although he was three for four at the plate with a triple and a stolen base to help his own cause, he lasted until only the fourth inning before moving to third base in favor of John Quinn.[20] Stillwater lost the game 12–8.

Stillwater turned the table on St. Paul the next day with a 10–6 win. Fowler came in from third base to finish the game as pitcher in relief of the starter, James McCue. Since the 0–16 start, Fowler and McCue had logged most of the innings and were the only effective pitchers during the next sixteen games, of which Stillwater won eight. It would be unlikely that the two would have continued at that pace without wearing down or breaking down, so on June 14 the Stillwater management signed John F. Quinn to become the ace of the staff.

There was already a John Quinn on the roster who mostly played outfield and pitched from the right side, but he was inconsistent. John F. Quinn was a left-handed pitcher who was residing in Canada when Stillwater signed him.[21] The team eased John F. into the pitching rotation but by the beginning of July made him the ace after one strong start after another. His best performance may have been a 2–1 twelve-inning win over Minneapolis on July 1.

The team continued to play at a .500 pace not only because of stronger pitching, but also from an improved lineup in the field. Johnny Peters, who played nine years in the major leagues, was added to the squad at shortstop. The club also signed Patrick Dealey, a catcher, and Otto Schomberg, a first baseman, from Milwaukee after the Wisconsin club decided to reduce the number of players on its roster.[22] Schomberg also was a strong hitter who rivaled Fowler as the top offensive force on the team.

Because of a revamped lineup and perhaps because of arm problems, Fowler played more at second base in July. He also filled in as catcher, but that requires a healthy arm that can make strong throws around the diamond. If he did have arm problems, he could play at second base and go many games without having to throw a ball farther than ninety feet. He continued to be strong at the bat as he went three for six with two doubles and knocked in the winning run in an 8–7 win over Minneapolis on July 2. The next day he combined with Schomberg, Peters, and Dealey for nine hits in support of John F. Quinn in a 10–3 win over Muskegon.[23] The win improved Stillwater's record to 15–30.

Just when things looked promising, Stillwater lost eight games in a row. John Quinn pitched well during this stretch, but John F. Quinn saw no action, and McCue was ineffective. Fowler was the most productive hitter, but he had only seven hits in twenty-seven plate appearances. Bud also was the starting pitcher in a game against Saginaw and lost 8–7. To make matters worse, he was fined $10.00 by the team for a wild throw that let two runs score. To get back on track, the team released five players during the stretch (McCue was the biggest name) and suspended another player for thirty days without pay.[24]

The team was down to nine players on the roster on July 17, but that is all they needed to beat Fort Wayne, 4–0. John F. Quinn was back on the mound, and he responded by going the distance for the shutout. Stillwater also slammed out eleven hits, but Otto Schomberg provided enough support for Quinn almost by himself, as he was three for four with a double and a triple.[25] Fowler was pounded by Fort Wayne the next day in an 11–1 loss, but John F. Quinn pitched and won the next four games to move Stillwater to 20–39. He gave up one, zero, four, and three runs in those games before losing to Grand Rapids, 8–3.

To give John F. some sorely needed rest, M. J. Bradley pitched against Grand Rapids on July 26. On the surface, things seemed to go well as Stillwater won 11–6. However, just before the game, Fowler was fined $50.00 and suspended for two weeks for refusing to catch Bradley.[26] It was never mentioned why Fowler would not catch Bradley, but the circumstance could have been similar to what happened with fellow black baseball pioneer Moses Walker. Walker was the first black to play in the major leagues when he joined Toledo of the American Association in 1884. He was a catcher who received acclaim for his skills behind the plate, yet his teammate, pitcher Tony Mullane, would not take signals from him because of his color. If Bradley was not following Fowler's signals and if team management would not support him, it is likely that he would have refused to catch for fear of bodily harm from the pitched balls. Catching is a physically challenging position normally; not knowing the intended speed, location, and spin of the ball could be dangerous.

The suspension ended up being shortened to two games in, perhaps, an act of necessity after John F. Quinn broke his right arm while pitching on July 28.[27] Not only did Stillwater lose the game to Grand Rapids, 10–0, but Quinn would never pitch in a high professional league again. With the release of McCue earlier in the month, John Quinn became the ace.

Perhaps the suspension also ended because the team management had second thoughts about who was at fault between Bradley and Fowler. Fowler played in the rest of the team's games that season, while Bradley never pitched another game for Stillwater even though they had just lost John F. Quinn. Bradley had only a 1–3 pitching record for the season, so the team management probably decided to go with the more successful of the two players even though that player was black.

The struggles on the field had affected the team's financial success all season, but the turmoil at the end of July and the first week of August cemented the team's fate. The team lost six games in a row by a combined score of 59–12 and fell to a record of 21–45.

Reports of dissolution circulated for weeks, doubtless making it hard for the team to stay focused. The *Stillwater Messenger* denied the rumors on June 28 when it claimed that the team was meeting expenses despite poor home attendance figures and traveling expenses. By July 12, it was admitted that the team would disband at the end of the season, but that claim took place at a time when players were not receiving their paychecks. The *Messenger* noted on July 26 that costs per game were $100.00 plus salaries, while home game receipts varied between $25.00 and $100.00. The directors voted to disband effective August 4, making Stillwater the fourth Northwestern League club to fold before the season ended. In all, the losses totaled about $7,500.[28]

Stillwater with its smaller population may still have had a difficult time compiling attendance figures that were competitive with the rest of the league even if the team got off to a successful start, but the club's struggles on the field compounded the issue. Although the ticket prices were twenty-five cents in accordance with the league norm, the team averaged fewer than three hundred spectators per home game. In comparison, road games at Milwaukee drew more than a thousand fans on two occasions, while a game at Bay City saw about 1,600 in attendance. The newspaper accounts of attendance figures are pretty sketchy, but the largest recorded home crowd was for a July 15 game against Bay City that more than six hundred patrons attended.[29]

The Northwestern League had all eight of its teams complete the 84-game schedule in 1883, but the league disbanded before any team finished the 110-game schedule in 1884. Despite having a superb 39–16 record and a chance to win the pennant, Bay City was the first to go when it folded on July 22. Evansville joined the league to replace them but played only five league games, winning four of them, before dissolving. Within three weeks, only Milwaukee, Minneapolis, St. Paul, and late-addition Winona were still fielding league teams.[30]

> "The great baseball rage is subsiding to quite an extent all over the country. Next year players will find it difficult to command the fancy prices they now do."
>
> **Grand Forks Herald, 1888**

Since the top four teams in the league standings were among the nine franchises that folded, the ones that survived—Milwaukee, Minneapolis, and St. Paul—started a new second season and added Winona as the fourth team to round out the league. However, the second season ended prematurely on September 2 when Minneapolis disbanded. There would not be another Northwestern League game played until the league reformed in 1886.

St. Paul and Milwaukee decided to keep playing in September and October 1884 and joined the outlaw Union Association near the end of the league schedule. Although it was in existence for only the 1884 season and threatened the other professional leagues by not joining the National Agreement and following the reserve rule, the UA was a major league while it lasted. (The league was organized on the premise that a player should be free to sell his services to the highest bidder when his contract expired. Not respecting the reserve rule was also their downfall as their own players were raided by other leagues.) St. Paul finished 2–6 in UA games, but they were only a combined 31–55 in the Northwestern League. Milwaukee had a record of 53–34 in the Northwestern League and also showed well in the UA, going 8–4. St. Paul and Milwaukee were two of twelve teams that played in the league at various points in the season.

Few members on the Stillwater roster had good seasons in 1884. Frank Jones led the team with a .302 batting average, while Fowler finished at .297. Otto Schomberg hit .279 with three triples and led the team with fourteen doubles. Fowler and John Pickett each compiled thirteen doubles; Joe Visner made up for his .243 average with eleven doubles, seven triples, and two home runs.

Fowler was the best of the pitchers with seven wins in his fifteen decisions, but John F. Quinn was the most effective in going 5–1 before he broke his arm. John F. also had the highest batting average on the team at .318 but had only twenty-two official at-bats. John Quinn and James McCue were each 4–9 on the mound, while Harry Yarnell and Peter Fries were winless at 0–8 and 0–5, respectively.

Although several of his white teammates were picked up quickly by other professional teams and six eventually played in the majors, Bud Fowler had to wait for another chance. He eventually signed for the 1885 season with Keokuk, Iowa, of the Western League along with Otto Schomberg; Joe Visner went to the Kansas City organization.[31]

Keokuk must have reminded Fowler somewhat of his previous situation at Stillwater. The Hawkeyes were a first-year team that was trying to establish itself in a high minor league. It was also a small city fighting in a league

Keokuk of the Western League in 1885: (seated, left to right) Kennedy, p, Van Dyke, rf, Dugdale, c, Hudson, p, Harter, cf; (standing) Schomberg, 1b, O'Brien, lf, Fowler, 2b, Corcoran, 3b, and Decker, c; Harrington, the field manager, is sitting in the middle.

made up of cities like Milwaukee and Indianapolis. Not only were some of the Stillwater players, such as Visner, Schomberg, and Fowler, in the league but the Milwaukee Brewers team from the Northwestern League re-formed as the Milwaukee Western League franchise.

The Keokuks had a good record against a schedule of semiprofessional and league games. Schomberg and Fowler did well while they played, but the entire league folded by the end of June. On July 15 *Sporting Life* noted the performance of the former Stillwater players, stating, "they played good ball with the Keokuks." For Schomberg, it was another bump on the way to the majors. For Fowler, it was another in a long line of short stays. He finished out the summer playing in Colorado.[32]

A new Western League formed in 1886 with teams from Lincoln, Nebraska; Leavenworth, Kansas; Leadville, Colorado; St. Joseph, Missouri; Denver,

Colorado; and Topeka, Kansas. This was one of Bud's best years in the high minors as he played the whole season for Topeka in a league that remained intact the entire season. As was the case for most of his career, Fowler responded to the consistent playing time with excellent numbers. He led the league in triples with twelve and was eleventh in hitting with a .309 average.[33]

Although Bud came into professional ball as a pitcher and catcher, by 1886 he was primarily a middle infielder, usually at second base, although he would still pitch an occasional inning or two. He always had speed in the field and running the bases, but he also started to be known as a base stealer. He had twelve steals in 1886 but registered much higher totals thereafter. That speed also helped his slugging percentage, as sixteen doubles, twelve triples, and three home runs in fifty-eight league games during that era was a productive total.

Instead of getting to return to play on a pennant-winning Topeka team in 1887, Fowler made the Binghamton, New York, team of the International League. Going into the season, he had reason to be excited as not only was the International League a top minor league, but he was one of seven black players in the league. The list included George Stovey, who won thirty-four games for the Newark franchise; Moses Walker, his catcher; and Frank Grant, the Buffalo second baseman, who led the league with eleven home runs.

However, instead of finding success and some amount of stability playing in a league that fielded other black players, Fowler ran into more problems than in his other seasons. The *Rochester Chronicle* reported on July 5 that despite hitting .350 and stealing twenty-three bases, "Fowler, Binghamton's second baseman, has been released upon condition that he will not sign with any other International club."[34] His career with the club lasted only thirty-four games.

More information came out on August 8 when the *Newark Daily Journal* noted, "The players of the Binghamton Baseball Club were fined $50 each by the directors because six weeks ago they refused to go on the field unless Fowler, the colored second baseman, was removed." The Binghamton franchise disbanded on August 20 after compiling a 27–46 record.[35] By that time Fowler was finishing out the season with the Montpelier, Vermont, team of the Northeastern League.

The *Rutland Herald* reported on August 24, "Captain Fowler of the Montpeliers is a colored man and a first class ball-tosser in every respect. He played a brilliant game yesterday on second and made two of the four runs for his club. . . . Fowler seemed to be the favorite with the spectators and was greeted with applause every time he stepped to the plate."[36] The next week the paper announced that Fowler had left for Laconia, New Hampshire. In eight games for Montpelier he hit .429 and stole seven bases.

The year 1888 brought more of the same level of mobility for Fowler as he began it in Crawfordsville, Indiana, of the Central Interstate League. The team was 21–21 on July 2 when the franchise moved to Terre Haute, Indiana. They started to play better, but the league folded in late July, and the team finished 32–26 while Fowler hit .294 with twenty-two stolen bases and six triples. Next Bud caught on with Santa Fe of the New Mexico League and hit .343 with eleven stolen bases and six doubles in twenty-two games.[37]

Fowler then moved to Greenville of the Michigan State League in 1889 and remained there the entire season. The *Grand Rapids Democrat* noted, "It is said he has played in nearly every state in the Union, coming here from Texas." In getting to play in ninety-two of the one hundred league games, Fowler hit .302 and stole forty-six bases.[38]

By 1890 Fowler was back in the Central Interstate League, playing for Galesburg, Illinois. He had one of his best days on May 2 when he collected six hits in seven at-bats and scored five runs as Galesburg trounced Peoria, 31–6. However, the team disbanded, and he jumped to Sterling, Illinois, of the Illinois-Iowa League. Later he rejoined Galesburg, which had regrouped and changed leagues, but he finished the season in Burlington, Iowa. The *Dubuque Daily Times* paid tribute to his four hits and stellar base running performance on July 28 at Dubuque, "Just think, five stolen bases off Jones in one game. As [league] President Atherton said yesterday, if only he had been painted white, he would be playing with the best of them."[39]

Fowler found no openings in white organized baseball in 1891, 1893, and 1894, so he spent those years in Findlay, Ohio, playing with an independent team. He went on barnstorming tours in the fall; in the off-season he continued to support himself as a barber.[40] In early 1895 he began organizing an all-black professional team, but support for such a venture was lacking in Findlay. As a result, he went to a rival town and found sponsorship for the team from the Page Fence Woven Wire Company of Adrian, Michigan. As part of the sponsorship agreement, the team became the Page Fence Giants and was given elaborate black-and-maroon uniforms and a private railroad car to use while barnstorming.

The Page Fence Giants had no home field and played continuously on the road as a full-time barnstorming team through six midwestern states. Their private railroad car not only eased traveling from town to town, but it came with a porter and a cook. The services they provided helped alleviate problems when the team needed to find a place to eat and sleep while in towns

Railroad car used by the Page Fence Giants

that observed Jim Crow ordinances. As the organizer of the team, Fowler played second base and was the captain, while fellow star Grant Johnson played shortstop. The team boasted five college graduates, forbade drinking, and paid the players $100.00 a month.[41]

The Giants made a big impact both on and off the field. In their first year they won 118 games and lost thirty-six while playing a wide range of minor league and independent teams. Besides their success on the field as an all-black team, the Giants also gained notice by riding bicycles through the town where they were playing to drum up excitement. Not only did they ride the bikes to sell more tickets, but their second big sponsor was Monarch Bicycles.

Fowler returned to Minnesota as the Giants made a trip in late April 1895 to take on the Minneapolis Millers and the St. Paul Apostles of the Western League. His team drew attention from the local papers for their palace railroad car and the bicycle parade through St. Paul on April 23, but more than anything, they received attention for being advertised as the strongest team of colored ballplayers ever organized.[42] It did not hurt the gate receipts in these Western League towns or the claim of being the strongest black team that the Giants beat the Western League member Grand Rapids Gold Bugs earlier in the season, 12–10.

Whereas Grand Rapids, Minneapolis, and St. Paul were all from the same top-level minor league, Grand Rapids was not successful in 1895. St. Paul (74–50) and Minneapolis (64–59) finished in the top half of the Western League, but Grand Rapids came in last (38–86). The difference among the three teams also showed in the results against the Page Fence Giants. Although the Giants had beaten Grand Rapids, they lost to Minneapolis, 25–2. The scores were a little more competitive against Charles Comiskey's St. Paul team, but the Giants still lost, 15–2 and 9–2.[43]

The team was a powerful black squad over the next few years. In 1896 they claimed the colored championship over the Cuban X-Giants by beating them ten games to one. In 1897 the team stated they had won eighty-two consecutive games, but they did not fare well financially and disbanded after the 1898 season.[44] Most of the squad reorganized in 1899 as the Chicago Columbia Giants, which went on to challenge for black baseball supremacy for a few more years.

Although he was the main force behind starting the Page Fence Giants, Fowler did not even finish the inaugural season in 1895. On July 15 he abandoned his creation to play for Adrian of the white professional Michigan State League. In thirty-one games between the Adrian and Lansing teams of the league, the thirty-seven-year-old Fowler hit .331 and scored forty runs.[45] It turned out to be his last opportunity to play in the minors. Significantly, his ten years of minor-league service were almost double the number that any other black player compiled.

By the 1890s it became increasingly difficult for blacks to play in organized baseball. Socially, it was more acceptable in white circles to permit segregation. The U.S. Supreme Court had a huge impact in making segregation the law of the land in a series of court rulings. Although part of the Fourteenth Amendment declared that all persons born or naturalized in the United States to be citizens and gave them the rights therein, there were several court decisions in subsequent years that allowed state laws to supercede national rights of citizenship. These rulings declared that state and national citizenship were separate, thereby allowing Jim Crow practices to be legal as long as they took place within state boundaries. Subsequent lower-court cases directly established the principle that blacks could be restricted to "separate but equal" facilities.

The economic downturn that eventually became the Panic of 1893 hurt black players along with everyone else. In an environment where some fifteen thousand businesses and banks failed while four million people lost their jobs nationally, the years 1890–94 also saw a severe reduction in the number of professional leagues due to fans having less or no money to spend on attending games. Black people were the first to be laid off in times of hardship in many industries, but it was even harder for blacks involved in baseball. Fowler and the other black stars had tended to get opportunities in white baseball only with struggling or newly formed teams that were desperate for talent. However, not only were there no new teams, but the teams that remained had many white unemployed players to choose from because so many leagues folded. By the time professional baseball began to expand again in the late 1890s, the white professional game was almost completely closed to blacks.

After 1895 Fowler played mostly with black teams, which, like the Page Fence Giants, he organized and managed himself. In 1904–05 he tried to organize a national colored baseball league but could not find the necessary financial backing.[46] He was reported to be ill and suffering financially by 1909 and quietly passed away at his sister's home in Frankfort, New York, on February 26, 1913. He was fifty-four.

Jim Crow laws and the barring of black players from white leagues at the turn of the century did not stop blacks from playing baseball. Much like other facets of their daily lives, blacks were forced to turn within their society to play professional baseball. Although the structure and financial backing of the Negro Leagues were never so sound as those of white-based organized baseball during the first half of the twentieth century, there is no argument that the Negro Leagues were talented, with Hall of Fame players such as Josh Gibson, Oscar Charleston, Buck Leonard, Satchel Paige, Rube Foster, Cool Papa Bell, and John Henry Lloyd. The Negro Leagues represent a colorful and heroic chapter in baseball history, as players were able to endure and fully develop despite major obstacles.

As great as the Negro Leagues were, the entire country was cheated of having the opportunity to see the great white and black stars play on the field together for a lengthy amount of time. There were many white and black baseball fans during the first half of the twentieth century who wondered whether black players were good enough to play organized baseball on the same field as the top white players.

Although Jackie Robinson, Willie Mays, Hank Aaron and other black stars of major-league baseball helped finally to change the perceptions of many fans in the 1950s, it does not reduce what Bud Fowler and other black baseball pioneers accomplished in the nineteenth century. Not only did Fowler achieve an outstanding record on the field in his years in professional baseball, but he fought to keep playing the game that was the passion of his life even though it would have been so easy to walk away or to play in environments that were less hostile and more stable. By persevering and continuing to play in spite of the growth of segregation, he made an impact as a pioneer not only in the integration of the game of baseball, but on the nation as well.

The Quicksteps Duel the Brown Stockings, 1887

The Minneapolis Millers and the St. Paul Saints have been well known in the history of baseball teams in Minnesota. The Millers began in 1884, at the same time that Bud Fowler played in Stillwater. The Saints evolved from an earlier St. Paul team, which had also been founded in 1884. Eventually, both teams became a part of the American Association in 1902. Baseball aficionados typically know these stories.[1]

Fewer people know about several black teams from the same decade. In 1887, three years after Bud Fowler departed from Stillwater, Minnesota's African Americans organized all-black teams in the Twin Cities—the St. Paul Quicksteps and the Minneapolis Brown Stockings. In 1887 the Quicksteps challenged "any colored base ball club" in the area that would show up, and the two squads would vie for the Championship of the Northwest.[2]

The Minneapolis team accepted the challenge, and the Brown Stockings dueled the Quicksteps in an August 1 game at Excelsior. St. Paul won, thereby claiming its team to be the "champions of the Northwest." The score is unknown because the newspaper account did not include it.[3]

A third black team, this one from the Fort Snelling military reserve just south of St. Paul, wanted a shot at beating the champion Quicksteps, and the ballclubs played each other on August 15 at the fort. The St. Paul team won the game by a score of 11 to 5. The game lasted two hours and fifteen minutes, after which the teams got to watch the dress parade of the fort's troops.[4]

Few traces of these teams remain. The roster of the St. Paul team contains none of the names of the players listed for the two black squads that played in 1876 (the Blue Stars and the Unions). We know of no photographs of any of the 1887 teams, and we do not know the names of any of the ballplayers from the Minneapolis or the Fort Snelling clubs. They are most likely forever lost to history.

However, the St. Paul *Western Appeal,* a black newspaper, printed the roster and the names of the St. Paul Quicksteps:

Roster: August 13, 1887			Lineup: August 1, 1887	
Jas. Duke,	P[itcher].	·	J. Duke,	P.
T. H. Long,	C[atcher].	·	T. *Young,*	C.
W. H. Brown,	1st B.	·	W. *N.* Brown,	1st B.
C. A. Lett,	2nd B. & Capt[ain].	:	C. A. Lett,	2nd B. & Captain
C. Wilkins,	3rd B.	·		
H. F. Newton,	L.F.	·	*A.* F. Newton,	3rd B.
A. Leboo,	C.F.	·	A. *Laboo,*	R.F.
W. H. Springer,	R.F.	:	W. H. *Spigner,*	L.F.
H. W. Fairfax,	S.S.	·	H. W. Fairfax,	S.S.
A. A. Cotton,	Sub[stitute].	:	A. Hester,	C.F.
W. D. Carter,	Man[ager].	·	W. D. Carter,	Manager

Note: The spelling of the players' names varied between the two lists; differences are marked by italics.

Drawing the Color Line on Walter Ball, 1890–1908

Jim Karn

innesota black baseball players from Bud Fowler in the 1880s through Kirby Puckett in the 1990s have had to deal with the reality of racial discrimination in baseball. Walter Ball's experience as a pioneer Minnesota black ballplayer mirrors the story of these individuals. He was forced by the color line early in his career to move from his home in St. Paul, Minnesota, ending up in the early heart of black baseball in Chicago in 1903.

By 1899 Walter Ball was acknowledged to be one of the top amateur pitchers in St. Paul. A move to Grand Forks, North Dakota, in 1900 marked the beginning of his professional career—pitching baseballs for a living. He pitched and played for seven different teams in North Dakota through the 1901 season. In 1902, Ball moved back to Minnesota and found great success as he pitched St. Cloud to the Championship of Eastern Minnesota.[1]

The story of Walter Ball as a ballplayer from 1890 through 1902 reflected America's treatment of its black population as almost all baseball from 1896 to 1946 was segregated. During this era the color of a man's skin was more important than his talent and skill. Ball rarely played with other black teammates from the beginning of his career in 1890 through the end of the 1902 season. Conversely, from 1903 when he moved to Chicago until the end of his career in the 1920s, he played and coached exclusively on all-black teams. Ball moved frequently from team to team in the years 1903 through 1914, playing for teams in New York, Philadelphia, Brooklyn, St. Louis, and Schenectady in an effort to earn a living from the game. It was said of Ball, "He was one of the best pitchers of the early years of Black baseball. He was a smart pitcher with good control, and made frequent use of the spitball, but was not a power pitcher."[2]

An examination of Walter Ball's life will help in understanding his baseball accomplishments in Minnesota during this racially charged period. Walter Ball was born in Detroit, Michigan, in 1880 and moved with his father, John, and mother, Ella, to St. Paul when he was eight years old. His father worked as a barber with his brothers Frederick and Walter and also as a porter for the Pullman Palace and Car Company. In 1893 the Ball family moved into a house at 818 Edmund Street in St Paul; this was to be Walter's home for the next five years. The family's house was not far from the Rondo neighborhood near the state capitol, where many of the black workers lived. At the time Walter was growing up, this area had a mix of nationalities, with Irish, Scottish, and German families living nearby. His neighbors included working-class laborers—shoemakers and factory workers—but also a few white-collar workers—collection agents and commission salesmen. Large families were common for the area, but the Minnesota state census of 1895 did not list Walter as having any brothers or sisters.[3]

The earliest reference found to Walter playing baseball was in a newspaper article dated August 4, 1896. He was the winning pitcher in a 26–25 game as the Nationals defeated the Tigers. Ball was a rising star on the local ball fields who began to get newspaper recognition for his pitching prowess. It appears that he had been active on school and amateur baseball teams since the early 1890s.[4]

The youth teams in St. Paul corresponded with one another in the 1890s through the columns of the numerous daily newspapers. Each day teams issued challenges to other teams of the same age group. A typical announcement was: "The Clovers challenge any club in the city under fourteen years. Address D. Lane 95 Valley Street. Would like a game for Sunday."[5] Teams arranged games and then played opponents. Newspaper reporters who wrote about the games usually listed the pitcher's and catcher's names in the line scores and sometimes included a box score. The articles had titles such as "The Amateurs" or "With the Amateurs" and covered literally hundreds of teams that filled the sandlots of the city from April to October. The stories rarely included the names of infielders and outfielders unless the player did something significant in the game. This practice makes it much easier to follow the career of a successful pitcher such as Walter Ball.

In 1897 the *St. Paul Pioneer Press* sponsored all-city amateur baseball tournaments. Teams competed in two divisions for trophies and medals. Players under the age of fourteen-and-a-half were in one division, and those who were under seventeen-and-a-half were in the other. The *Pioneer Press* gave plenty of publicity to promote the summer contests. Accordingly, Walter Ball's name was mentioned a number of times beginning in May. He started the season playing for the New Homes team but soon moved to the Funks Exports. He struck out 15 batters in a victory over the Shakopee Browns junior team and followed that with an 11-strikeout performance against the

Emmerts Bocks. Walter was an up-and-coming pitcher who was in demand by teams made up wholly of white players and had no problem in moving from team to team for a better situation.[6]

The *Pioneer Press* Junior Championship was scheduled to be played in early August in the brand-new Lexington Ball Park, home of the St. Paul Saints of the professional American Association League. The thrill of playing on a real field after coping with hardscrabble vacant lots of various conditions must have been exciting for the young players. Walter Ball and the Funks Exports were one of six teams chosen for this event.

The Funks Exports, with Walter pitching, lost the first game of the tourney in extra innings, 9–8. Walter had struck out eight batters and helped his own cause with two doubles while at bat. A newspaper reported that a falling out among team members occurred after the loss and charged that Ball had used foul language in the post-game ruckus. The *Pioneer Press* responded to this charge and defended his actions: "Walter Ball . . . has decided to sever his connection with that [Funks Exports] club. . . . Ball is a well educated young fellow, as well as a clever player, and those who know him need no assurance that he did not use the language attributed to him."[7] Ball signed on with the rival Young Cyclones that was also competing in the tournament. There was no indication that other teams objected to this change or that the final arbitrator, the *Pioneer Press,* did either. Ball pitched the final two games for the Young Cyclones, ironically against the Funks Exports, for the St. Paul City Championship. He pitched magnificently, striking out 14 former teammates in the first game and 13 in the next as his team claimed the championship.

As a result of the win, the Young Cyclones were matched in a Twin Cities title game against the Minneapolis champion, the Adam Street Stars. Walter did not start as a pitcher and was used only in relief late in the game. Since he had been the only pitcher used by the Cyclones at the end of the season, it seems odd that he was not chosen to start this important game. Although he played in the field, starting at first base and batting in the cleanup position, it is possible that he was not named to pitch for reasons other than sound baseball strategy. This slight by the Young Cyclones appears to be an instance of racism—a problem that he was to encounter a number of times as his career moved him away from the playgrounds of St. Paul. It may have been another insult that in a team photograph of the Young Cyclones that appeared in the *Pioneer Press* Walter Ball was the only one not wearing a team uniform. A long article summarizing the 1897 season accompanied the picture, but it omitted mention of Ball as one of the main reasons for the Young Cyclones winning the city championship.[8] Nonetheless, he had a remarkable season. His pitching record for 1897 (from available records) featured 13 wins against only two losses.

The next year brought great changes. According to the 1898 *St. Paul City Directory*, Walter's father, John M. Ball, had relocated to Montreal, Canada. This move left Walter to earn a living on his own. That year he played baseball with a number of local ball clubs—L. G. Hoffmans Caterpillars, The Bostons, and the Dreies Club. Thus baseball became a full-time summer job for him. A typical story in the newspaper stated: "The Dreies . . . will cross bats next Sunday . . . for a purse of $15.00. The batteries for the Dreies will be Ball and Dolan." The *Pioneer Press* published several photos and articles about Ball's teams, including a solo picture of Walter in a pitching pose. The caption summed up his career to that point, noting that: "Walter Ball the pitcher of the Caterpillars and of the Bostons, is one of the best young players developing among the St. Paul Amateurs. In spite of his youth, he has been pitching more or less for ten years. He has terrific speed, good control, and all the curves. He has made this year a record of twenty strikeouts in one game against the Merrian Park Crescents. Ball has lost none of the games he has pitched this year and in 1897 he lost but one game, a ten-inning contest when he pitched for Funks Exports against the Young Cyclones."[9]

In the 1899 season Ball began to travel. "The St. Anthony Park Mfg. Company defeated the Duluth ball club on Sunday . . . at Duluth . . . batteries—St. Anthony Ball and Ritter." He was developing into an all-around ballplayer and becoming a clear favorite of the sports columnists at the *Pioneer Press* and actually played for a team sponsored by the newspaper. He was quite a hitter, and in one game, "Ball, of the Pioneer Press team" swatted "a home run, two three baggers and a single out of four times at bat."[10]

Baseball enjoyed great popularity at the turn of the twentieth century, and the sheer number of teams playing in St. Paul and throughout Minnesota was impressive. Demand for talented ballplayers increased, as a notice in a newspaper at this time revealed: "Wanted—baseball players to go west, first and second basemen, shortstop and pitcher. Must be fast and recommended. Apply in person room 146 Hotel Nicollet, Minneapolis."[11] Ballplayers could make a living at it if they were willing to travel and forego a home life and a stable job. But black ballplayers had fewer options for playing opportunities than white players enjoyed due to the color line that had been drawn in the late 1890s. Semiprofessional and amateur baseball were open to a black ballplayer, but he needed to be an *exceptional* player, not just a *good* player, to hire on with one of these white teams.

It was significant, therefore, when the following notice appeared in the August 19, 1899, *St. Paul Pioneer Press*: "Walter Ball, the promising young colored pitcher is organizing a colored nine for a two months tour this fall through Minnesota, Iowa, Illinois and Wisconsin. He already has some eight players on his list and wants eleven to complete the organization. Colored ballplayers who can really play ball can communicate with Walter Ball at 204 Martin [Central] Street. It will be a fast aggregation and will make a lot of semi-professional nines hustle."[12] The organization of all-black teams had already begun in Chicago and New York but was unknown in Minnesota. This attempt to form a black-only team was a natural reaction to the color line in baseball.

"The sun of our perfect freedom is rising in this Northwest."

Fredrick L. McGhee, 1891

This article represented one of the few that identified his race to the public during the time he played in St. Paul. The fact that little mention was made of his race seems to indicate that he was being judged mainly for his ball-playing ability. In the next three years, however, as Walter moved farther and farther from St. Paul, this race-neutral reporting would not always occur.

By the end of August 1899, the amateur baseball columns of the various St. Paul newspapers contained no mention of Walter Ball. The most plausible explanation for this absence was that he was able to get his "colored" team off the ground, and he started touring the Midwest. The St. Paul newspapers did not print his tour itinerary, and it is hard to track his path. But even if this team did not get organized, one can see that he was thinking of ways to make a living from his ball-playing skills. That Walter Ball attempted to organize a black team in the Twin Cities illustrated organizational skills that would serve him well in the years to come.

At the start of the new century, Ball sold his services to the highest bidder and moved from St. Paul to Devils Lake, North Dakota. He pitched in June against the Larimore, North Dakota, team, recording a victory.[13] Shortly thereafter, on June 16, he signed on with the Grand Forks, North Dakota, team. Grand Forks had recently had a local black player on its town team. Bishop ("Bish") Dorsey started playing for Grand Forks in 1893 and continued through the 1899 season.

Dorsey had "lived in Grand Forks since childhood," and had played baseball in the area "ever since he was old enough to handle a ball" and was considered "one of the star players of every first-class Grand Forks team." But he got into deep trouble in 1899. While working at Dan Sullivan's East Grand Forks saloon, he served a customer named John McCabe who objected to him and used a racial slur. Dorsey punched McCabe from across the bar and got slugged in return. Onlookers broke up the fight immediately, but Dorsey left the building and came back and struck McCabe with a big piece of wood, killing him. Dorsey fled but turned himself in to the authorities later that night, telling them that he "had no thought whatever of killing the man."[14]

A crowd of men reportedly gathered near the saloon that night, looking for Bish Dorsey, and had he "been within reach," there was "little doubt he would have been lynched," according to a Crookston newspaper. Since a black man had been lynched in Grand Forks by a vigilante mob in 1882, there was a chance that it could happen again, but there was a real effort by the police to prevent just such a reoccurrence.[15]

Dorsey went on trial for murder, and several prominent citizens of Grand Forks testified in his behalf about his good character, which was publicly known from his baseball career. The judge listened and sentenced the defendant to twenty-one years in Stillwater State Prison. The emotionally charged trial occurred just six months before Walter Ball began playing baseball in Grand Forks in the summer of 1900.[16]

Walter Ball made sacrifices to play in North Dakota. He was a married man, and he decided to take time off from the team in July to go to St. Paul, where his wife gave birth to a baby boy. The local newspapers tended to paint a generally positive picture of Ball. The city and its citizens seemed to like him; for example, a reporter wrote that "H. S. Chase offered Walter Ball a new pair of baby shoes for that young heir of his for every man he strikes out after the game had progressed a few innings. Ball won shoes enough to last his boy for the next two years."[17]

Walter Ball had an extremely successful year pitching for the Grand Forks team, with 11 wins, two losses, and one tie. At the end of the season, the team held a banquet to honor the players. As the *Grand Forks Herald* summed it up, "The fans must not forget to give Walter Ball a great deal of credit for his playing this summer. He was, early in the season, the club's mainstay in the box and did the work that kept the team to the front when it was in need of help in the pitchers box. He could have joined the Devils Lake team at good pay and when he preferred to join the locals he took chances on not getting a cent for his work, for the local management pay no salaries but divide all earnings pro rata at the finish of the season. Ball was the only pitcher the team had during most of the season and he worked hard for the team's success. He is a first class ballplayer and the management will do well to hold on to him next season." At the conclusion of the season, Walter Ball and his family stayed in Grand Forks for the winter. He spent time at his residence on 514 South Fourth and worked as a porter with the Great Northern Railroad.[18]

Walter Ball (sitting, left) and the Grand Forks team, champions of North Dakota in 1900 with a twenty-nine and three record

The beginning of the 1901 season brought a rude awakening to Ball when the color line reared its head. A letter to the editor of the *Grand Forks Herald*, written by "A lover of the Game," revealed agitation against Ball by his white teammates from the previous year: "The writer has been informed by a rumor of sufficient force to give it credence that there is a feeling and intention upon the part of some of the other players of last year to prevent . . . players from belonging to this year's team. . . . Ball is a good pitcher, a magnificent fielder who is always wide awake, a good batter and fine base runner, and then too, his conduct upon the baseball field has always been exemplary. . . . Any intention to select players for the local nine for any other reasons or motives . . . will greatly injure the sport in Grand Forks."[19]

Two days later in the *Daily Plaindealer,* a reporter put the problem of Walter Ball's place on the team in language plain enough for all its readers to understand: "Considerable feeling has been worked up among the baseball enthusiasts of the city over Ball . . . being left off the Grand Forks team this year. Ball is a colored boy, but that should certainly not mitigate against him. He is acknowledged to be one of the very best players in the state. As far as the sentiment expressed has shown there is nothing under the sun against Ball excepting his color."[20] Despite this plea, the color line had been drawn by the Grand Forks team, and Walter Ball had to search for another team for the 1901 season. Even after this treatment by his teammates, he continued to make Grand Forks his home.

Six weeks later, the reporter for the *Daily Plaindealer* rubbed it in on the team's management when he opined, "It does seem queer though, that after turning down . . . local players who are in every way qualified to fill the position, that it should be found necessary to seek financial assistance to procure . . . men, whom it is doubtful, are any better than Ball. . . . Why then, it is asked has he not been given a place? Simply that several of the players objected to his presence on the team and their objection had more weight with the manager than the wish of the public who patronize the games."[21]

After Grand Forks rejected him, Ball played for seven different teams, the longest for the Lakota, North Dakota, squad. On May 29, 1901, he probably became the first black athlete to play for the University of North Dakota in Grand Forks. He pitched seven innings against the Fargo Agricultural College (now North Dakota State University) in a 13–3 loss. Always looking for a way to make money, Walter agreed to umpire a game between two teams in the same league in which he pitched. In this contest, Devils Lake squared off against Langdon, and the report stated, "Ball was the best ever, and no one kicked, not even the visitors."[22]

Ball appeared willing to take any available work, especially to support his family. According to an account published by Frank Leland, Ball captained a team at York, North Dakota, in 1901. This series of games for York occurred in the middle of the season that he played with the Lakota team. To be a captain of a team was an unusual honor for a black ballplayer, especially on an all-white team at the turn of the twentieth century; indeed, being chosen as the captain of a team at that time was a significant honor for any ballplayer.[23] The incomplete record for Ball in 1901 shows him with a 9 and 9 record, which was not up to the standards that he had established in his years of pitching in St. Paul or for Grand Forks. Ball and his family stayed in Grand Forks at the end of the 1901 baseball season, and he again found work with the railroad as a porter.

After a season with seven different teams, Ball searched for a more solid place in spring 1902. He appeared to find one in Duluth, according to news reports: "Walter Ball has signed with the Duluth team, which was a very strong one, but disbanded when it was announced by one of the leading ministers of that place that he would wage a constant and unremitting warfare against Sunday ball."[24]

The Grand Forks club, in the meantime, signed a contract to run a team in the professional Northern League for the 1902 season. Joining the league in its inaugural season fit the progressive image the city was trying to project. But the management of the Grand Forks team did not immediately understand that the Northern League excluded black players as a general rule. This was illustrated by an article in the *Grand Forks Herald*: "Ball came here [from Duluth] with the expectation of signing with one of the Northern League teams, and there is no doubt that he will get in the game as he is one of the fastest ball players that ever stepped on a diamond in this neck of the woods. He has not made any arrangements as yet, as none of the managers knew he was to play in the league, but he will have no trouble in signing with one of the clubs."[25]

At issue was the National Agreement that the Northern League had signed with professional baseball, which prohibited teams from hiring black baseball players. Accordingly, Ball was "not picked up by a Northern League team" at that time, as Grand Forks soon learned.

But Ball caught a break when he received a telephone call from Manager Wenzel of the St. Cloud semiprofessional team. They were interested in him and wanted him to pitch for them starting immediately. St. Cloud had explored joining the Northern League, but they were not successful in raising the required money or public interest. The St. Cloud manager knew Walter because he had pitched a game against them in June the previous year. Ball had been hired by the Cass Lake team to pitch against St. Cloud as they vied for a purse of $100.00. In that contest, "Ball struck out thirteen and allowed six hits."[26]

Before St. Cloud called Ball, the team had shown an interest in signing Billy Williams, another black ballplayer from St. Paul. Williams had played amateur baseball in St. Paul against Ball in·the 1890s. He was one of the best black ballplayers at the turn of the twentieth century in Minnesota, starting with his stint at Chaska in 1900. At that time he was given a chance to sign a professional contract if he would try to pass himself off as an Indian. He refused to go along with this charade, and with his rejection went his opportunity to play league baseball.[27]

Despite their best efforts, St. Cloud failed to sign Williams for the 1902 season, and he played for other teams instead. He was on the roster of the Royalton ballclub that faced St. Cloud and showed what he could do with a bat: "with two men out Williams . . . swatted the first ball pitched." He "reached up in the clouds with the end of a wagon tongue that he was using for a bat. He caught it fairly and eased it over the right field fence" for the only home run of the game.[28] By 1904 he was working full time for the governor of Minnesota as an aide. He was reappointed by every governor, both Democrat and Republican, until he retired in 1955 after 51 years of service.

The St. Cloud club seemed happy to sign Walter Ball. A newspaper writer praised him: "He has plenty of speed and is able to land them as deceptive as any one."[29] They hoped that Ball could help them compete with the Waseca team, the prior season's state champion, which was led by black pitchers George Wilson and William (Billy) Holland. A number of cities in Minnesota were anxious to hire ballplayers of any color as long as they could win ball games against rival cities. Defeating a neighboring town gave cities of all sizes a civic boost.

Because African Americans were not numerous in Minnesota, especially in cities outside of St. Paul, Minneapolis, and Duluth, a black ballplayer was a real curiosity in many parts of the state. The novelty factor involved in having a black player had the tendency to increase attendance, and a few players found teams willing to hire them for a single game, a series of games, or for the entire season.

Ball's first game with St. Cloud was an unqualified success as he pitched well against the St. Cloud Redmen and won the support of his teammates. The writers in the local newspapers described him as "Ball, the colored gentleman" or "Ball, the colored lad." By May 23, though, there were few references to Walter's race in the local newspapers. Statements such as "Ball is what we have been looking for. He is not only a first class pitcher but plays the game in all its stages. His . . . work in the ninth was the salvation of the game. Ball has won a happy home in St. Cloud."[30] This last comment came after he defeated the Globe Trotters, a professional team representing the cities of St. Paul, Minneapolis, Duluth, and Red Wing.

Ball became St. Cloud's main pitcher, and he started most of the games. He won a May 30 game, pitching all nine innings in a 3–2 victory. The next day, he pitched three innings in relief of the starter and picked up another win. On June 2 he again started and pitched nine innings, striking out 12, but losing a 3–2 game. In that game, he developed "a very sore finger that precluded him from doing quite an effective work in the curve line."[31] Ball was perhaps being overworked, but as the star hired pitcher, it was assumed that he would throw most of the innings in the team's games. In that era, pitchers were expected to fill in at other positions on the days they were not on the mound. Nearly all teams carried only ten to twelve players, and anyone who planned to play baseball for a living needed to be versatile.

Walter Ball again looked for ways to supplement his income. He purchased the right to rent cushions for grandstand seats at the ball park, charging "five cents per game." This cushion concession was a way for management to increase Ball's salary without incurring any extra cost to the club. Walter needed the money because on June 5 his wife and young son joined him from their Grand Forks home. The newspaper noted that since their arrival "the ballplayer is happy."[32] The nomadic life of a ballplayer made the establishment of a home life extremely difficult for both spouses. St. Cloud in 1900 had a black population of only eighteen, seven adults and eleven children, so having his family join him was important for Walter.

The St. Cloud team attempted all kinds of promotions in order to raise enough money to pay the players' salaries. The New England Bloomer Girls, a perennial attraction that was booked by management in many Minnesota towns, were scheduled to play a baseball game in St. Cloud. "The game will be an innovation in Balldom, inasmuch as it will be played by electric lights, fifty arc lights being necessary. . . . Frank James a brother of Jesse James is a feature and will umpire the game." Afterward the local newspaper said that "Gasoline lamps were hung about three sides of the diamond and the play was horseplay and nothing else."[33]

On June 15, St. Cloud played Anoka, and Walter was in top form as he struck out 17 batters and allowed only two hits. By June 26, he had been with the St. Cloud team for six weeks and had a record of 8 wins against two losses.

A highlight of Ball's season came when he pitched against the Grand Forks team of the Northern League. The contest provided him with a chance to show that he belonged in their league. As the game was an exhibition, it was acceptable for a semipro team with a black pitcher to compete against a professional one. "The St. Cloud team will play the Grand Forks league team at Cass Lake on Sunday, 6–29, the day following the close of the Northern Minnesota Fireman's tournament at Cass Lake."[34]

St. Cloud's team was undergoing a management shift at this time. According to a newspaper article, "A meeting of the Baseball Association bondholders has been called . . . the management of the team has not been satisfactory." By the end of the meeting, a reporter stated that "the ball fund now amounts to almost $260 and the salaries are all paid to June 16. With some good games it is hoped to increase the fund." The Little Falls newspaper speculated, "It was rumored that Ball, the phenomenal pitcher had been released on account of demand for increase in salary, this however is not true."[35]

The Great Northern Railroad ran an excursion train from St. Cloud to Cass Lake for the big game, and the City Band enlivened the trip with music. The teams were to play for a purse of $100. The headlines in St. Cloud afterward told the sad story: "Was a case of Larceny" and "A Victim of Pickpockets." St. Cloud lost the 10-inning game by a score of 5 to 4. Ball struck out 10 batters, and it was agreed that he "pitched a magnificent game." The Grand Forks newspapers were even more gracious, stating, "Ball, the colored pitcher for the Saints and an old favorite with Grand Forks fans, was heartbroken over the defeat and wanted another game for $200 a side. Manager Callahan [of Grand Forks] assured him that it was like stealing money from his grandmother."[36]

On July 2, St. Cloud defeated Royalton, a small town north of St. Cloud, even though Royalton had loaded their team with outside players. Ball played centerfield, and his "fielding was a feature of the game. He made a dash for a high fly, covering a long distance and got the ball on the dead run." On the Fourth of July, St. Cloud played at Brainerd where Ball pitched 13 innings on this traditional ball-playing day, earning a solid 4–2 victory. It was a "hot day" that "warmed him up so that he pitched one of the best games." It seemed that "thirteen innings were only an exercise for him."[37]

But trouble came for Ball just two days later when the Saints lost a double-header to the Twin Cities champions, The Gannymedes. The local newspapers sharply criticized Ball for his pitching, saying, "it was the general opinion if he had done his usual good job it would have been a shut out." In the second game, a 13-inning 3–2 loss, the paper blasted the whole team for playing "like a lot of dope fiends who had run out of the drug the day before." Ball was a target of abuse because he "dropped a fly" in centerfield. It appeared that "some changes" were due to improve the team's play. Team manager J. B. Pattison fined Ball five dollars because he had "muffed an easy fly and loafed while going after the ball." Ball was "at first inclined to object to the fine" but decided pay it and "stick with the team and play the good article of ball he had been playing up to a few days ago."[38] While the St. Cloud newspapers noted that all the players had played poorly in the doubleheader, Ball was the only one singled out by name and the only one who had to pay a fine for poor play. In the next scheduled game, against the strong Waseca team, Ball was not in the lineup for the first time since being hired by St. Cloud.

The Waseca EACO Flour team had been one of the best in Minnesota in 1900 and 1901 due to the one-two pitching duo of George Wilson and Billy

Holland, veteran pitchers who had played for the greatest Chicago-area black teams of the late 1890s. Waseca had also hired Robert Footes, a veteran black catcher from Chicago, to handle these ace pitchers. Wilson had started his baseball career in 1895 with the Adrian, Michigan, team of the professional Michigan State League. He compiled a fantastic 29–3 record that year while also batting .327. One of Wilson's teammates while he was with Adrian was Honus Wagner, the future Hall of Fame shortstop who went on to a brilliant career with the Pittsburgh Pirates. In 1896 as the color line slowly closed professional baseball to black players, Wilson was forced off the Adrian team, and he began pitching for the famous barnstorming black team, the Page Fence Giants.

In *A Game for All Races,* Henry Metcalfe says, "The Page Fence Giants were a team without a home, but they had a sponsor whose name—The Page

The Waseca EACO Flour team in 1900, with George Wilson (seated, front row, right) and Robert Footes (standing, left)

Wire Fence Company of Adrian Michigan—was emblazoned on the side of the opulent sixty-foot railroad coach where the players lived during their never ending road trip. When the team arrived in a town for a game, the players disembarked with bicycles (donated by their other sponsor, the Monarch Bicycle Company) on which they went door-to-door selling tickets to the day's game before reconvening on the main street for a pre-game parade. The Giants also hammed it up on the field to the delight of the crowd."[39]

The Page Wire Fence team ended up with deep financial difficulties and folded in 1899, forcing George Wilson to find another ball club, and he joined the newly formed Chicago Columbia Giants. Two of Wilson's opponents while he was with the Columbia Giants became his Waseca teammates in 1902—Robert Footes and Billy Holland. These three veteran players left Chicago for Waseca and led the team to the mythical Minnesota State Championship in 1901 when they defeated Litchfield at Lexington Ball Park in St. Paul before a large crowd.

Billy Holland was called "one of the top pitchers of the era" who "played with many of the best black teams . . . including the famed Page Fence Giants" and the Algona, Iowa, Brownies. Holland's career in black baseball ran from 1894 to 1908. After his playing days, he became an umpire in the Negro League during the 1920s. Robert Footes, the catcher, had a career that "bridged two centuries, playing with teams in both the East and the West for fifteen years. He began his career in 1895 as the regular catcher with the Chicago Unions."[40]

St. Cloud desperately wanted a victory against Waseca. "Interest in the two games" was high, and a large crowd came to the contest. In the first game, with Wilson pitching, Waseca took a 7–0 victory. But in the second game, Ball turned the tables, pitching an 8–5 victory over the "Champion of three states." A local writer believed that Ball had "redeemed himself handsomely" with his winning effort. He had also handled his bat well. According to a news report, "Wilson, Waseca's star twirler, told a St. Cloud man Monday on the train that Ball's three bagger in the Sunday game was the best hit that had been made off him for years. He is not used to allowing that kind of a blow at the ball."[41]

Shortly after the Waseca games, the manager of the team in Watkins, located thirty miles south of St. Cloud, tried to arrange a match with the Saints, but only if Walter Ball did not participate because the Watkins management was "understood to draw the color line in deference to local sentiment."[42] The race issue that was always close to the surface bubbled over in this case. St. Cloud had just defeated a Waseca team that included two black pitchers and a black catcher and did not schedule a game with the Watkins team with those preconditions in place. The newspaper left unsaid whether the games were not played because of principle or simply because no suitable date could be found.

At the same time that Watkins was making their offer, manager Pattison received a letter from the all-black Algona Brownies looking for games with St. Cloud. Unfortunately the teams were unable to agree on a date. The Algona Brownies were one of the best black teams outside of Chicago or New York in 1902 and 1903. Several players from the Chicago Union Giants had gone to Algona, including Billy Holland and George ("Rat" or "Chappie") Johnson.[43] In 1902, Algona played a number of games with the Waseca EACO Flour team, splitting the games evenly. Algona wanted to play St. Cloud, particularly after St. Cloud defeated George Wilson's Waseca team, to show that they were the best team in the three-state area, and, probably more important, they anticipated a good gate.

St. Cloud's players had several days off each week when there were no games scheduled. On July 14 a reporter stated that "Members of the . . . team were driven to Meadow Lawn Stock farm where they spent the afternoon inspecting the Clydesdale horses." But it was not all relaxation on their days off as it was noted on July 16 that "The ballplayers are at work at the park improving the diamond. No. 2 shovels look well in the hands of the tarriers." At times, St. Cloud's ballplayers were loaned out to other towns when there were open dates on the schedule. Such was the case when Walter Ball played for Royalton in a game against Long Prairie on August 15.[44]

Ball and his team played a game against Stillwater on July 27. Stillwater was the town where Bud Fowler, the pioneer black ballplayer, pitched in 1884. With Ball throwing a fine game, St. Cloud beat Stillwater in a 3–1 decision. He struck out 14 batters and allowed only two hits. After the game, according to one story, "a number of baseball enthusiasts raised quite a sum of money today and presented it to the members . . . as an appreciation of good work done on the diamond. . . . Sunday's game made a number of fans mighty glad, financially and otherwise."[45]

By late July the team had financial troubles. To save money, the management moved the players from hotel rooms and found lodging for them in private homes.[46] Most amateur and semiprofessional teams faced chronic problems with funding in the early 1900s, as do such teams in modern times.

By the middle of August, Walter Ball had been quite successful as St. Cloud's main pitcher, winning 14 games and losing just 5. He had pitched often and he had pitched well, allowing two or fewer hits in a game four separate times. Additionally he had struck out 10 or more batters in a game 10 times. Within a four-day span from August 17 to August 21, Ball pitched two terrific games but lost by a 1–0 score each time. He then turned around and pitched three games from August 24 to August 30, winning all three.

By season's end, St. Cloud's record was 29 wins against 12 losses. Walter Ball's personal record was 17 victories and 7 defeats. In these 24 games, he had pitched 207 innings, striking out 217 batters. Playing in all but two games during the season, Walter batted .307, with 18 doubles, five triples, and one home run. He could look back at the 1902 season as a success for him personally, professionally, and financially. In St. Cloud he appeared to have found a home where he could play baseball for more than one season without the color-line issue being raised.

But no sooner had the season ended on September 2 than local newspapers began speculating on the potential involvement of a St. Cloud franchise in the new professional leagues that were being formed in the region. Newspapers reported that "Plans will probably soon be announced for the organization of the International baseball league" and "the Northern baseball league . . . [will] if possible add Brainerd and St. Cloud."[47]

With a family to support, Walter Ball could not just wait for the next baseball season. He needed income immediately after the last game had been played. On September 8, he rented a building and opened a "Turkish Bath room and gymnasium." The bath was "fully equipped with all the modern appliances," and local citizens were said to have assured him of their "generous support for the undertaking." The new enterprise supposedly boasted the "best tub baths in the city" and could be used for a fee of twenty-five cents.[48]

Walter also actively recruited ballplayers in St. Cloud for the 1903 season. A reporter stated, "Wilson may come." In the midst of speculation that Wilson would "probably be at Waseca or Duluth next season," Ball worked "to secure Wilson for the St. Cloud staff of pitchers," because Wilson was a "world beater." Wilson might even become a partner in the Turkish bath parlors.[49]

Walter Ball and his family seemed to be comfortably settled at St. Cloud, but in early December 1902, he sold his Turkish bath parlors. Although his family was still making St. Cloud their home, he obtained "a position in the commissary department of the Great Northern."[50]

In early February 1903, St. Cloud baseball enthusiasts met on a regular basis to determine the type of team they wanted to have in the new season. Professional baseball was attractive to the town for the prestige it imparted because it had the highest status of all the levels of baseball that could be played in the region. But continuing in semiprofessional baseball was still a strong possibility because it did not require the same financial commitment that professional baseball needed. St. Cloud baseball fans contacted local businesses to see what amount of money was available, and by March 1903, $500 was in hand, and they hoped to raise $800 before the season started. This was considerably short of the money needed to start a professional baseball team, however.

Walter Ball moved back to Grand Forks in January 1903 and started making inquiries about baseball jobs for the new season. He also wrote a letter to St. Cloud to his old manager, J. B. Pattison, asking "for a place with the local baseball team as a pitcher." No doubt Ball was dismayed when he learned that the team had "decided that the 'color line' will be drawn this year in the make up of the team and it is not likely that Mr. Ball will be given the position."[51]

With professional baseball dangling as a possibility for St. Cloud, it appears the team was hedging their bets in not giving him his pitching job back. The use of the term "color line" in their rejection of him was a real slap in the face and indicated that his status of star pitcher did not protect him from the racism that simmered within the St. Cloud community. In the meantime, Ball, who was again engaged in work as a sleeping car porter for the Great Northern, took time to contact other teams and had hopes that he might be employed by the team in Stillwater.[52]

Meanwhile, George Wilson and Billy Holland had hired on with the Duluth Fashions. This club later combined with another one in Duluth and joined the professional Northern League. A writer put it bluntly about Duluth using George Wilson for the 1903 season: "Van Pragh has signed Wilson, the colored pitcher, and under the rules of the league he will not be allowed to play. . . . A year ago the color line was drawn and a rule to that effect incorporated in the by laws. From practically every town there is objection to the playing of colored men. . . . Wilson is one of the best pitchers that ever visited the northwest or any other country for that matter."[53]

So Ball, Wilson, and Holland were all out of a job due to the drawing of the color line. Wilson took the initiative at this time to write to manager Pattison asking to "pitch in St. Cloud for $100 a month."[54] The irony of this request was delicious, as St. Cloud had just dropped Walter Ball from their team because of his color.

A Grand Forks newspaper reported that "Walter Ball is negotiating with the Chicago Unions and may decide to go to the windy city for the season. The team is one of the heaviest outside the [professional baseball] league, and out of nearly 120 games played last year, but 13 were lost."[55] This was the first time that there was a mention of Walter Ball moving out of Minnesota and going to Chicago to play baseball.

Frank Leland in his 1910 booklet on Chicago baseball history stated that "he wrote to Walter Ball and succeeded in signing him in 1903 on the Chicago Union Giants, which was the first colored team he had ever played on." Just as he was making the decision to move, Walter Ball and his wife received a crushing blow. In late April "the 2 ½ year old child of Walter Ball and wife died as a result of an attack of convulsions. It was their only child and the blow is a hard one for the bereaved parents who have the sympathy of many friends in the city. . . . The funeral will be held from the home at 2:30 Friday afternoon. Mr. Ball is employed on the Great Northern as a sleeping car porter."[56]

With the death of his son on his mind, along with the decision to move to Chicago, Walter played just one game after the funeral. He pitched for the York, North Dakota, team before he left Grand Forks. In that game, a reporter stated that "Ball in the box . . . made an excellent showing . . . allowing but three hits." In the middle of May a local writer reported that Ball left for Chicago to play "with the Chicago Unions. Ball is a pitcher whose equal is not found every day, in or out of league circles." He passed through St. Cloud on his way south and "said to a St. Cloud man that he would give all he possessed if he could be with the city team this year."[57]

Walter Ball had come to a crossroads in his baseball career. Year after year he had been successful pitching for semiprofessional teams in Minnesota and North Dakota, but each time he had been released at the end of the season because the imposition of the color line had barred him from his team. He now headed to a city where he had never played and to work for a team he had never seen. The only thing that he knew was that he would not have to worry about being released due to his skin color; on a black team, only his talent on the ball field would determine his fate.

Meanwhile, George Wilson signed a contract with St. Cloud when the team did not join the Northern League. News reports were positive about Wilson, just as with Ball the year before, stating, "were it not for his color, he would be in one of the big leagues." His contract reputedly called "for a nice fat salary." In the 1903 season, Wilson put up fantastic numbers for St. Cloud, winning 21 games against three losses and one tie. He pitched 227 innings, struck out 251 batters, and ended with an ERA of 1.59.[58]

A high point of the 1903 season for Wilson and the St. Cloud team was a month-long traveling series of sixteen games against a team from Glencoe. The teams toured together all over Minnesota and eastern North Dakota, playing one another. One of the players on this Glencoe team was a black pitcher named Robert "Doggie" Woods, who had been with the Algona Brownies in 1902.[59]

Walter Ball arrived in Chicago, and it did not take long for him to establish himself as a first-rate pitcher. He had an excellent summer in 1903 for the Chicago Union Giants, and many of the top black teams soon were bidding for his services. After the season ended in Chicago, he was recruited by the Algona Brownies, becoming one of a number of Chicago ballplayers who finished the 1903 season with the Iowa team.[60]

In 1904 the manager of the famous New York Cuban X Giants recruited Walter Ball, and he left Chicago. He pitched for the X Giants when they defeated the Brooklyn Dodgers on June 6 in Atlantic City, marking the first time a black team ever won over a white major league ball club. After a successful season with the X Giants, he started 1905 with the Brooklyn Giants but left midway to finish the second half with the Chicago Union Giants. Ball was responsible for helping the team win 48 straight games. The New York Quaker Giants signed Walter in 1906, but this team folded by July 1, and he ended the season in Chicago with the Leland Giants.[61]

In 1907 Ball returned to Minnesota, where he helped to form and manage a black team in St. Paul. In May, he recruited players for the St. Paul Colored Gophers. The *Pioneer Press* welcomed him back to his hometown, reminding readers that Ball "learned to play ball in St. Paul and was well known in local circles six or seven years ago, when he pitched for the 'New Homes' and other local teams. Ball has played with colored organizations in all parts of the country, and he says that his present team will compare favorably with all of them." He was to be both a player and a manager.[62]

Walter pitched a game against the Calumet, Michigan, team on May 6, 1907, but lost a close 5–4 decision. Calumet was the 1906 winner of the Northern Copper Country league, the successor of the Northern League of 1902–05. The newspaper reporter stated that he "pitched gilt-edge ball but was not given the support that the Calumet pitchers got." By the end of May, Walter was enticed back to Chicago to play for Frank Leland's team. He was becoming a genuine star player with the black teams in Chicago and New York, and they actively recruited him. The highlight of the 1907 season with the Leland Giants occurred when "Ball made a phenomenal catch in right field that won the championship for the Lelands." This great catch occurred in the final game of a six-game series that the Lelands played against the All Stars at Chicago White Sox Park: "Over 22,000 persons witnessed the games, which were . . . the record for semi-pro ball."[63]

In 1908 Ball returned briefly to Minnesota when Kidd Mitchell, the black owner of the all-black Minneapolis Keystones, hired him to pitch for the ball club and help prepare the team to compete with the St. Paul Colored Gophers. But Frank Leland engineered Ball's release from his contract with the Keystones, and Ball again finished the season with the Chicago Leland Giants.[64] Ball's connection with Minnesota diminished with the years, except for the famous series of games that the Leland Giants played against the St. Paul Colored Gophers in 1909. The career he was carving out in black baseball was his main focus from 1909 until he finished his playing career in 1923.

Walter Ball at the age of twenty-nine was at the peak of his pitching prowess, and his career was in full bloom as he led the Chicago City League in pitching with a 12–1 record in 1909. The Leland Giants was the only black ball team that was admitted into the prestigious Chicago City League. One of the teams in this league was Anson's Colts, which was run by Adrian "Cap" Anson, the one person who has been personally blamed for blacks being excluded from professional baseball starting in the 1890s.[65]

At the end of the 1909 season, Walter pitched and played in a famous series of games the Lelands Giants had arranged with the Chicago Cubs of the National League. He pitched in the first game and lost a tough 4–1 decision as he was matched against the famous Hall of Fame pitcher Mordecai "Three Finger" Brown. In the last two games of the series, Ball played in right field. Bill James in *The Historical Baseball Abstract* rated Walter Ball as the best black baseball pitcher in all of black baseball for the 1907, 1908, and 1909 seasons. Alex Irwin, a contemporary black player, evaluated Ball's overall play, saying that he was an "A-1 batter, good thrower, lightning on foot and very heady."[66]

In 1910 and 1911 Ball pitched for the Chicago Giants as one of the top hurlers in the league. At this same time, he was one of the pioneer black ballplayers to play winter baseball in Cuba. He spent the seasons of 1908, 1909, and 1911 in Cuba and was called a "great pitcher . . . a famous pitcher from the Negro leagues." In 1912, according to author James A. Riley, Ball "pitched with the St. Louis Giants, where he won 23 straight games against all levels of opposition." John McGraw, the crusty manager of the New York Giants, said in 1912 that "it was too bad that Walter Ball was colored" or he would have been able to pitch in the major leagues.[67]

By 1913 Ball was splitting his time between the Brooklyn Royal Giants and the Schenectady Mohawk Giants. He pitched "against the white Trenton, N.J., club. . . . [and] won that game 2–0 after striking out 15 batters and the game was over in 53 minutes—a record for that day." The following year he played for the New York Lincoln Giants and the Lincoln Stars of New York. This was the last time that he left the Chicago area to play for a baseball team.[68]

Rube Foster was able to get Ball back on his Chicago American Giants team in 1915. They played a West Coast series of games that started in California, went to Seattle, and ended on the Canadian border. After 1916 he continued his association with the Chicago Giants, which was not considered one of the top teams in the league. By 1920 Walter was playing again with a number of former teammates, starting as far back as 1908— Charles (Joe) Green, John Beckwith, Frank Wickware, Clarence (Bobby) Winston, and his old St. Paul Gopher teammate from 1909 Johnny "Steel Arm" Taylor, to mention just a few. In 1920 Rube Foster succeeded in organizing the first Negro major league, one of the most important events in black baseball history. Ball was near the end of his career as a pitcher, and the last statistic for him that has been found is a 0–3 league record in 1921. Some sources indicate that he continued to pitch through the 1923 season.[69]

Publicity photo of Walter Ball in a Minneapolis Keystones uniform with a north-woods studio backdrop, 1908

Walter Ball's career did not end when he stopped league pitching. He remained active in running baseball teams as late as 1930. During this year a reporter for the *St. Cloud Daily Times*, noting a visit by Walter to St. Cloud, stated, "Walter Ball, a pitcher for the St. Cloud Baseball team . . . was in the city yesterday, renewing old acquaintances. . . . Ball has not been in St. Cloud for many years but yesterday walked into the Thielman Hardware store and asked, 'is the paymaster here?' Mr. Thielman immediately recognized Ball as the former chucker who was rated as high as any in the northwest 25 years ago. At present he has a ball club traveling through Canada."[70]

The year 1937 saw Walter Ball still in uniform and active as a member of the Negro East-West game, the most important black ballgame of the year. This game regularly sold out Comiskey Park in Chicago in the 1930s and 1940s, sometimes rivaling the white Major League All-Star game in attendance.

Walter was a coach on this midseason all-star team, which included Bingo DeMoss, Willie Foster, Turkey Stearnes, Willard Brown, Double Duty Radcliffe, Bullet Rogan, and Hilton Smith.[71]

Walter Ball died December 15, 1946, in Chicago, and the *Chicago Defender* sportswriter Faye Young wrote an extensive obituary. Ball was buried in Lincoln Cemetery in south Chicago. His death in 1946, after enduring countless instances of racial discrimination in his career and the juxtaposition of Jackie Robinson's signing of a professional contract to break the color line in 1946, closed one chapter in baseball history and opened another for black ballplayers.

Trying to define Walter Ball's place in Minnesota black baseball history with the sparse amount of information available is not possible. We know that he was one of the best of the pioneer black ballplayers who bridged the early years of the twentieth century until the start of organized black baseball in 1920. We know also that he was, starting in 1908, one of the earliest ballplayers who played winter Cuban baseball. Sol White, one of the first and best of the nineteenth-century black ballplayers and a recognized expert on early black baseball, called Walter Ball a "great pitcher" and stated that "in naming a few of the many colored players of Major League caliber . . . there are many colored pitchers who would no doubt land in the big league. McClellan, . . . Holland, . . . Ball." James A. Riley in his *Biographical Encyclopedia* wrote, "At the end of the first decade of the [twentieth] century, he [Ball] . . . was considered 'head and shoulders' above other moundsmen."[72]

Walter Ball played a total of twenty-four years against great white and black players and teams. He was a member of teams in New York, Florida, California, Washington, Cuba, and most of the United States between the two coasts. He endured discrimination due to his race on numerous occasions, but this prejudice did not defeat him. Unlike others who were noted for their rowdy reputations, he was an exemplary ballplayer and role model wherever he played or coached. Walter Ball toiled in the shadows of the more publicized white teams with patience and a quiet dignity that is hard to imagine today. His career, after a century has passed, has been forgotten in Minnesota, his home state and the state where he began his career.

Rube Foster, known as the "father of the Negro Leagues," has a burial site in Lincoln Cemetery with a large granite tombstone to mark his grave and has earned a place in the Baseball Hall of Fame. Walter Ball, a ballplayer who played in the shadows of baseball all his life, is buried near Foster. But Ball has no place in Baseball's Hall of Fame, and no monument or marker remains to show where he is buried, only an open grassy area that lies in the shade cast by other monuments.

Opposing the Color Line in Minnesota, 1899

When southern states adopted Jim Crow laws in the 1890s, Minnesota's African American leaders worked hard to prevent the passage of similar laws that would segregate the races within the state. In 1899, Governor John Lind signed an act that prohibited the "drawing of the 'color' line in any public place of entertainment or business." Known as the Minnesota civil rights law, the act banned the exclusion of persons "from full and equal enjoyment of any accommodation, advantage, or privilege furnished by public conveyances, theaters, or other places of amusement, or by hotels, barber shops, saloons, restaurants, or other places of refreshment, entertainment, or accommodation . . . [on] account of race or color." The state thus joined Wisconsin and other northern states in opposing the color line.[1]

An editorial in a local black newspaper, the *Afro-American Advance*, in 1899 stated that Minneapolis, and by implication Minnesota, was perhaps a bit better place for African Americans than were other locations: "There is not another city in the Union where the white people are so friendly disposed toward Afro-Americans who manifest the least anxiety to make something of themselves, as in the City of Minneapolis." If a black person was "honest, upright, businesslike and true," he would be judged "from a standpoint of merit." In St. Paul in 1901, "a larger percentage" of the city's black population owned homes "than in any other city in the country."[2]

Archbishop John Ireland of the St. Paul Roman Catholic archdiocese spoke often about racial matters in Minnesota. As far back as 1891 he protested the actions of southern states in discriminating against African Americans when he stated, "I would say let all people in America be equal socially and politically." He contended that "color [was] the merest accident." He asked, "Why select one color and place a bar upon it?" All the Jim Crow laws were "baseless prejudice." He felt "proud to call all men my brothers," proud that he was "able to rise above prejudice." Ireland requested that Minnesotans "give them their opportunity" in society and "admit the blacks on the same principle that you admit the white brother."[3]

Private businesses in Minnesota, including hotels and restaurants, sometimes did discriminate against individuals, depending upon the morality and character of a business proprietor or landlord. Baseball, as a form of public entertainment, could not prohibit African Americans from buying tickets to games. However, baseball leagues were considered to be private enterprises, and leagues set up ground rules that usually banned African Americans from teams, as was the case for Walter Ball in St. Cloud and in Grand Forks.

African American men, in general, had to have "black wisdom" in order to identify quickly places of business that would accept them as customers on equal terms with whites. It might not be hard to tell if a business owner was hostile toward a black customer. Sometimes waitresses at a restaurant refused to wait on black customers, as occurred in 1901 in Minneapolis (the white restaurateur was fined twenty-five dollars).[4] A hotel clerk might turn away black lodgers, saying that no rooms were available, when the hotel barely had any guests at all.

A small incident in a saloon in East Grand Forks spoke volumes about the problems of being black in Minnesota in 1899. James Godetts, a tall and powerful man, trained as a professional boxer and known for his "neat dress and good manners," had moved to Bemidji in the late 1890s after eloping with a white woman from a wealthy family in Michigan. Godetts was in town on business and somehow got into a saloon altercation, whether with a bartender or a white customer is unclear, and attempted to protect his person by brandishing a knife, his great equalizer. A police officer quickly arrived on the scene and arrested Godetts as the troublemaker. Godetts ended up being found guilty of the offense of "resisting an officer," and his penalty was to pay a one hundred dollar fine or serve a ninety-day jail sentence. Godetts hired attorney Charles Scrutchin, Bemidji's African American lawyer, to submit an

The St. Paul Colored Gophers, late in the 1907 season: bottom row, left to right, Sherman "Bucky" Barton, cf, Willis Jones, lf, Clarence "Dude" Lytle, rf and p, Phil "Daddy" Reid, president and manager, Frank "Bunch" Davis (?), ss, Jesse Sheffer (or Schaeffer) (?), c, Thomas Means, p; top row, Sammie Ransome, 2b, Johnny Davis, p, George Taylor, 1b and captain, Fred Roberts, 3b

appeal, and with Scrutchin's help was cleared of the charge. Scrutchin proved that the case did not have "facts sufficient to constitute a public offence."[5]

There had been racial trouble in East Grand Forks and in Grand Forks, just across the Red River, in 1882. The only case of an African American man being lynched in North Dakota occurred in that year when a man by the name of Charles Thurber, employed as a blacksmith's assistant, was hanged by a rope suspended from the bridge connecting the two cities. Thurber had been accused of sexual assault against Minnie Taska, a young woman who probably had a consensual relationship with Thurber. Thurber contended that "she had frequently permitted his caresses." The reality of the case may have been only that Thurber had "made indecent proposals" to another woman, the wife of a railway conductor. A lynch mob, including a number from the Minnesota side of the river, tore Thurber out of the Grand Forks jail "after a desperate fight" and lynched him. The local newspaper deplored the mob action, reporting that the sight was "sickening and disgusting" and that the mob "passed around the bottle" after the horrible deed had been done.[6]

Was Minnesota a better place for African Americans than were other states? The Red River lynching would be remembered as a shameful blot upon the history of East Grand Forks, but the incident was not well known throughout the region. Still there were occasional incidents later in Minnesota's history when violence lurked beneath the surface calm of racial harmony and accepted roles. Restraint by both blacks and whites was the usual theme, and on Minnesota's baseball fields, peaceful coexistence predominated. All was not equality on the ball diamond, as pitcher Walter Ball knew firsthand. There were a few close calls, with angry confrontations, but no violence in the next decade in Minnesota.

Bobby Marshall, the Legendary First Baseman

Steven R. Hoffbeck

He was a tall man, often standing head and shoulders above his teammates, white or black. He had a longish face with narrowed eyes. His figure was rangy and strong, like a pillar upholding his team. Bobby Marshall was distinctive in looks and in character. As one of the few college-educated black baseball players, he was a man of great presence who was qualified to bear the title of "attorney" but who turned his back on the profession, preferring to wear the label of "professional ball player." He played for so many seasons that he became the patriarch of black baseball in Minnesota, beloved by his brethren of the diamond and respected by white players and fans alike.

There was a time when just about everyone in the Upper Midwest knew the name and the fame of Bobby Marshall. He was, simply put, the greatest athlete who ever grew up in Minneapolis. Minnesota baseball fans applauded him as the "star slugger" of the St. Paul Colored Gophers. One sportswriter rated Marshall as "the best playing colored first baseman" of his era. Another writer knew him as a clutch hitter "renowned for his long bingles at opportune moments."[1] He was versatile—playing first base and in the outfield and pitching when needed.

Marshall's professional baseball career began at the time when Minneapolis and St. Paul founded its first truly professional black teams, modeled on those of Chicago. It was the era when black community leaders responded to the color line in baseball by creating teams that might beat the white ballclubs if they could meet on a level playing field.

Bobby Marshall's paternal grandfather and great-grandfather had been slaves in Richmond, Virginia. His father, Richard Marshall, eventually moved north to Wisconsin. There he met and wed Symanthia Gillespie in the late 1870s. She was the daughter of Ezekiel Gillespie, a railroad porter. Mr. Gillespie was a former slave reputed to have assisted the Underground Railway in the 1850s and who became a civil rights pioneer in Wisconsin when he tried to vote in 1865, was rejected, but had his right to vote upheld by the state supreme court in 1866. Ezekial and his wife, Catherine, a mulatto with German-Jewish heritage, helped found the first African Methodist Episcopal Church in Milwaukee.

The Gillespie relatives had been leaders in the black community in Wisconsin. Richard and Symanthia Marshall's first child, Robert Wells Marshall, was born on March 12, 1880. Within two years, Richard Marshall moved his family to Minneapolis, where he worked in a lunchroom.[2]

Bobby Marshall grew up in Minneapolis on East Eighteenth Street, on a block where there were several other black families and a Swedish family, the Gundersons. As a child, he learned to play football just two blocks away on East Sixteenth Street with a neighbor boy named Sig (short for Sigmund) Harris. Harris was the son of Marks Harris, a partner in Harris Brothers, junk dealers, and Harris Machinery Company. This African American kid and this Jewish boy and the other neighborhood lads "grew up together, played, camped and fought" their way through the grades at "ancient" Madison Grammar School. They honed their skills at baseball in their "Sand Lot days at Park Avenue and Franklin." They learned boxing, holding their own tournaments in an old barn on Sixteenth Street. Harris and Marshall, along with Roger Gray, organized the Madison grade school football and baseball teams.[3]

Marshall and the neighborhood kids went on to excel in sports at Minneapolis Central High School. In their four years on varsity, with Sig Harris at quarterback and Bobby Marshall at end, the football team suffered only one loss and won the state championship for three years in succession. Marshall was a wonderful athlete. In his prime, Bobby Marshall stood six feet, one inch tall and weighed 180 pounds. His long arms could hold off blockers in football and nab high throws to his first-base position. Marshall was an all-around athlete, as a contemporary noted, "He could play all sports, and play them well." He played football, baseball, tennis, and hockey as mainstays and indulged in track, basketball, wrestling, boxing, and bicycling. High schools held regular bicycling meets at Inter City Field Days, and Bobby was said to be "some punkins as a bike racer."[4]

Yet even as he won adulation, Marshall had to face the realities of life for African Americans at the dawn of the twentieth century. His father had worked his way up to being a janitor by 1900. His mother, Symanthia, passed away on February 19, 1900, at the age of forty-nine. Described as a "devoted Christian" and an "earnest church worker" at St. Peter's A.M.E. Church, she was "one of the leading race women" in Minneapolis, "taking part in every motion to help the interests of the people." Her family and a "host of friends" mourned her loss. At age twenty, Bobby helped hold the family together, working as a janitor, like his father, to help support siblings Sarah, Alice, and Lewis.[5]

Bobby Marshall graduated from high school in 1901 and followed Sig Harris to the University of Minnesota in 1903, taking up the study of law and joining the football team. The young man continued playing all the time he studied in law from 1903 through the spring of 1907. Marshall was known as an "outstanding student" as well as an "outstanding athlete," being named an All-American end. In 1904 the Gophers were the disputed Champions of the West. He made front-page headlines (in 1906) in the *Minneapolis Tribune* after he kicked the winning 48-yard field goal against the University of Chicago: "Bob Marshall Saves Day By Place-Kicking Goal." Marshall also led the blocking for the tying touchdown against Michigan in the game that gave Minnesota the Big Ten title and started the Little Brown Jug rivalry in 1903. He was the first baseman on the championship baseball team at the U of M in 1907.[6]

So it was that Bobby Marshall established himself as one of Minnesota's heroes. The talented Marshall fit well into the University of Minnesota partly because he was so fair-skinned that he could get by in white society.[7] People all across the state knew him as a Gopher football star, a black man on a team that featured a Jewish quarterback (Harris), Swedish or German linemen, and a Native American captain (Ed Rogers), and as an athlete who earned "7 M's"—seven letters (baseball in 1906, 1907; football in 1903, 1904, 1905, 1906; and track in 1907). He was also the first black professional hockey player in the United States, playing with a Minneapolis team from 1905 to 1910.

When Marshall completed his studies at the University of Minnesota in 1907, he came to a major crossroads in his life. Although he had chosen the legal profession as a career, other opportunities beckoned. At a testimonial dinner for Marshall after his last season as a college football player, all of the leading lights of the Twin Cities black community were present, including all the lawyers. Attorney Fredrick L. McGhee, a founder of the Niagara Movement and the NAACP, had spoken on the topic "What Next?" for Marshall's future. Attorney William R. Morris talked about "Afro-American Athletes." The problem for Marshall was that there was only enough business available for three or four African American lawyers in Minnesota. There were a limited number of African American clients to serve—and whites mostly preferred going to a white attorney. Marshall eventually came to understand that the law profession was "not a lucrative thing" for a black man nor a good way "to support the family." Nevertheless, he was listed as a lawyer in the 1908 Minneapolis city directory with an office in the city's Metropolitan Life Building, starting as an assistant to another black attorney, William Franklin, his law classmate.[8]

The University of Minnesota baseball team of 1907; Bobby Marshall is in the back row, second from the left.

Sports, on the other hand, offered several options to the well-known university athlete. His "unconquerable love for athletics" led him to divide his time between the law office and the athletic field. Beginning in 1907, he played baseball in summer, football in fall, and hockey in winter. He got his first taste of professional baseball, segregated as it was, that year, filling in for the regular catcher on a newly formed black team, the St. Paul Colored Gophers, for one game. It was a May day, just before he left on a road trip with the University of Minnesota baseball team to play Notre Dame, the University of Chicago, and other teams. In the contest versus the Austin-Westerns, a St. Paul semipro team, Marshall got a Texas leaguer to right field, scoring a run in a 3 to 1 Gophers' victory. Significantly, he came through in the clutch. The *Minneapolis Journal* sportswriter said Marshall's work at catcher "was a feature" of the game, but the *St. Paul Pioneer Press* writer opined that "Bobby's forte is evidently football," stating that he "catches fairly well but cannot throw or bat." In later seasons, Marshall would show him to be wrong.[9]

In 1908, Marshall joined the Minneapolis Keystones, a black team that challenged the St. Paul Colored Gophers for the top spot in Minnesota semiprofessional baseball. In his first full pro season, he began a friendship with one of the best players of the era—William Binga. Binga, an established veteran, was a third baseman and one of the best hitters on the team. Binga had played with the elite teams in black baseball, including the Page Fence Giants, the Columbia Giants of Chicago, and the champion Philadelphia Giants of 1906. A contemporary described his fielding ability as "instinctive"; he seemed to "know just where the batter is going to hit. He never forgets a batter, how and where he hits." Binga had often made "4 or 5 hits in a game," due to his ability to "place his hits."[10] Minnesota became Binga's baseball home for the next fifteen years.

In 1908, Bobby Marshall generally played in right field, but he filled in as catcher and first baseman when needed. He also pitched against lesser opponents. He pitched eleven games for the Keystones in 1908, winning ten of them. Marshall usually batted second or fifth in the lineup.[11]

That season had several highlights for the Keystones and for Marshall. While touring in Iowa, the Keystones met the Oelwein town team, strengthened by the addition of a "spit ball artist" pitcher from West Union, Joe Hovlick (who later pitched in the major leagues from 1909 to 1911). In what was said to be "the greatest game of base ball ever pulled off in Northern Iowa" and "one of the greatest semi-professional games ever played in Iowa," Hovlick struck out seventeen Keystones in seventeen innings. Even though the spitballer appeared to outduel Charles Jessup, allowing only four hits while Jessup gave up fourteen, the Keystones finally won, 5 to 3. Hovlick's spitter betrayed him. Two runs scored on each of two occasions when a spitball made its dive, hit the front of the plate, and bounced high over the grandstand. Marshall scored from second base on the first wild pitch in the third inning, and in the fourth, Alex Irwin singled, stole second, and scored when the wild pitch landed behind the grandstand on North Frederick Street. The local editor asked, "Did anyone ever hear of such a happening in base ball?" The spitball's high bounces became legendary, and the games were "great for the fans." The local newspaperman stated that Bobby Marshall was a "hit with the fans as he showed himself to be a great athlete."[12]

In 1909, Marshall joined the lineup of the St. Paul Colored Gophers, a team that proved to be the greatest black team in the history of Minnesota. The Gophers' management raided the roster of the Minneapolis team, signing Marshall in their major publicity coup. The Gophers also stole William Binga, the best player the Keystones had.

But it was Marshall who became the most popular Gopher because he was a Minnesotan and because he always seemed to propel his team to victories on the ball diamond. In a big game or a vital series, Marshall would find

The St. Paul Colored Gophers at Hibbing's hardscrabble Iron Range ballfield on May, 22, 1909: front row, left to right, Sherman "Bucky" Barton, Arthur McDougal, unknown, William McMurray (?), unknown; back row, unknown, unknown, George "Rat" Johnson, Phil "Daddy" Reid, Felix Wallace (?), William Binga, Bobby Marshall. The Gophers won, 17 to 2.

a way to win. He was a tremendous first baseman, noted for his long "reach, fielding ability, and fearlessness," for "nothing but a locomotive" could hurt him in a collision near the bag. He was "a big hit" all over the Upper Midwest because fans remembered his past glory as an All-American end on the University of Minnesota football team. He was greatly admired, too, for his "wonderful fielding stunts around first base." He was lauded by the local black press as "the Idol of the Gridiron, the Star of the Diamond, the Pet of the Lady Fans."[13]

That summer, Marshall helped the Gophers win the season series between the rival Twin Cities black ballclubs. In the first July matchup, the Gophers won 5 to 2, with Marshall slugging a home run and a triple (going two for five), while Binga got a couple of hits and stole two bases. In the second game, the Gophers again beat the Keystones, this time 8 to 4. The Gophers pounded out thirteen hits, with Binga going three for four and Marshall batting two for four with a double and a sacrifice fly.[14]

Much later, in a September rematch, the Gophers defeated the Keystones again, in an "easy game," 9 to 7.[15] These games, held in the Twin Cities stadiums, were vital to the financial success of the Colored Gophers and the Keystones because the travel expense was minimal. The large crowds that typically turned out from the black communities in both St. Paul and Minneapolis lent hopes that a black sports franchise could be a successful business.

Marshall got his introduction to big-time colored baseball in the summer of 1909 when the Colored Gophers played the Chicago Leland Giants, the premiere team of black baseball-dom. This was the great series of the season—the Gophers played a five-game matchup against the Leland Giants for "the championship of the country." The Chicago team had "a galaxy of stars" that could not "be found on any other colored club"—including future Hall of Fame pitcher Rube Foster, who was the manager. All of the games took place at Downtown Park in St. Paul, giving the Gophers a home-field advantage.[16]

The Colored Gophers needed every advantage they could get against the Leland Giants, which had "the greatest trio of Afro-American pitchers ever seen on one team" up to that time. The stars were Walter Ball, the Minnesotan, and William Gatewood, both of whom had previously pitched for the Colored Gophers, and Charles (Pat) Dougherty from the West Baden, Indiana, team. The Leland Giants were hyped in the local newspapers as "unquestionably the greatest team of Afro-Americans ever assembled" and "far-famed as the best in the land."[17]

The Gophers countered with "one of the strongest 'semi-pro' pitching staffs in the country" in pitchers Johnny Davis, Johnny "Steel Arm" Taylor, Robert "Buster" Garrison, and Julius London. Garrison had not lost a single game in May or June.[18]

The Gophers literally caught a break. Rube Foster suffered a broken leg on July 12 and was not available for mound duty. Despite all the talk about pitching, the first game was, oddly enough, a slugfest. The Gophers got twenty-two hits off the Giants' aces Gatewood and Ball. The Chicago team also hit well, stroking fourteen hits off Julius London and Johnny Taylor. The Gophers' James B. ("Candy" Jim) Taylor, playing at shortstop, went five for six at the

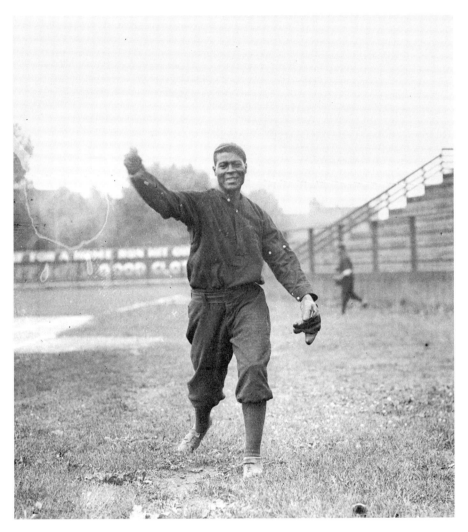

William Gatewood of the Leland Giants, throwing a baseball, 1909

plate. The game went into extra innings after the Giants tied the score at eight-all in the ninth. It looked bad for the Gophers when Chicago got a run in the top of the eleventh inning and even worse when Eugene Milliner grounded out to second to lead off the bottom of the eleventh. But William Binga singled, Rat Johnson doubled, and then Bobby Marshall came to the plate. The tall first baseman swung at the first pitch and sent the ball high into the air in center field. The ball soared over the wall, over the cigar sign, and into the lots across the street. Marshall got only one hit in the game, but it was a clutch hit off Walter Ball to win the game 10 to 9. The mammoth

The Colored Gophers borrowed Foster from the Leland Giants for a game against Hibbing in 1908; he pitched a no-hit, 5–0 gem.

home run, in the "dead ball" period, became another part of the stuff of the legend of Bobby Marshall. It was a great moment in Minnesota baseball.[19]

Attendance was good, with over a thousand, mostly black, fans but with "a goodly sprinkling of white ones." It was a nice crowd for a Monday ball game.[20]

Even more folks came to the Tuesday game, with about 1,500 showing up for the 3:30 P.M. start. Pat Dougherty, the Chicago left-hander, proved to be too much for the Gophers, striking out nine. Johnny Davis matched Dougherty through six innings of a scoreless game, but the Giants counted three runs in the seventh off two Gopher errors and then scored three in the eighth and two more in the ninth. The Gophers were "helpless," getting just four hits off the southpaw and escaped a shutout by scoring a single run in the last of the ninth.[21]

Things looked good for the Gophers in Wednesday's matchup, as Johnny "Steel Arm" Taylor got a one-run lead in the first inning and shut out the Leland Giants for eight innings. He mystified his opponents with his pitching motion, throwing his "arms and legs about in bewildering fashion," knotting up suddenly "like a porcupine," and then dangling and shaking his toe in the air, bringing the ball around his toe. Taylor struck out six before he tired in the "fateful" ninth inning, when the Leland Giants struck suddenly for five big runs, including a home run by George (Ed) Wright, the shortstop.[22]

It was a heartbreaking loss for the Gophers. They had the lead over Walter Ball of Chicago, who had worked eight innings before giving way to Dougherty and Gatewood. Even worse than the loss, the Gophers had to play without their catcher, Rat Johnson, after he suffered a sunstroke and "had to be carried from the field in the fifth inning." Eugene Milliner also hit the fence after making a great catch in left field in the fifth, colliding with the boards with such force that a "thud was heard in the grandstand." The eight hundred fans in attendance had to be stunned just as badly as Milliner by the sudden turnaround in the ninth, putting the Gophers down in the series, two games to one.[23]

The fourth game was a classic, and the Gophers jumped on Gatewood, Chicago's starting pitcher, for two runs in the first inning. Felix Wallace led off with a single, "Candy" Jim Taylor was out when he hit to the pitcher, but McMurray got a double to deep center, and then Milliner shook off his injury of the prior day and hit a drive to deep center field, legging it into a triple through "some of the speediest footwork ever seen on the diamond." The Gophers managed two more runs in the third without getting a hit; Wallace reached base on the third baseman's error, "Candy" Jim Taylor also reached on an error, and then both scored on a wild pitch by Gatewood. Julius London shut down the Chicagoans, scattering four hits. The Leland Giants came back, getting a run off London in the fourth on a walk, a single, and an error. Johnny Davis came on in relief in the seventh and gave up another run in the eighth on a hit, an error, and an outfield fly. Davis survived a scare in the ninth. Chicago's Talbert flied out, but Moore reached first on an error by Milliner on a fly to left. Wright also reached base on an error when "Candy" Jim "fumbled his grounder" to third. But Davis bore down, striking out Charles (Joe) Green and getting Gatewood to ground out to short. The Gophers were outhit, four hits to three, but got the key victory.[24]

The Colored Gophers' catcher George "Rat" Johnson posed with an admiring young fan in 1909.

The series finale brought Pat Dougherty to the mound for the Leland Giants against Johnny Taylor for the Gophers. It looked like doom for the Gophers, as Dougherty held them hitless through seven innings. Taylor was almost as good, giving up just one run in the third and another in the eighth. Trailing two to nothing, salvation came for the Gophers in the eighth as Eugene Milliner repeated his heroics of the previous day. Milliner hit a drive to deep center field and legged it out for a triple on a hit that would usually be just a double in Downtown Park. Binga followed with a single, Marshall flied out, but Johnny Davis came in as a pinch hitter and got a single. Johnny Taylor got the lead for himself by hitting a single, driving in two runs.[25]

With a 3–2 lead, Taylor faced the Leland Giants' last gasp in the top of the ninth. Chicago tried every trick known to ballplayers to get a run to tie the game. They had Gatewood come in as a pinch hitter, they "tried to bully-rag the umpire," but all in vain, for they could not get anything more off Taylor. Even though Dougherty had struck out seven Gophers, Taylor had outduelled him by giving up only two hits to the Leland Giants. The Gophers were honored as the Champions of Colored Baseball by taking the cliff-hanger series, three games to two. Had Rube Foster been physically able to pitch, the outcome likely would have been reversed.[26]

Marshall and his Colored Gopher teammates found glory that summer as Champions of Colored Baseball, but they also faced the realities of life on the road. The Gophers had a grueling schedule, traveling an estimated five thousand miles by railway. It was similar to the life of a traveling salesman, being away from home for long stretches of time. Owner Phil "Daddy" Reid contemplated the purchase of a special car but did not have enough money for such a thing. The longest tour was from June 14 to July 16, in which the team played thirty-eight games in thirty days. In this "strenuous trip" the Gophers won thirty, lost seven, and played to one tie. The team had another road trip from about August 1 to September 17 in which they journeyed through southern Minnesota, Iowa, and Wisconsin. The Gophers won twenty-eight of the thirty-two games played.[27]

The traveling team roster listed only twelve men—eight position players and four pitchers, which meant that the pitchers had to be able to fill in at other positions when needed. All of them had to be iron men to withstand the demands of travel to play over a hundred games in a season. Bobby Marshall was one of the iron men for the Gophers, as well as one of its feature attractions; as one newspaperman wrote, "The fame he attained in athletics at the Varsity makes him a big favorite in every town and hamlet the Gophers appear."[28]

These iron men also were expected to be gentlemen. Each man was to conduct himself in a manner acceptable to white baseball fans while also serving as a role model of racial pride among African Americans. Each player had to have a personality that could absorb a certain level of racial abuse from fans and from the opposing players. The team members had to use "black wisdom" to know how and when to hold one's tongue and to know how far they might be able to go to deter racial epithets and slurs. One of the catchers, William McMurray, was an expert at making "fine sport with the spectators" at games, always "keeping his temper" but "being ever ready with repartee."[29]

Bobby Marshall ascended to the heights of black baseball in 1909 and 1910. Rube Foster, who later founded the Negro Leagues, liked the first baseman's talent and competitiveness. When Foster asked Marshall and teammate Felix Wallace to join his Leland Giants roster in 1909, after the Colored Gophers' season had ended, Marshall went to Chicago in October. It was the best pay he ever received for playing baseball— fifty dollars per game (non-pitchers would typically get twenty dollars per game in 1909). He played well against several white city-league teams there.[30]

But Marshall got a rude awakening in Chicago. He participated in just the first game of a three-game, black-versus-white series against the Chicago Cubs. The Cubs, winners of one hundred games and runners-up in the National League that year, had already beaten the Chicago White Sox for the championship of the Windy City and had a strong lineup, featuring the double-play combination of Joe Tinker to Johnny Evers to Frank Chance. Marshall dropped the ball twice for two errors to give the Cubs a big inning, and the Cubs won that first game by a score of 4 to 1. He could not get a hit against the Cubs' Mordecai "Three Finger" Brown, a future Hall of Fame hurler. Marshall sat out the final two games. Had he not committed those two errors, he might have remained in the top echelon of that era's black baseball.[31]

"A base ball fan is an animal which is almost human in some respects. It runs wild between May and September and flocks together between 3 and 6 o'clock P.M. The rest of the year it lies dormant. This animal has lungs as powerful as a rhinoceros and has a wonderful, unfailing eyesight; which enables it to see better than an umpire. It is an omnivorous animal but lives principally on peanuts, pop, and tobacco."

Leeds [N.Dak.] *News,* 1907

Bobby then became a witness to the ruthlessness of the color line in baseball as game two of the series played out. The Cubs faced the masterful hurling of Rube Foster and were losing, 5 to 2, entering the ninth inning. Foster, who had just recovered from his broken leg, began to tire, and the Cubs tied the game at 5–5. With runners on first and third and two outs, Foster went to the dugout to get a relief pitcher. He asked the umpire for the official score, and the umpire objected to this delay. The Cubs also objected, and a group of Giants and Cubs gathered around the umpire in "conversation." At that time, the runner on third stole home, while Cubs players were on the field and in the way of a possible throw home. The umpire ruled that time had not been called and that the runner was safe at home. The Cubs left the field with a 6–5 victory. Foster protested vociferously, noting that Cubs were on the field and he was not on the mound. The umpire let the run stand. The Giants' fans wanted to attack the umpire, but two policemen gave him an escort from the field. The Cubs won the last game, 1–0. Burned by the thought that the Cubs had to cheat to defeat him, Foster wanted a rematch, but the accursed Cubs had too much to lose against him and nothing to gain by playing his team again.[32]

The Colored Gophers had been dubbed the Champions of Colored Baseball and had a marvelous won-lost record in 1909, but the challenge of barnstorming baseball weighed heavily on owner Phil Reid. By the time the 1910 season rolled around, Reid was in deep financial difficulty. He announced his intention not to reorganize the Colored Gophers in April, and his best players signed to play with teams elsewhere. Bobby Marshall, Felix Wallace, Rat Johnson, Jim Taylor, and Johnny Taylor were spirited away by Frank Leland to join the Chicago Giants—a rival to the Chicago Leland Giants now controlled by Rube Foster. Marshall was paid well for his time with the Chicago Giants, receiving a salary of forty dollars per week, plus expenses. A highlight of Marshall's time in Chicago came in two of three games against the Cuban Stars, both losses, when he played errorless defense but got no hits.[33]

Marshall went on the Chicago Giants' road trip in April and May, traveling through the Deep South to the Gulf of Mexico and back to Chicago. He experienced the best and worst of life with a touring baseball team, being part of one of the better black teams of that time. The Chicago Giants played against black teams in Houston and Dallas; against the New Orleans Eagles; and in Mobile, Alabama, and Pensacola, Florida. According to Marshall, the Giants won thirty-five games on the way south but lost three games on the trip home to Chicago. Marshall recalled that some of the players had been "celebrating too much," and the carousing interfered with their on-field performance.[34]

Marshall returned home in early June to reclaim his Minnesota roots and, one could speculate, to resuscitate his law practice. It would appear that the Chicago Giants spent too much time on the road to suit Marshall. Thus ended his short association with Chicago's black teams. He had built his connections in his home state, and his greatest opportunities appeared to be there. Jim Taylor also returned to the Colored Gophers.[35]

The 1910 Colored Gophers team, plagued by financial difficulties, proved to be weaker than in previous years. This showed up not so much in road games with local white teams but in competition for the highest honors in colored baseball. The biggest series for the Colored Gophers came in July against the Chicago Giants, and the Chicago ballclub dominated the Gophers in St. Paul, four games to one. Marshall led the Colored Gophers in hitting, getting five hits in thirteen at-bats, including two doubles and a home run, but it was not enough to offset the superiority of the Giants—who outhit, outfielded, and outpitched the St. Paul team.[36]

Still the Gophers and Bobby Marshall had a fine overall record in 1910. But the financial state of the team deteriorated by August. The distances of the trips from town to town in Minnesota were too great for the Gophers to play just one game in a town. Hence, the Gophers scheduled a six game series against their rivals in Hibbing, but the Hibbing fans got tired of seeing the Gophers for that many games in a row, and the attendance declined. Second-baseman George Bowman had to be released because he had lost interest and wanted to quit. The Gophers were using only nine men by late August, and the pitchers got less rest, having to play every day in the field. As a consequence, Hibbing won four of six games from the Gophers. Even Chisholm beat the Gophers twice, and the team nearly disbanded. Overall, though, the Gophers won six of eleven games against the Hibbing nine.[37]

By the end of the 1910 season, Bobby Marshall, now thirty years old and no longer a young man, had to decide which road to take. He could build bridges of understanding between the separate worlds of white and black Minnesotans by his popularity and athletic prowess or he could be an attorney. Either way, in the parlance of the era, he might serve to "uplift the race." Clearly his time spent as an athlete hindered his chances for success as a lawyer. In 1908 he had had his own law office next door to attorney William H. H. Franklin, another black class of '07 graduate from the University of Minnesota. Two years later Marshall had no office and carried on any legal work from his father's house. This part-time status changed by September when he turned away from coaching and joined with Otto A. Pitzke and Franklin in a law firm called Franklin, Pitzke, and Marshall. The firm dealt in the general practice of law and also "collections, real estate, insurance, personal injury cases." At some time after 1910, perhaps early in 1911, he did some legal work with the "office of Nash and Armstrong, a firm of well known white attorneys."[38]

He did not forsake sports, however. In 1911, when the St. Paul Colored Gophers failed to field a team, Marshall reorganized the outfit, naming it the Twin City Colored Gophers and arranging its schedule from his law office. Daddy Reid was finished as the owner and left the baseball scene entirely. Marshall became the manager and was also the recruiter, journeying to Chicago to hire several players from the black teams there. He signed a few of the lesser players and spread the word—more hype than real hope—that he had signed Rube Foster. Marshall did manage to obtain the services of veteran pitcher Bert Jones, formerly with the Algona Brownies. Harry Brown, said to "have played with the leading negro clubs of the East," pitched for the Gophers (and played third base).[39]

But the Colored Gophers were not as good as they had been in previous summers. After the Alexandria, Minnesota, team swept a four-game series from the Gophers, a local sportswriter commented, "The Colored Gophers are not playing as classy ball as they did two or three years ago."[40]

The last year of existence for the St. Paul Colored Gophers (and for the Minneapolis Keystones) came in 1911. It was also the last year that Bobby Marshall attempted to practice law. It was clear that William Franklin had a firm hold on the clientele of a black lawyer in the Twin Cities and that Marshall's chance had passed him by, supplanted by the "call of the pigskin and the lure of the diamond." He attempted to "make athletics his profession" at a time when an African American was not particularly welcome in any occupation. As Bobby said, "I love games of all kinds from tennis to football. Anything to be fighting to win a game. It's what I live on." Rather than continue an ineffective, part-time status as an attorney, Marshall accepted a permanent, stable (if unglamorous) position as a grain inspector, working for the state of Minnesota, in September 1911. A civil-service position with the government was considered to be a "good job" in the days when most black men were working as laborers, railway porters, barbers, or janitors.[41]

And so, as the 1912 season began, the Colored Gophers and Minneapolis Keystones were no more. But Bobby Marshall organized and became the captain of a new team, the Hennepin Clothing Company's colored team, known as the Hennepins. William Binga stayed around as did Johnny Davis, but most of the other players went to other fields in other cities. Joe Davis, a pitcher and probably the brother of Johnny Davis, joined the team. Marshall once again went to Chicago to sign players from the roster of the Leland Giants, garnering the services of a couple of lesser players (one of them a shortstop known only as Selden). Bobby spread word that he had signed Rube Foster again, but he had not. It was said the clothing company's team was "outfitted" in "first class style," but the glory years for black baseball in Minnesota were over.[42]

After 1912, black teams would come and go in the Twin Cities as sponsoring businesses founded teams and the teams foundered. But Bobby Marshall was a mainstay of black baseball in Minnesota, playing for most of the best teams in the period from 1912 to the 1930s. In 1913 the Minneapolis team changed its name to the Hennepin Negro Giants, with Bobby Marshall still as the leader. William Binga continued playing, as did pitchers Johnny Davis and Joe Davis.[43]

In some years, Marshall played for white teams. In 1913, the St. Cloud Pretzels semipro team recruited Marshall away from the Hennepin Giants in late July to play second base, right field, and shortstop in weekend games. He did well and helped the St. Cloud nine defeat a touring black team from French Lick Creek, Indiana—the Plutos—in two of four games by getting four hits. The Plutos had lost just seven games out of seventy-nine that season. Marshall led his team in hitting with a .495 average in the last four games, as St. Cloud won thirteen out of nineteen games that season.[44]

Marshall again played for St. Cloud in 1914, and his Pretzels defeated the touring French Lick Plutos 11 to 3, a game in which Bingo DeMoss, the great black athlete, got two doubles and a single. The teams did not play a series because many of the local fans were "wearied of the oft repeated appearance of the blacks" and wanted to see a "neighboring team" or have a "free Sunday" without baseball.[45]

In 1915, Marshall played for the small town of Cokato, just fifty miles west of Minneapolis, on weekends, helping the team fill the little Westside ballpark. Marshall rode his motorcycle to Cokato to join a team of paid pros that included "Rube" Ursella (a pro football player and former Gopher who often played football with and against Marshall). It became common for Minnesota teams in the outstate areas to hire the best ballplayers from the Twin Cities for Sunday games. A "good semi-pro pitcher" would receive "from $7.50 to $20 per game," while a skilled catcher could "get up to $12.50 a game." Outfielders were paid "an average of $5 per contest" and infielders about $10 per game. It was good money for the time.[46]

Not much is known about Marshall's personal life. After his father died in 1917, the mantle of family patriarch fell to Bobby. The following year, at the age of thirty-eight, Bobby married Irene Knott, a beautiful eighteen-year-old. Irene's family had originated in the South but had migrated to Montana where she and Bobby met. His extensive touring in baseball and football had hindered his ability to develop a family life but helped him find Irene. The couple settled down in Minneapolis and eventually had four children—Robert, Jr., William, Donald, and Bette.[47]

In the years following World War I, things changed in Minnesota. Minneapolis surpassed St. Paul in population of African Americans and in prominence. As increasing numbers of southern blacks migrated to the northern states, "racial attitudes began to harden" in the Twin Cities. All pretense of a delicate balance of racial harmony in Minnesota evaporated. Fears of Reds, foreigners, and migrating African Americans brought a different climate to the Upper Midwest, increasing discrimination in employment and housing.[48]

Marshall's work with the State Grain Inspection Department allowed time off from work only on the weekends and holidays, and his days of extended touring throughout the Upper Midwest ended. He continued to play semiprofessional baseball on summer weekends, albeit for teams of variable quality, picking up a few extra dollars to supplement his wages. Occasionally he joined a team in outstate Minnesota or in North Dakota that was willing to pay him pretty well for his talents. For example, in 1919, he played for the Mott and Regent teams in North Dakota. In 1921, Marshall and his friend Joe Davis spent a summer playing baseball at Estevan, Saskatchewan, and Bobby reportedly hit .450 in fifty-seven games. Then Marshall was the captain (and

The Askin and Marine team in Cokato, probably in 1922. Marshall (third from the right in the back row) wore a Buffalos' uniform.

a player) for the Askin and Marine Colored Red Sox in 1922, when the team won thirty out of thirty-nine games. In the fall he played professional football and was well known in the region for his pro football involvement with Minneapolis teams during the 1910s and in the early 1920s, playing for the Duluth Kelleys NFL team in 1925. In winter he "kept in trim by playing a smashing game of hockey, the most dangerous of sports."[49]

Throughout the 1920s, Marshall continued going to games with his friends Lee Davis, a catcher, and Joe Davis. In 1923, Marshall was the first baseman, catcher, and second baseman for the Uptown Sanitary semiprofessional team. He and the team would often meet at Lee Davis's house in Minneapolis and then ride together to the games in outlying towns near the Twin Cities.[50] In 1925 he was the first sacker for Potts Motor Company.

Marshall gained respect from his fellow black ballplayers as one of the experienced veterans. In a spring game in Long Prairie in 1925, the "old-timer" got a big, fat, easy pitch from the great black pitcher John Donaldson when the two faced each other. Donaldson "pitched easily to Marshall," and Bobby "accepted the smiling John's invitation to hit one" by smacking a double into the cars parked in center field, driving in the lone run for Marshall's Colored Gophers that day. Bobby often said after he got home to Minneapolis, "We didn't make a lot of money, but we sure had a lot of fun."[51]

The St. Paul Uptown Sanitary team in 1923; Johnny Davis is third from the right and Marshall is sixth from the right.

Occasionally, former university teammates Sig Harris and Fred Chicken would gather at Marshall's house to play the piano and sing, not very well, but they would all sing together. He played plenty of poker with his buddies also.[52]

Marshall became a leader of the black sports community in Minnesota. In 1922, for example, he played a significant role in negotiations with Rube Foster to create a Negro League franchise in Minnesota. Foster planned to bring the Twin Cities into his league, founded in 1920, and sought out Bobby Marshall and his Colored Red Sox team as members. The talks were not fruitful, and Marshall and his team played out the year away from the national spotlight that being a part of the Negro League would have brought them. Marshall no doubt was a part of the renewed effort in 1925 to establish a franchise in Minnesota when Foster tried to have a club play in Minneapolis at Nicollet Park when the Minneapolis Millers were on the road.[53]

By 1932 Marshall was called the "grand old man" at first base for the St. Paul Monarchs, still going strong. He finally retired from the game in 1938 at the age of fifty-eight. For the Twin Cities African American community,

Bobby Marshall was "the image, the mentor, the star," from 1908 into the 1930s, according to Harry Davis, the son of Lee Davis.[54]

The Gopher great lived a long life, long enough to witness the erosion of the color line in baseball in the 1940s. The rumors of change came first in 1942 when three Negro League players were invited to a tryout by the Pittsburgh Pirates organization. A prominent Minneapolis sportswriter, George A. Barton, hoped that the players would "decline the invitation" and continue to play in "their own leagues" and on all-black teams or in "semi-pro teams made up of whites and Negros." Barton interviewed a local black preacher who believed that colored players should not play where "we are *not* welcome." The preacher used Bobby Marshall as an example of a great African American ballplayer of the past who "would not have accepted offers from teams in organized baseball," but the preacher made no effort to contact Marshall concerning the subject—and neither did the sportswriter. The article contained a photo of Bobby Marshall and tried to persuade the public that Minnesota's black athletes would have been opposed to the plan of major-league baseball to admit black players. The preacher declared that Marshall would have been "too intelligent" and had "too much pride to court humiliation from the white players in major and minor leagues" and to go where black people were "not wanted."[55]

The response of the Twin Cities black press was immediate and wrathful. The editor of the *Minneapolis Spokesman* asked why Barton did not "obtain the opinion" of Bobby Marshall on the subject when his photo accompanied the article. The editor noted that blacks were not welcome in boxing before Joe Louis created opportunities for African American boxers to make a "legitimate living in the ring." He pointed to the way that black people opened up industries by insisting upon equal opportunities, not waiting until they were welcomed. The editor surmised that Barton did not seek Marshall's opinion on the topic because he realized that Marshall and other great athletes had been "robbed of thousands of dollars by the prejudiced anti-Negro practice of organized baseball," which Barton condoned. Barton had a "record of years of fair and friendly appraisal of the Negro athlete" before the unthinking article appeared, but he should have been advocating for opportunities in baseball for all racial groups. He pointed out that the "glaring inconsistency of calling professional baseball a national game" while "barring one-tenth of the country's population from full democratic participation in it" was "something of which we should all be ashamed." It was truly time to let go of the "moth eaten racial taboos" that had "kept worthy Negro American men out of big-time baseball all these many years." The flap died down when the Pirates withdrew the offer, and African American players had to wait another five years, until 1947, when Jackie Robinson, a college-educated man like Bobby Marshall, integrated major-league baseball.[56] Marshall let the editor of the *Spokesman* speak for him, much as he had to let his glove and his bat do his talking on the baseball diamond.

Marshall lived to see integration in Minnesota baseball when Roy Campanella broke the color line in the American Association in 1948. In his old age, the Minneapolis Millers awarded him a lifetime pass to their games, so he was able to witness the on-field talent of Ray Dandridge and Willie Mays and the other black players who came to his home city of Minneapolis.[57]

Marshall retired from the Grain Inspection Department in 1950, after thirty-nine years of service, and the local union membership gave him a testimonial dinner at a hotel in Minneapolis. Among the six hundred friends who attended were some well-known people, including Governor Luther W. Youngdahl, the main speaker, Gopher coaching great Bernie Bierman, and old friend Sig Harris—truly a tribute to Marshall's sports career.[58]

The testimonials to Marshall at his farewell banquet told of his on-the-field accomplishments and of his contributions to the people of the Twin Cities. He inspired great devotion due to his character and concern for those around him. An old Central High teammate, Walter C. Robb, wrote that Marshall was "really [like] one of my older brothers." Sig Harris called Marshall a "true friend."[59]

Those who knew him well called him "the outstanding man of the Minneapolis African-American community." Marshall believed in being a good role model, and his fellow African Americans acknowledged that he was a "great man because he spent so much of his time sharing his knowledge with younger people." For example, he was a coach at the Phyllis Wheatley House, a settlement house in Minneapolis. Marshall also helped by officiating at youth games. He coached his three sons in boxing, and the youngsters won "many titles" in the ring. He was called upon to deliver a speech to the track club at the Phyllis Wheatley House in 1926, seeking to inspire youngsters to gain "good sportsmanship and clean living." In 1933 and 1935, he gave inspirational speeches to Twin Cities high school football players for the Sterling Club, an African American men's club; he was honored at a Big Brothers banquet in 1936. Bobby also showed spiritual leadership as a member of long standing at St. Peter's A.M.E. Church in Minneapolis.[60]

In the 1950s, Marshall showed signs of the onset of Alzheimer's disease. He began to forget things; several times when he attended a Minneapolis Millers ball game, he left his car near the ballpark and took a bus home, forgetting that he had driven. Sometimes, Sig Harris or other well-to-do university alumni would hire a chauffeur-driven limousine to pick up Marshall to go to the Millers games. His racial background limited his opportunities to prosper, but he was rich in friends. Marshall died in 1958 at the age of seventy-eight. The newspaper tributes by then were short and devoid of the recognition due one of Minnesota's greatest athletes, as if the new generation of writers had lost some of the collective Minnesota memory.[61]

In 1910 Marshall had already become known as "an old favorite" and an "all around athletic star," as a reporter for the *St. Paul Pioneer Press* wrote. Some went even further in their assessments; Marshall was "one of America's greatest all-around athletes," according to sportswriter George Barton. Marshall was unforgettable in his lifetime, but after his death, sportswriters came to suffer from a "very strange lapse of memory," rarely mentioning "one of the greatest of them all—Bobby Marshall." He became a "neglected . . . star."[62]

Indeed, Marshall has received little mention in the histories of black baseball in America, despite being judged to be good enough to play first base on one of the greatest Negro teams in history, the 1909 Chicago Leland Giants. Marshall's St. Paul Colored Gophers of 1909 also have to be considered among the best teams of black baseball in their era. Had Marshall been able to bring a Negro League franchise to Minnesota in 1922, his name would have been known as much nationally as it was regionally. Still, he struggled to gain recognition for black baseball in his region just as others did elsewhere, albeit with less acclaim than men such as Rube Foster.[63]

In 1999 a prominent Twin Cities newspaper rated Bobby Marshall as number fifty-one among the Top 100 Sports Figures of the twentieth century, listing him as the tenth greatest football player in Minnesota's history. Most of the modern-day experts knew only a summary of his accomplishments; the man and the details were largely forgotten. But Harry Davis, whose father had played baseball with Marshall in the 1920s and 1930s, made sure that Marshall was on the list. In 1991 the University of Minnesota included Marshall in its Athletic Hall of Fame as a member of the Pioneer Group, alongside Bronko Nagurski.[64]

Bobby Marshall was not just a great African American athlete, he was a great American athlete. He played every position in baseball over the course of his thirty-year career and loved the game. The image of Marshall at first base was impressive. A Hibbing sportswriter wrote in 1910, "He is a tall, rangey fellow and spears the ball with one hand when they come high."[65]

It has been said that sports not only builds character but also reveals character. A look at the life of Bobby Marshall shows that he was a dedicated player who excelled in clutch situations, that he could be counted on by his teammates in the height of competition, that he loved athletics, and that he stayed true to his family and his home state of Minnesota. Marshall always played to win, even when he was coaching children, causing his daughter Bette to ask, "Daddy, why don't you let them win sometimes?" Bobby replied, "I can't let them, it would get me out of practice."[66]

Bobby Marshall used the same bat for thirty years. To preserve it that long, he gave it a new layer of paint at the conclusion of every season. The many coats of paint made Marshall's bat heavy and covered its wooden core. It was probably as hard as iron after several years. His bat never broke. His character was much like his bat, strong and able to endure.[67] Season after season he played baseball in Minnesota, each year building on his reputation as a gentleman and a sportsman, but also adding another coating to his exterior. He had endured his share of racial slurs, but he did not retaliate to those catcalls, keeping his dignity intact. He earned respect from his fellow Minnesotans, white and black, by the way he played baseball. Although Marshall was limited to having his bat speak for him, he remained never broken, like his bat.

Barnstorming Teams, 1909–1920

A number of black baseball teams toured Minnesota, especially in the years between 1907 and 1920. Chief among them were the St. Paul Colored Gophers and the Minneapolis Colored Keystones, who put outstanding teams on the field but vanished from the scene after a few seasons. From 1907 to 1909, the Colored Gophers played 365 games, winning 311, going up against the "best teams in the country outside of the big leagues." The Gophers' winning percentage was said to be "a record never before equaled by a professional Independent team in America."[1]

The Keystone season records are harder to trace than those of the Gophers. The owner and manager of the Minneapolis Keystones was Kidd F. Mitchell, an African American and the proprietor of a saloon in the Keystone Hotel. The secretary who arranged the schedule was a man named Eddie Davis. Mitchell supposedly had "big financial backing," and he hired pitchers Walter Ball and Charles Jessup from the Chicago Leland Giants. Jessup became the mainstay on the mound that season, while Ball returned to Chicago after a short time. Mitchell then brought in a gigantic pitcher named W. J. Freeman, who stood six feet, six inches tall and weighed 245 pounds and who had played with Omaha, Kansas City, Chicago, and the Anaconda and Butte teams of Montana. William DuBerry (or Dewberry) from Chicago and Charles "Slick" Jackson also joined the pitching rotation. In 1908, the Minneapolis team reportedly won eighty-eight games and lost just nineteen, with two ties.[2]

The 1909 Keystones purportedly won thirty-nine of the first forty-four games they played, but the team faded after July and was unable to match the winning percentage of its first season. The pitching staff consisted of Jessup, Jackson, and newcomer Archie Pate. That year the team acquired Willis Jones, the diminutive outfielder who had played previously with the best Chicago teams and with the Colored Gophers.[3]

The ballclub encountered financial difficulties and moved its operations out of state, joining the Texas Baseball League in 1910. The Keystones returned to Minnesota for the 1911 season, but information regarding their schedule is scanty, and research has uncovered the results of only twelve games, with the Keystones winning five and losing seven. In its final season, 1911, the most notable new arrival was Hurley McNair, a man who later became a star player with the Kansas City Monarchs in the Negro Leagues by the 1920s. The roster for the Keystones tended to be rather unstable, with players constantly arriving and then leaving through the team's four years of existence.[4]

Midwestern teams wanted to play against the Gophers and the Keystones for several reasons. The first was to see how the local nine measured up to an elite semiprofessional black team, hoping to get a victory. Second, both the Keystones and the Gophers were desirable feature attractions. Small towns, especially, hired the Keystones to give exhibitions, using the game as a fundraising venture to refill the coffers of the town team. The black teams were a novelty, and the games were sometimes a part of a local festival. When the Keystones played at Granite Falls in 1908, the local newspaperman commented on the expense of bringing the visitors to town, hoping that the fans

Willis Jones, at bat for the Chicago American Giants, 1911. Jones used a split grip on his thick bat to punch the ball and spray his hits to all fields.

would help meet the cost. In Arlington, Minnesota, the Keystones' game was a part of a monthly Market Day, and farmers flocked to town to get supplies and to enjoy a baseball game on a Monday. Similarly, Zumbrota scheduled the Keystones to take on an area team in conjunction with its annual Street Fair, played at "Priebe's pasture past the [famous] covered bridge." The Keystones won, 7 to 3. A number of clubs "did not expect to defeat" the Keystones but planned to put up a respectable fight.[5]

Underneath the competitive aspect of barnstorming baseball lurked the idea that fans wanted to see a baseball "battle between the whites and the blacks." The Keystones, apparently, were willing to profit from this scheme. It appears that the black teams sometimes made sure to lose the first match of a multiple-game series, thus giving the local white team the feeling that the Keystones were not as good as their reputation. This might bring fans to the ballpark to see the local nine take apart the "colored wonders" and would attract heavier betting on the hometown favorites. The Keystones would agree to the bets and then shut out or shut down the local hitters, taking a healthy amount of cash with them on the train to the next town on the schedule.[6]

The success of the Keystones and Gophers spawned imitators. One barnstorming team that arose in 1909 was the Colored Giants ballclub from Duluth. A local boxer named Walter Whitehead, who was black, organized a team in mid-July. The Walter Whitehead Colored Giants were to play a white team from nearby Cloquet on Sunday, August 1, on Cloquet's diamond. The "husky Duluth fighter" was to be the catcher, and the pitcher was to be "an imported [Colored] Gopher from St. Paul." The team had been "practicing steadily every night," and the players were said to be "in shape to take the measure of the [Cloquet] lumber town nine." The result of the game is unknown as is whether the team played any more games. The Duluth newspapers did not follow through with a report of the match.[7]

The Keystones and Gophers competed for scheduling dates in the Upper Midwest with other barn-storming clubs of varying levels of quality and novelty. For instance, a sports story in the *Minneapolis Journal* in 1910 mentioned that a new team had arisen in neighboring South Dakota, in Aberdeen. The ballclub, named the Hub City Browns and managed by Billy Patterson, advertised to arrange games with "outside teams." Little more is known of this organization. Buxton, Iowa, also had a black baseball team, the Wonders (circa 1900–1914). The Keystones vied against the club in 1908, and the Colored Gophers played them in 1909.[8] In 1911, the Tennessee Rats, an all-black ballclub, came to Minnesota, and the All-Nations team, with several African American players, toured parts of the state in 1912.

Competition for the Keystones and Gophers came from more than all-black teams. White teams from various leagues barnstormed to make extra money after the regular season ended. Such teams included Chicago City League teams, the Logan Squares, and Cap Anson's Colts. Most unusual among these touring clubs of white players was the Fat Men's Ball Team, from Waterloo, Iowa, in 1910. Also labeled the Two Ton Base Ball Team, it featured Frank Knee, weighing 450 pounds, as the manager, and "Baby" Bliss, the "largest man in the world" at 650 pounds, playing catcher. The smallest player listed on the regular roster was Pinkey Howry at 325 pounds, and the grand total for the fourteen-man squad was listed at 4,847 pounds. The lineup consisted entirely of heavy hitters.[9]

> **"The Westerners are baseball mad. It is baseball seven days of the week. . . . They prefer going to a ball game to going to church. They go by train, trolley, and auto, scores of miles. When they return home they are so full of the feats of the heroes of the diamond they can think of nothing else."**
>
> *Fargo Forum,* 1911

There were also a few Native American baseball teams that barnstormed. In 1908 the Haskell Indians (or National Indians), a team from Lawrence, Kansas, played games in Iowa, being billed as "the Great American Indian[s] playing the Great American Game."[10]

The baseball field at Kerkhoven, about 1915, shows typical small-town playing conditions faced by the barnstorming teams, with fans seated around the infield and cars parked at the edge of the outfield.

John Wesley Donaldson, a Great Mound Artist

Peter W. Gorton

The decade of the 1920s brought new ideas and new heroes to Minnesota. The First World War redefined the United States as it became a world power. Prohibition of alcohol challenged the moral values of the populace; radio carried information and conveyed a sense of connection from ocean to ocean. Racial lines were blurred with the introduction of the new "jazz" music, originally American and originally black, while at the same time Ku Klux Klan sympathizers flourished. Spectator sports appealed to the masses. More people had more money than ever before, spending it on consumer goods—radios, refrigerators, and cars. Others freed up time for vacations and disposed of their disposable income. Business boomed and investors brought a bull market to Wall Street.

The age of the million-dollar drawing card dawned. Babe Ruth rose as the greatest national sporting icon, revolutionizing baseball with his home runs and his uppercutting swing. The Babe had risen from poverty in his boyhood in Baltimore to star status. Henry Ford, renowned for producing the affordable Model T, became so well known that some people urged him to seek the presidency in 1924. Minnesota's own Charles Lindbergh, Jr., became an aviation celebrity and an international hero.[1]

Lindbergh was a symbol of the Roaring Twenties. When Lucky Lindy flew his single-engine airplane across the Atlantic Ocean in 1927, Minnesotans cheered with delight. They adored the Little Falls man for his daring feat. The nation honored him with a ticker-tape parade down the avenues of New York City. Lindbergh had redefined how Minnesotans, and Americans, would view themselves throughout the world. He was truly Minnesota's pride and joy, and Little Falls meant to do him proud by hosting a Lindbergh Homecoming Festival in August.

Fifty thousand people came to the central Minnesota town for the all-day event that featured band concerts, a street dance, and a magnificent parade consisting of nearly more bands than floats. The parade included a float depicting the Statue of Liberty and the Eiffel Tower with a replica of the *Spirit of St. Louis* tethered between the virtual New York and Paris. The bands came from all over Minnesota—Brainerd, Glenwood, Royalton, Sauk Centre, and many other towns accompanied by numerous drum corps, including ones from Red Wing, Chisholm, and Hibbing. More than five hundred school-aged children marched in the parade waving "Welcome Home Lindy" flags honoring their hero.[2]

A baseball game was also part of the All-American festivities for the All-American Lindbergh. The game featured a semiprofessional team from the tiny town of Bertha and the barnstorming, bearded House of David ballclub from Benton Harbor, Michigan. Both squads had stellar records, and both could appeal to the crowds because of their ballplaying skills and distinctive styles. Bertha had played twenty-one games thus far and won nineteen, including a victory over the House of David in late June. The House of David had dominated small-town midwestern teams on a regular basis for several years.[3]

It is not known if aviator Lindbergh attended the game, but six thousand others paid fifty cents each for general admission and an extra two bits for each grandstand seat to witness the matchup. The Little Falls mayor, Austin L. Grimes, threw out the ceremonial first pitch, then watched a talented black pitcher named John Donaldson take the mound that afternoon. Some fans knew just how great a mound artist Donaldson had always been. No one except Donaldson, though, knew what it was like to be a baseball star who played in obscurity nearly all his career—pitching in towns such as Brower-ville, Akeley, Lismore, Good Thunder, Fulda, or Clarkfield. He had mowed down batters from teams like the Joliet Prison All Stars, the Hibbing Colts, the St. Paul Patocks, and the New York Mills Millers.

Some folks called him "Cannonball" Donaldson; others referred to him as "the famous colored twirler" or the "coal tar colored heaver." Whites some-times called him a "colored boy" or "southpaw black boy"—others called him worse things. Whatever name they used, they learned that he could really pitch, leading the Bertha team to the championship of semiprofessional baseball in Minnesota in 1924.

Bertha's ballclub had two other black players that day. One was a catcher by the name of Sylvester "Hooks" Foreman. He had been in the big-time Negro Leagues with the Indianapolis ABC's and the Kansas City Monarchs. The management had hired another black pitcher especially for the Lindbergh Festival game; his name was Lefty Wilson. That was not his real name; he had changed his name from Dave Brown several years before when he fled from a New York murder scene.[4]

The House of David, a religious community, had eleven players with long unshorn locks of hair, gloves and bats blessed through their distinctive ceremonial practices, and fundamental baseball skills. They were odd but they were very good at baseball.

The day proved to be a great one both for Lindbergh and for Bertha's team. Donaldson started the game and shut out the House of David for two innings, and then Lefty Wilson took over the pitching duties for the final seven innings of a 1 to 0 ball game. Donaldson and Wilson combined to throw a six-hit shutout of the hard-hitting House of David nine.[5]

Donaldson's star did not shine as brightly as Lindbergh's that day. Lindbergh was, after all, the lone son of a well-known Minnesota congressman and politician, Charles Lindbergh, Sr. Lindy became a spokesman for the aviation industry and remained an international celebrity until the end of his days. Donaldson, in contrast, continued to pitch for Bertha, then moved on to teams in Minneota, Madison, Lismore, Melrose, Arlington, and St. Cloud before starting his own touring team in Fairmont for the 1932 season. Both men had links to Minnesota and kept those ties for the remainder of each man's lifetime. Minnesotans remembered Lindbergh; they largely forgot about what Donaldson had done in the state.

John Wesley Donaldson originally came from Missouri. He was born in the town of Glasgow on February 20, 1892. As a child he expressed the wish to "be a globe-trotter" and to "learn all about the world." He earned free tickets to the theater by working at odd jobs for the traveling entertainers. Later in life, his ball-playing exploits fulfilled his curiosity about travel and seeing the world.[6]

Young Donaldson showed a remarkable talent for playing baseball, starting with the kid's game called "one old cat." Donaldson was "always called upon to pitch for he could throw the ball the farthest." He became the pitcher for the Evans grade school team and, by sixth grade, led his teammates to a regional championship. Unfortunately, his mother was "strictly against his participating in the national game" and strongly opposed playing baseball on Sundays because she was a very religious woman. She believed that Sundays should contain no work, just church and prayer. They agreed John could play only on weekdays.

Soon after, Evans school played for a championship, and the game was to be on a Sunday with John Donaldson pitching. He went to the diamond without his mother knowing of it. When she got wind of what was going on, she hurried to the ballpark with the "intention of whipping John and sending him home." Arriving at the game at a "critical moment," and hearing the crowd cheering her son, she relented and became his most loyal fan.

Donaldson was a dedicated student, graduating from Evans high school with high honors in a mixed class of "both white and colored pupils." According to historian James Riley, Donaldson attended George Smith College in nearby Sedalia for a year before focusing on baseball as a way of life. The game provided a way to see the country, just like the traveling entertainers he had seen in Glasgow.[7]

Donaldson's professional career began in 1911 when he pitched for the Tennessee Rats barnstorming ball club. He pitched forty-four games that season, losing only three. Donaldson "became the talk of the fans in every place he played," and he was the main "drawing card" and "money maker" for the Rats. It was said that he "received absolutely nothing" for his pitching and "was forced to sleep in opera houses, [or] barns" and seldom got a room in a hotel, "unless circumstances called for respectable treatment." He made his first appearance in Minnesota in September of that year, but it is not known if he had to sleep in a hotel or in a barn.[8]

Sometime in the 1911 season, a sharp baseball entrepreneur named J. L. Wilkinson discovered Donaldson's all-around baseball abilities and signed him for the All Nations traveling ballclub for 1912. That season he gained a reputation—he pitched at Deerwood in early August, winning 20–0, but was noted for striking out the first twelve batters he faced.[9]

This was where the real John Donaldson started to become the legendary hurler. Within two years, the story would be told of a game in which the hard-throwing colored left-hander would be "jeered and otherwise abused" by prejudiced local-yokel fans. He would accept "the abuse with a gracious smile" and then prove himself as a man and a pitcher "by striking out the first twenty-one men up to bat" and by winning the game in a shutout performance. Twelve batters in reality had grown to be twenty-one in myth, and the black pitcher established himself as a phenom who pitched no-hitters and shutouts in amazing numbers in the hinterlands of the Upper Midwest.[10]

The All Nations team, based in Des Moines, Iowa, was owned by J. L. Wilkinson, a white man who was nonetheless accepted by black players and known later for his Kansas City Monarchs Negro League team in the 1920s. The team was composed of players of several different nationalities, having a "Scotchman, an Indian, an American, a Jap[anese], a Mexican, a Turk, an African, a Greek, and a Chinaman." Contemporary sources indicated that Wilkinson had patterned the All Nations team after the model of the earlier Hopkins Brothers touring ballclub and that he also controlled the Boston Bloomer Girls baseball club.[11]

The All Nations team played about twenty-five games in Minnesota in 1912, and Donaldson took his turn on the mound, alternating with the great Cuban black hurler Jose Mendez and two other pitchers, Thomas Means and Art Dunbar. Mendez was the mainstay of the Cuban Stars (1909–12) team that toured in the United States and of the Almendares team of the winter Cuban League. Mendez was the right-handed ace and Donaldson was his left-handed counterpart; together they were two of the best black pitchers from 1910 to 1920. With such a talented pitching staff, the All Nations won ninety-two games, losing only twenty-two, with two ties in 116 total games.[12]

Donaldson dominated the amateur and semiprofessional teams he threw against for eight seasons from 1911 through 1917 when he was one of the best pitchers in black baseball. His won-loss record for his first two years with the All Nations was eighty wins and five losses, for a winning percentage of .941. His legendary prowess grew. He faced a ballclub in Marshall and struck out the first eleven men. He "gave the greatest exhibition of pitching ever seen here," wrote a local newsman, "striking out the entire team, nine men, and then starting over again and striking out two more" for the total of eleven. He later struck out seven batters in a row in the same game. Fantastic reports of Donaldson's exploits preceded the arrival of the All Nations in every Midwest town. John was said to have mowed down thirty-five Sioux Falls batters in an eighteen-inning game and to have struck out twenty-six hapless opponents in another ballgame.[13]

The All Nations club traveled in its own private Pullman railway car (nicknamed "Loretta" in 1912, then a new one called "Jeanette" in 1913) and had its own cook who journeyed with the team. Thus the players did not have to worry about being refused overnight lodging or meal service along the way. Riding the rails from town to town, contest to contest, payday to payday was a way of life for the team.[14]

Wilkinson's All Nations ballclub brought technological advancements to the rural towns of Minnesota. In 1914 he introduced an arrangement of electric arc lights called the Swaine system. When draped around the diamond, they provided 50,000-candlepower of light that was said to make the field "light as day." The attraction of literally lighting up the darkness drew fans from around the area like moths to a beacon lamp.[15]

Towns all over the Land of 10,000 Lakes anticipated the arrival of Donaldson and the All Nations as a social event. Wilkinson promoted his 1913 squad as "a bunch of professional players, made up of Americans, Cubans, Indians, Japanese, Negroes, French, Hawaiians and Mexicans," minus the Turk from the

John Donaldson traveled throughout Minnesota with the All Nations from 1912 to 1917 and 1920 to 1923.

year before. The team at one time even carried a wrestler named "Cyclone" Ben Reeves, a champion 175-pound wrestler from Iowa. He was known to grapple any man who dared to think he could beat him.[16]

In 1912 the All Nations had barnstormed with a person called "Carrie Nation," a woman (or a man impersonating a woman) who played first base. Wilkinson borrowed the name of the saloon-smashing, anti-alcohol crusader as a means to showcase a female as part of the All Nations team. The All Nations consistently drew crowds of five hundred spectators throughout their railway travels in Minnesota.[17] Anywhere and by any means that the team could draw a crowd, it would.

John Donaldson spent all or part of seven seasons traveling throughout the United States and Canada with the All Nations, presumably because he could make good money at it. Black baseball in that period had a few great teams but no well-organized Negro League. There were a few dominant teams in Chicago (Rube Foster's club), St. Louis, and New York, while other teams arose and then faded away. Wilkinson moved his base of operations to Kansas City from Des Moines in 1916, and his All Nations became a part of the Western League of black teams. Kansas City was a convenient base for

Donaldson, just one hundred miles from his Glasgow hometown, and he flourished there. The 1916 season was a highlight of Donaldson's entire career, when the All Nations had the best record in the Western League and the league named him as the left-handed pitcher on the West All-Star Team. As one of the best colored pitchers that year, he was chosen to play Florida resort baseball with the Poinciana club that winter. Baseball historian John Holway rated Donaldson as the best pitcher in black baseball in 1916, listing him as the George Stovey Award winner for that year.[18]

In 1917 the All Nations ballclub dissolved when players were drafted into the military, and Donaldson was among those who served a tour of duty in World War I. It was also the year that he married Eleanor Watson. In 1918 he returned from Europe to pitch for two all-black teams in New York—the Brooklyn Royal Giants and the New York Lincoln Giants—and with the Indianapolis ABC's before being signed by the Detroit Stars in 1919.[19]

Donaldson found a place within the newly established Negro National League (NNL) when it commenced in 1920. The Negro League, the brainchild of Rube Foster, was the first successful national organized baseball league comprised of all-black teams. Again, J. L. Wilkinson was his benefactor, signing him for his Kansas City Monarchs. The other founding clubs in the West included Foster's Chicago American Giants, the Chicago Giants, Cuban Stars, Dayton Marcos, Detroit Stars, Indianapolis ABC's, and St. Louis Giants.

Donaldson spent the seasons from 1920 through 1923 with the Monarchs. Wilkinson built the team around players he knew, including the great Mendez and Donaldson. Having encountered serious arm troubles, Donaldson became the regular centerfielder but was still able to fill in on the mound. Good with the bat, he was the leadoff hitter initially and then was moved down in the batting order year by year as he got older; still he had "exceptional speed from the batter's box to first base."[20]

The veteran Donaldson became teammates with outfielder Hurley McNair (1888–1948) and catcher Sylvester "Hooks" Foreman, forming a bond that would last throughout his career. McNair was a speedster who led the West in doubles and triples for several seasons and hit for high average. Foreman was breaking in as a back-up catcher. One of the highlights of this period was a 1922 exhibition game between the Monarchs and a Babe Ruth team of barnstorming players in which Donaldson garnered two hits in four at-bats in a Monarchs victory.[21]

Donaldson's Minnesota story resumed when, prior to the 1922 season, he signed an independent semipro contract with the Browerville, Minnesota, ballclub. The Browerville organization sent transportation to receive Donaldson a few days before the start of the season, but he failed to appear, choosing instead to stay with the Monarchs. In June 1922 Donaldson returned to the All Nations, traveling with yet another installment of the barnstorming stars.[22]

After the 1923 season, Donaldson left the Monarchs to play in Minnesota. The veteran lefty signed a contract with the Bertha ballclub for $325 per month, a contract painstakingly arranged by the board of directors and lucrative enough to lure him to central Minnesota. The man who became the guiding force behind the team was manager Ernie Fisher, keeper of the local pool hall, and his name became synonymous with the team. The club became known as the Bertha Fishermen, and Ernie was the "Fisher" in Fishermen.[23]

It would seem unlikely that a big-name black pitcher would play in Bertha, a farming community of only six hundred white people known chiefly as the "The Butter Center of Todd County." It seemed even more unlikely that the team would be a success, but Fisher had the moxie effectively to advertise Donaldson as one of the best drawing cards in the region and the ingenuity to make the enterprise fly. Why not cash in on the Donaldson fame? The left-hander's name had been known around central Minnesota since the time that he had first pitched in Little Falls, Bertha, Melrose, and Deerwood in 1912 and in other places in subsequent years. Tiny Bertha became a place where Donaldson proved his worth not only as a ballplayer but also as a man.[24]

There were several reasons why John Donaldson agreed to play in Bertha. Probably most importantly, his wife, Eleanor, had her father living in the Twin Cities and the Donaldsons could often get together with family. Furthermore, John was well acquainted with Minnesota from his touring days in the state with the All Nations. Certainly his guaranteed contract provided a stable work environment, something that had been lacking throughout his career. And so the Bertha experiment began. John and Eleanor left their home in Kansas City on April 27, 1924. They stayed in Minneapolis at first, and he traveled by rail to Bertha for the weekend games. General manager Ernie Fisher eagerly anticipated Donaldson's arrival. He hoped to bring baseball notoriety to the small community, and he wanted this business venture to turn a profit.[25]

The Bertha Fishermen played a fully independent semipro schedule, choosing not to be a member of the nearby Central Minnesota League—one that had barred all colored players.[26] This league included other area teams, such as Long Prairie, St. Cloud, Sauk Rapids, Sartell, Crosby-Ironton, Clear Lake-Clearwater-Becker, and Cold Spring. When various leagues drew the

Posters, such at this one advertising a game at Moorhead in 1925, brought fans out to see Donaldson pitch. It noted that Bertha had the "fastest" team in Minnesota and the "greatest colored" pitcher.

color line, black players who wished to make some money playing ball in Minnesota had to go to smaller and smaller towns. Hence Bertha could hire a black player like Donaldson while Long Prairie, just seven miles distant, could not and would not hire a black man in the 1920s because its team belonged to the league. This decision went against the precedent in that town; Long Prairie had hired George "Rat" Johnson as a catcher in 1908–09. However, other teams that had not yet drawn the color line would be willing to play against Bertha's independent ballclub.

There were certain fundamentals for the Bertha management. They scheduled games wherever they could draw the most gate admissions. The team would usually split game receipts with their opponents, the winner receiving

60 percent and the loser 40 percent. Admission to games was generally fifty cents for an adult to watch the ball game, with grandstand seats extra. Other fans paid to park their automobiles just beyond the outfield to view the action.[27] Most small-town ballparks lacked an outfield fence to mark home-run clouts, and the cars provided a boundary. If the ball was hit into the parked cars that surrounded the outfield, the batter was automatically limited to a ground-rule double.

Fisher understood that his Fishermen could only make money if they drew big crowds and fielded a winning team, and Donaldson filled both bills. Some newsmen from neighboring towns attempted to discredit Bertha's team by calling attention to Donaldson as a "ringer," while other towns depended on "home talent." Jealous writers publicized the outrageous salary Bertha paid to the interloper. The *Wadena Pioneer Journal* conveyed its message this way: "See Donaldson, Bertha's negro twirler. The boy Bertha is paying $325.00 to do the twirling. He's either a wonder or a lemon." But fans wanted to see the "wonder" pitcher so often mentioned in the papers: "That it pays to advertise and that every knock is a boost was plainly shown by the 1,000 fans that attended the Bertha-Wadena game at Wadena" on May 11, 1924.[28]

Manager Fisher cared less about the insults thrown at Donaldson than the size of the crowd he drew. He scheduled games solely with teams capable of

Fans parked their cars in foul territory of Bertha's treeless ballpark, about 1925.

properly advertising the contests and generating large gate receipts. It took only several weeks for John Donaldson to convince Fisher that he was worth every penny paid to him.

On May 30, 1924, he proved his value as a drawing card. The Minnesota-Dakota Indians arrived in Bertha with a squad of Native American talent from the plains. This traveling team featured a few former minor leaguers, but all were of Native American descent. Ernie Fisher hired the Staples Area Band to provide entertainment before and after the game and between innings in the hope of stirring up a crowd. It worked—a total of nearly a thousand watched, and John Donaldson excelled.

The *Long Prairie Leader* described Donaldson and the matchup in crude racial terminology:

Donaldson pitched a no-hit, no-run game and every Bertha player got at least one hit and one run. Just 29 men faced Donaldson and Bertha errors permitted one to reach first and one got as far as second on two consecutive errors. Several times a Brave was a good waiter and would have three balls and not a strike, but the next three would be strikes whether he wished it or not, and when the game ended Donaldson had 20 Redskin scalps dangling from his strike-out belt. . . . During the middle of the game there appeared Busby's All-Star Colored Minstrels, consisting of 18 Plantation raised Jazz Hounds, several of whom were friends of Donaldson's. The troupe had been playing at Staples and when they heard that Donaldson was in Bertha they came unsolicited, paid their 35 cents admission and rendered free music consisting of "Big Olio Vaudeville Oddities." The Staples 24 piece band had been hired by the baseball association and if there are any who think they did not get 35 cents worth let them call on V. E. Bartlett and get a free pass to the next performance.[29]

It took some courage for John Donaldson to make Bertha his home base for baseball in the 1920s, for racial tensions had been running high. Conditions had deteriorated after a dreadful lynching of three black circus workers in Duluth in 1920 and because of ongoing agitation of the Ku Klux Klan in Minnesota. The Klan had ten active chapters in Minneapolis and vigorously promoted its "white supremacist" ideologies. News reports of a cross-burning incident at Staples, just fifteen miles from Bertha, at a spot between the baseball park and the cemetery went simmering through the minds of the region's Catholics, recent immigrants, and blacks. Reports of Klan meetings in Bemidji and in Deer River, north of Bertha, were widely disseminated.[30]

Despite the racial climate and the fears, it appears that John Donaldson was able to build upon an earlier legacy of touring black players and teams. The good will and competition fostered by the St. Paul Colored Gophers and Minneapolis Keystones from 1907 to 1911 continued as various all-black

Twin Cities' teams toured small-town Minnesota. The skill of George "Rat" Johnson as a catcher had been readily apparent in nearby Long Prairie in 1909, and the talent of Donaldson was plain to see in 1924. It was generally accorded in the 1920s that Donaldson gained the respect of the local people whom he encountered in Bertha and elsewhere. He was regarded not only as a great ballplayer but also as an upstanding citizen. A black ballplayer like Donaldson could get along in Minnesota if he conducted himself with professionalism wherever he went and did not participate in drinking, smoking, or cursing. However, a black ballplayer could hope to transcend race by awing the white crowds with talent. A fan pointed out that a local ballgame was "attractive, for it had the great and mighty John Donaldson in it," a pitcher who "mowed down" the local batters "fair, square and decisive." He insisted that the moundsman was the "big attraction" and that two-thirds of the "large crowd of people" turned out because they "wanted to see Donaldson, the great." The big crowds were not there to see the other players, "they wanted to see Donaldson, the master of base ball."[31]

Donaldson's skills drew such big crowds to Bertha that by the summer of 1924 Fisher had to expand the bleachers at the local park to hold them all. The black newspapers in the Twin Cities were hearing of, and began reporting on, the successes of Donaldson. The *Northwestern Bulletin* called him the best-known colored baseball player in the world.[32]

The *Park Rapids Enterprise* described its local encounter with Donaldson and his Bertha teammates on July 6, 1924:

Bertha has the reputation of being the fastest ball team in this part of the state. From the exhibition they put up here it seems that they have a pretty fair team and one star Donaldson, the famous colored man, at one time with the All-Nations team. He coaches, runs the team, stars in the pitcher's box, plays to the grandstand and tries to run the umpires. Sometimes he gets away with it all.[33]

Donaldson's showmanship was never more evident than in an August game at Battle Lake when he and the Fishermen found themselves without a catcher at game time because R. W. Bottemiller was getting married that day. A stranger in town, Kenneth "Zonie" Personius, shouted from the crowd, "I'll go in and catch the game."

"Are you a catcher?" asked Donaldson.

"Maybe not," said Zonie, "but I grab 'em and hold 'em."

Zonie was told to grab a catcher's mitt, and after he caught just one warm-up pitch from Donaldson, the great pitcher allowed, "All right, you'll do, get into that suit."

Thus on that August afternoon, amateur Kenneth Personius helped perpetuate the legends concerning John Donaldson. The Bertha team won the game 1 to 0, with Donaldson notching nineteen strikeouts.[34]

After Donaldson joined the team, financial solvency followed. A public report on the finances of the ballclub for the last four games of 1924 revealed the impact of having an outstanding black pitcher on Bertha's side. Those games versus Gary (at Detroit Lakes), Pelican Rapids (at Fergus Falls), and Browerville were all wins for the Bertha club. Donaldson averaged eleven strikeouts, and the Bertha club outscored its opponents 19 to 8. Since the winning team earned 60 percent of the gate receipts, Bertha got a total of $1,420.97 for just four games. The cash covered the expenses, the largest of which was Donaldson's salary. The numbers tell the story. Donaldson received $1,478 for the season while the rest of the Fishermen shared $1,460. Not only was his salary more than that of his teammates put together, he also was paid more than the total earned by all the visiting teams that year (a sum of $1,104). After all the expenses were met, the organization realized a profit of $205.99, putting it on the plus side of the ledger.[35]

Hiring a black pitcher was definitely worth it, for the Bertha Fishermen claimed the Central Minnesota and Northwest Minnesota State championships. The ballclub finished with an overpowering record of twenty-one wins, five losses, and one tie. Donaldson won all twenty-one games, losing only three, which gave him a winning percentage of .875. In his twenty-five appearances he struck out 325 batters, averaging 13.5 strikeouts per game. His 325 strikeouts came in just 211 innings pitched. Even if most of these opponents were small-town players, the numbers remain impressive. Donaldson also led the team in hitting, sporting a .439 batting average. Financially, the team made money, and it extended Donaldson a contract for the following season—with a raise in salary to four hundred dollars per month.[36]

Bertha's baseball fans loved John Donaldson. In 1925 he helped coach the local high school baseball team, arriving in town in late April prior to the opening of the season. His knowledge of baseball was apparently more important than the color of his skin, and he helped teach youngsters the basics of the game. His social status as a star pitcher permitted him access to a position of responsibility that another black man probably would not have been offered.[37]

The eve of another tremendously successful season was at hand, inspiring a fan to write this poem in homage to the 1925 Bertha nine:

The Bertha Fishermen in 1924: (front row, left to right) August Thias, "Getty" Geithman, Red Westergren, W. K. Bottemiller; (standing, left to right) Gust Kassube, George Johnson, Elwyn Anderson, John Donaldson, Milton Abbott, Oscar Wagner

The Bertha Fishermen in 1927: (left to right) Carl Gregerson, Al Theis, August Thias, George Johnson, John Donaldson, manager Ernie Fisher, Earl Plummer, unknown, Sylvester "Hooks" Foreman, Ole Wald, Pete Briere

Our dear old Mr. Donaldson
Is back again, I see
For he must think it's lots of fun
To pitch for us, by Gee.
How good it is to see him back,
Among our happy boys,
And he can show you how to whack
That ball, with happy joy.
Our team, they say, he's going to call
"The best team in the state,"
Because they truly can play ball
As good as leaguers great.
You see we have the strongest team,
Of any town nearby,
And we will show them how it seems,
To cheer as we pass by.[38]

The much-anticipated second season for Donaldson and Bertha began with the Fishermen winning eleven of their first twelve games. In these early games Donaldson had performances marked by eleven, thirteen, fifteen, and sixteen strikeouts. The club drew two thousand fans in St. Cloud, where Donaldson won by striking out fifteen men. Perhaps he sent a message of dominance to a team that played in a league that prohibited all black players.[39] This was a sign of things to come. The year would find John Donaldson pitching in more matchups, to larger audiences, and to additional all-star aggregations trying to knock him off.

Newspaper reports from 1925 praised the veteran left-hander: "His control was perfect, and he kept his strike-out ball in reserve for the final batter, five of his six strike-outs being delivered as the means of retiring the side."[40]

"Donaldson was simply invincible and cut the Millers down like grass falling before the mower. Of the first nine men up Donaldson helped retire eight, five by the strike-out route and three by tossing the ball to first base."[41]

"Donaldson may not be the whole Bertha baseball team, but he does appear like the tail that wags the dog."[42]

A Paynesville fan who attended the Bertha–House of David game June 30 wrote, "We think lots of Mr. Donaldson here in Paynesville, not only for his good baseball, but for his clean-cut sportsmanship, both on and off the diamond, and I think he has won the favor of the people wherever he has appeared."[43]

The value of a John Donaldson pitching performance to the Bertha team was never more apparent than in a Fourth of July weekend series with St. Cloud. The Fourth was traditionally a big day for baseball throughout the state as crowds gathered for patriotic parades and for holiday hoopla. Donaldson was scheduled to hurl the Saturday game, and another of Bertha's pitchers, Len Schroeder, was to start on Sunday. Saturday's crowd to see Donaldson was an impressive 2,850. So many were packed into the grandstands that "it was with great difficulty that everyone could get a view of the diamond." The receipts for Donaldson's game totaled $1,200. The Sunday event brought a thousand fans and a gate of only $400. Donaldson proved himself to manager Ernie Fisher time after time. The Bertha team finished the season with a record of twenty-four wins and ten losses. John Donaldson had twenty-three wins and five losses and a batting average of .387. He threw a one-hitter and a two-hitter and had a pair of eighteen-strikeout games.[44]

Immediately after the close of Bertha's regular season in 1925, Donaldson agreed to play with at least three other small-town teams in southwestern Minnesota—at Minneota, Madison, and Lismore. Minneota hired him on two separate occasions. John had ties to Minneota through his younger brother James, who played for the club that season. James Donaldson was an outfielder, shortstop, and pitcher who gained a loyal following in the tiny town just north of Marshall prior to falling ill and returning to their parental home in Missouri.[45]

Tragically, James's condition grew serious in late August, and John was called to his mother's home in Glasgow, where James subsequently passed away from what the doctors described as brain fever. As a tribute to his departed brother, John Donaldson returned to Minnesota to pitch for Minneota against the undefeated Lismore Gophers in early September. He pitched where his now fallen brother had graced the mound earlier in the season. On that Sunday, Lismore ultimately won the game 3 to 1, due to fielding errors by Minneota. Donaldson completed the game with fourteen Gopher strikeouts to his credit.[46]

In addition Donaldson played for the local nine in Madison. Pitted against archrival Clarkfield, Donaldson and the Madison team lost in eleven innings despite Donaldson's nineteen strikeouts. Poor fielding by the inexperienced Madison club caused the game to swing in favor of Clarkfield, 6–2.[47]

John was then hired by the Lismore ballclub for its game against the all-black, traveling Tennessee Rats (his former team) in September 1925. The Lismore Gophers, usually composed of all-local talent, including the town butcher, printer, barber, drayman, banker, and billiard-man and a couple of local farmers, now had the edge. The *Murray County Herald* described Donaldson in superlatives: "Donaldson – the invincible John – not only the greatest colored player that ever lived but also one of the best pitchers of all time is to pitch for Lismore." Once again, the inexperience of the local team brought defeat, but the game was close because of Donaldson's thirteen-strikeout performance, and Lismore fell to the barnstorming Rats by the score of 2 to 1.[48]

The chance to have Donaldson for more than just one game led the Lismore team's management to offer him an excellent contract for the upcoming 1926 season.[49] A newspaperman chronicled Bertha's loss of Donaldson under the headline: "Bertha's Big Smoke Signed up with Lismore Club."

John Donaldson, America's premier colored baseball pitcher, who worked for Bertha the past two seasons, has been lost to that village this year and has signed up with the Lismore, Minn., club. This is the greatest setback to the Bertha baseball team that could happen for the "big smoke" was the greatest drawing card that club could obtain. Through Donaldson's prominence Bertha gained wide publicity and cashed in heavily on the black boy's name. Unless Bertha is exceedingly fortunate in its selection of its next headliner it faces a loss from which it will never be fully able to recuperate.[50]

The offer of $450.00 per month lured Donaldson away from his Bertha home base and granted him an increase of $50.00 per month over his previous year's salary. Lismore's contract included the use of a furnished house for John and Eleanor. The increase in salary and extra fringe benefits enticed Donaldson to make the move.[51]

Apparently no hard feelings arose between Donaldson and the Bertha ballclub as local newspapers printed reports of Donaldson returning to visit friends in Bertha.[52] He left the city on good terms and often visited there while traveling with other clubs.

The 1926 Lismore Gophers had attracted the biggest name in independent baseball to throw for them. John pitched the entire year with less-talented players than he had previously known at Bertha; the Gophers had a less-than-stellar record of twenty wins and twenty-four losses with one tie. The biggest difference between the 1926 season and the previous ones was Lismore's maintenance of a more prolonged schedule, which overworked its ace hurler. Donaldson appeared in all but six games for the Gophers. He still managed to carry a walloping .448 batting average. In a stretch from July 14 to August 15, he pitched ten games, having a pair of three-hit contests and strikeout totals of fourteen, fifteen, seventeen, and eighteen.[53] The thirty-four-year-old Donaldson dominated at times, but the overall result was less than magical.

Bertha's manager Ernie Fisher brought Donaldson back to the Fishermen for the 1927 season. Fisher recruited new semipro ballplayers for the team, including the key element—black catcher Sylvester "Hooks" Foreman, who had previously played in the Negro National League with the Indianapolis ABC's and with the Kansas City Monarchs. Foreman was known as a showman behind the plate as well as a great catcher and hitter.[54] With Foreman in the fold and a respectable team assembled around him, John Donaldson and the Bertha ballclub again dominated semiprofessional baseball in Minnesota.

> "Curve them when they think they're coming straight, straighten them out when they are expecting a curve, lob them when they are set for fast ones; and come on with the speed in a pinch."
>
> **George Edward "Rube" Waddell, pitcher**

The Fishermen opened the 1927 season in front of 2,600 fans at a packed park that had been expanded in order to accommodate more automobiles in the outfield. The first opponent was the St. Paul Armours, the 1926 amateur state champions. Carloads of baseball fans from all parts of the state ventured to the little town in the woods, coming from as far south as New Ulm, as far north as Duluth, and as far west as Wahpeton, North Dakota; one car even had New York state license tags.[55] The Bertha franchise enjoyed wide coverage among local newspapers. Representatives from the *Long Prairie Leader, Eagle Bend News, Sauk Centre Herald, Verndale Sun, Parkers Prairie Independent, Clarissa Independent, Wadena Pioneer Journal, New York Mills Herald, Grey Eagle Gazette, Browerville Blade, Henning Advocate, Sebeka Review, Menahga Journal,* and *Staples World* attended the game.

Although Bertha lost 7–5, Donaldson struck out twelve, and with that the old Donaldson was assuredly back, at the ripe old age of thirty-five. The gate receipts bulged as the Bertha management kept a handsome total of $395.30. Despite the initial loss, the Bertha ballclub embarked on a run—winning an amazing string of twenty-four games with but a single defeat. Fans continued to flock into Bertha from all over, and sportswriters delivered favorable reviews: "Two auto loads of fans came from Aberdeen, South Dakota, last Thursday forenoon, a distance of 190 miles. They stopped on the highway, sent a man to the gate to ask, 'Does Donaldson pitch today?' and when the reply was 'yes' all paid their 50 cents each to see Donaldson in action."[56]

According to another newspaper story, "Herman O. Sonnesyn, former editor of the *Bertha Herald*, who has now been at Bessemer, Michigan, three weeks, is still hearing and talking Bertha baseball. 'Sonny' writes in part as follows: 'Must tell you something I heard about John Donaldson. The fellows here knew I had been in Bertha and would you believe it knew all about our baseball record. Was never so surprised in my life as the other night when I heard a fellow discussing the Armour game. . . . So you see the world is small. Here I am in Michigan and the first crack out of the box I hear about John Donaldson.'"[57]

The two biggest dates in 1927 happened within a three-day span in August. In two games more than eleven thousand people would see the Bertha team play. The first was the Northern Minnesota Fair in Bemidji, where five thousand fans took in the contest that pitted Bertha against an all-black team, the Gilkerson Union Giants from Chicago. Bertha won the game 5–3 behind a fourteen-strikeout performance from Donaldson.[58] The other event was the great day of the Lindbergh Festival in Little Falls.

One week after the Lindbergh event, the Bertha Fishermen traveled to Fargo-Moorhead to battle the rebuilt and more powerful Twins, beefed up with the addition of the Southern Minnesota League All Stars. As was often the case, opposing teams hired out-of-town talent for contests against Donaldson, as one sportswriter stated, "Reports from Fargo are that they have scoured the entire state and northwest for players to beat Donaldson's crew." As the 1927 season progressed, the normal hometown teams grew tired of losing to Bertha. Consequently, they bolstered their lineups in hopes of limiting the dominance of a supreme black hurler.[59] Donaldson ended up holding Fargo-Moorhead to no earned runs or hits in their game on September 5, while the all-stars from the Southern Minnesota League nipped Donaldson 4 to 3 giving him only his second loss in twenty-five tries.

The 1927 Bertha team finished the season with a record of twenty-eight wins and only four defeats. Bertha played teams from all over the state including New York Mills, Pelican Rapids, Battle Lake, St. Paul, Belle Plaine, Hutchinson, and Alexandria. Other games were held in the neutral cities of Breckenridge, Melrose, Sauk Centre, Bemidji, Little Falls, and Long Prairie. Donaldson ended with a final record of twenty-two wins and four losses and a batting average of .440.[60]

Then it happened to Bertha again; it lost Donaldson to a higher bidder, as a news story headlined it: "Donaldson Returns His Contract."

John W. Donaldson, for three years Bertha's premier mound ace, has returned his contract to the Bertha management with the request to have same cancelled. He has offers from several other places which will bring him much more money than Bertha can afford to pay, hence the resignation which the Bertha Baseball Committee had to accept reluctantly.[61]

Donaldson began the 1928 season pitching for the Scobey, Montana, ballclub, a team that featured the play of Swede Risberg, banished from baseball for his role in the Black Sox Scandal of 1919. Scobey had made a serious effort to entice the lefty away from Bertha in 1927. In order to cash in on the pitcher's name recognition, the Scobey ballclub toured Minnesota as John Donaldson's All Stars, a title that promised a larger gate. The team opened in Melrose, where Donaldson defeated the local club 3 to 0 before a crowd of 1,600.[62]

The All Stars next went to Little Falls where Donaldson lost. They were then scheduled to play Melrose at Breckenridge. Donaldson, after being offered a contract by Melrose, changed teams and played for Melrose. He continued there until his release from the club in late August, compiling a record of nine and six while Melrose finished the season with seventeen wins, fourteen losses, and one tie.[63]

After being released from Melrose, Donaldson offered his services to the Arlington nine. The town long held a reputation as a hotbed of small-town Minnesota baseball enthusiasm and talent. Arlington had hired a black pitcher earlier in its history when it signed George H. Wilson in 1903, and the town was looking to Donaldson in a match against Melrose on the Melrose diamond in early September. He lost to his former team by a score of 6–2, striking out only one batter.[64]

In the 1928 season, Donaldson influenced the course of black baseball in Minnesota by personally recommending a battery to Little Falls for its semiprofessional team. According to a contemporary account:

E. V. Wetzel, manager of the Little Falls Independent baseball team was notified late yesterday by John Donaldson that the colored battery from Chicago will sign a contract with the local organization. A letter will follow the wire message, giving the names of the players and other details. They probably will be signed up within a week.[65]

The black players that journeyed to Little Falls were Webster McDonald and John Van. McDonald went on to become a pitching star for the Little Falls organization for the next four seasons, compiling an astounding record of seventy wins, nine losses, and one tie and creating a baseball powerhouse in the Morrison County city. Van played catcher for Little Falls for only one season and was replaced at catcher by Sylvester "Hooks" Foreman for the 1929 season. Some sources indicate that John Van had to leave town after he allegedly winked at a white woman in the bleachers after a game.[66]

The 1929 season proved to be a marvelous chapter in the annals of Minnesota semiprofessional baseball history. The year witnessed a great expansion of semipro teams in the center of the state modeled after Bertha's success, as various teams hired players from the Twin Cities to come up by train or auto, play on the weekends, and then return to their jobs in the metropolitan area. This competition for the dollars of the baseball-watching public, along with Donaldson's departure from Bertha and, finally, the onset of the Great Depression, led to the dissolution of the Bertha semipro franchise. The Twin Cities players took their earnings back to their homes, spending little in Bertha.

Donaldson, in his declining years, took his glove and his bat and went on the road, joining the barnstorming Colored House of David team for the 1929 season. These black players claimed to be from Havana, Cuba, but were from all over, and that season they traveled throughout the Midwest and into Canada. The team used the famous "House of David" title on their jerseys but had no association with the Benton Harbor, Michigan, sect. The playing tour took him to only a smattering of games in Minnesota that year.[67]

Donaldson returned full time to Minnesota in 1930, taking up residence in St. Cloud. The St. Cloud Saints, a semipro team, arranged for Donaldson, now thirty-eight years old and an aging veteran of Minnesota baseball, to become affiliated with the ballclub. A local writer maintained that "Although Donaldson . . . is well along in years, he has taken an auspicious start. . . . The St. Cloud management is under no permanent obligation to the colored artist and he comes here with the understanding that he must deliver the goods in each game he starts." Donaldson accepted the contract in order to continue his career. With the advent of the Depression, black players were eager to play wherever they could get a contract. Certain of his ability, John took the mound on St. Cloud's terms.[68]

Donaldson started out eleven and two with the pair of losses coming against the archrival Little Falls club, which again employed McDonald and Foreman as battery-mates. Donaldson proved himself again in St. Cloud and pitched the entire year with the team. His season ended with a disappointing performance, however, when he pitched seven innings in an 8–1 loss to the American Association's St. Paul Saints.[69]

The 1931 season found Donaldson once again playing for his former team, the Kansas City Monarchs. The depths of the Depression sent the Negro National League into disarray. Teams needed to travel and rely, even more than before, on barnstorming. The Monarchs scheduled games across the Midwest, taking on all comers, and the team's travels brought it to Minnesota. On July 19, 1931, Donaldson and the Monarchs stopped in Crookston. They proceeded to shut out the team of all-stars assembled by Crookston businessmen 6–0 with Donaldson playing centerfield. Local newspapers featured him in articles promoting the game and, with John Donaldson appearing, the crowds came in droves.[70]

After spending the 1931 season on the road, Donaldson embarked upon an ambitious venture for the 1932 season. He knew of a ballpark south of Fairmont, on the shores of Silver Lake, called Hand's Park, having played several games at the park over the previous years. He approached the Hand family about wanting to start a new team, one that played an independent schedule with the home games to be played at the dilapidated grounds. Ernest Hand, Sr., was receptive to the idea, and Donaldson bought the old park and called Fairmont his home for at least part of the season.[71]

Donaldson's initial plans called for permanent lights for the diamond because night baseball might attract large crowds. He wanted to play as often as possible, night or day, regardless of the day of the week.

Donaldson then organized an all-black baseball team. One by one the players arrived in Fairmont in the spring of 1932. Donaldson had arranged accommodations for the players with Mr. Hand so they could stay in resort cottages located on the grounds of Hand's Park. Donaldson brought in friends from his wide-ranging past and recruited talented younger players to fill the lineup of his newly minted version of John Donaldson's All Stars. He landed Hooks Foreman to share the catching duties with a former Kansas City Monarch, Chappie Gray. To help with the pitching for his club, Donaldson

The *Fairmont Daily Sentinel* featured Donaldson and the All Stars at Hand's Park in an article on June 10, 1932; front row (left to right) Hurley McNair, George Jones, Chappie Gray, Charlie Hilton, ? Anderson; back row (left to right) John Donaldson, J. Moore Allen, ? Cunningham, Robert "Piggy" Hawkins, Bill Freeman, Joe "Jellyroll" Barker, Buzz Boldridge.

signed Bill Freeman, who had been working with semipro teams for the last few seasons throughout Minnesota.[72] His best player was the veteran Hurley McNair, who had started his career with the Minneapolis Keystones in 1911 and who had led the Negro Leagues in several hitting categories in the 1920s while with the Kansas City Monarchs. The elder players—Donaldson, Gray, and McNair—became mentors for the younger players.

Harry J. Earle, a sportswriter at the Fairmont newspaper, the *Daily Sentinel*, supported Donaldson to the utmost, writing regularly about the new additions to the All Stars: "Manager Donaldson brought 'Bill' Freeman, husky pitcher, back with him Sunday night. Freeman is said to be quite a hitter and John says that's what wins ball games. 'I want hitters,' said John 'and I think I have acquired some in "Jellyroll" Barker, "Piggy" Hawkins, Hurley McNair, Charlie Hilton and Chappie Gray.' That bunch should break a lot of pitchers' hearts this summer."[73]

The team spent the month of May repairing the grandstands and working on the infield grass, including rebuilding the pitching mound. Eleanor Donaldson stayed with her husband and prepared the meals for the players. After the diamond was ready, the field opened with a game on May 22.[74]

Donaldson's team then played host to a full schedule of contests against teams from Minnesota and Iowa and a couple of barnstorming clubs. Donaldson had assisted in the revival of the sport in Bertha, Lismore, and Melrose and was willing to add Hand's Park to the list of successful venues. But this time he managed his own team, his own ball park, and, most importantly, the gate receipts.[75]

Why would black players play in Fairmont? Hard times had befallen all of black baseball in the Depression, and ballplayers simply needed someplace, oftentimes anyplace, to earn some money. The prospect of playing for John Donaldson, among the best-known and most-respected players of the day, was appealing to the brotherhood of black baseball.

Probably the highlight of the season came early in the All Stars' run at Hand's Park. On May 22, 1932, the All Stars returned baseball to the refurbished park with an 8–1 victory over Corwith, Iowa.[76] Donaldson pitched the full nine innings, striking out eleven of the Nighthawks, never being in any danger. Charlie Hilton, the club's second baseman, went four for five with three doubles.

Donaldson's club charged forty cents admission to home games at Hand's Park. As the season progressed, the gate receipts increased gradually but eventually would not be enough to sustain the All Stars at their home field. Accordingly, Donaldson's All Stars left Minnesota just after the Fourth of July for a barnstorming tour to play teams from Missouri, Iowa, South Dakota, Nebraska, and Oklahoma.[77] They never returned for another season in Fairmont or in Minnesota.

Donaldson finished his playing days in the 1930s with the Kansas City Monarchs and became a coach; Satchel Paige was on the team. He spent his later life teaching baseball to children in the Chicago area. Ultimately, he finished his career in organized baseball as a scout for the integrated Chicago White Sox. He died in 1970, at age seventy-eight, and was buried in an unmarked grave at Burr Oak Cemetery in Alsip, Illinois. Until 2004 his gravesite was forgotten and unrecognizable, but, due to the efforts of history sleuth Jeremy Krock, an engraved stone and a bronze likeness of Donaldson now grace the final resting place of the talented pitcher who knew no respite during his barnstorming baseball days.[78]

Minnesota played an integral role in the baseball life of John Wesley Donaldson. He first arrived in the state in 1911 as a member of the barnstorming Tennessee Rats. An outstanding record with the tiny country town of Bertha followed, as well as stints with several other small Minnesota towns. He created much publicity and struck out fistfuls of hitters, garnering success wherever he went. In 1927, the year of Lindbergh's historic crossing of the Atlantic, he was the starting pitcher for the hero's hometown homecoming celebration game. His fame and reputation helped ultimately to pay his salary.

Donaldson's career stretched from 1911 to 1934. He deserves examination as a potential Hall of Fame ballplayer, but this gifted left-handed pitcher played in the wrong time period, beginning when there was a lull in the national black baseball scene corresponding to the time when he was in his prime. His peak performances came prior to the founding of the Negro League in 1920. Donaldson had a stellar reputation, but he spent too much of his time barnstorming in the 1910s and too much time in Bertha, Minnesota, in the 1920s to gain the recognition he might otherwise have received.

The 1920s was an era of the million-dollar drawing card. In his own way, John Donaldson used, and was used, for his famous name. He was a black pitcher who managed to make a living playing baseball in the Land of 10,000 Lakes. He must be remembered not only as the "greatest pitcher in the world" during his career, but as one of Minnesota's all-time, premier pitching talents.

The Mystery of Lefty Wilson

Peter W. Gorton

he strange saga of Lefty Wilson began in San Marcos, Texas, in 1896. That was the birth year of Dave Brown, the fourth son in a family of eight. He grew up dirt poor and made his way in life by playing baseball. At age twenty-one, he entered the history of black baseball as a pitcher for the Dallas Black Giants.[1]

In 1919 Brown was convicted of highway robbery. Fortunately for him, Rube Foster, the patriarch of black baseball and a fellow Texan, posted bail and got him out of jail on parole. Foster brought the left-hander north to be the ace of his Chicago American Giants in 1920, the inaugural year of the Negro National League. It was a big step away from his small-town roots, with plenty of big-city temptations in the age of Prohibition.

For the next three seasons, Dave Brown gained recognition as the "best left-hander produced by the Negro Leagues," according to baseball historian John Holway, as the American Giants dominated the league. In the off-season, he competed in Cuba (where alcohol and other activities illegal in the United States were not prohibited), posting a record of seventeen wins and twelve losses.[2]

The Eastern Colored League, formed in the winter of 1922–23, raided the Negro National League for many of its stars. Brown was among the players who jumped, signing with the New York Lincoln Giants. His record in New York did not match the glory of his Chicago days, and his career there ended in 1925 when he ran afoul of the law again.

On May 1, 1925, Dave Brown pitched his last game on the national stage, scattering seven hits as he held the Bacharach Giants to a single run in a 6 to 1 win. After the contest, Brown and two team-mates, Oliver Marcelle and Frank Wickware, went to a speakeasy in Harlem. Brown got involved in a late-night street brawl; perhaps there were illegal drugs involved, the facts of the case were unclear. But eyewitnesses claimed that a man named Benjamin Adair, a resident of Harlem, ran up to Brown and his two friends, shouting, "Now, I've got you." The man was brandishing a revolver. Shots rang out and Adair lay mortally wounded. He died in a Harlem hospital.[3]

Law officers showed up on the baseball field the next day, looking for the three ballplayers. Brown was nowhere to be found, having fled the city. Authorities sought him, but he went into hiding in the middle of the nation. Thus began his life on the run, a life spent in small towns similar to the ones of his childhood.

Brown showed up in Minnesota in July 1926 with Gilkerson's Union Giants, a traveling troupe of black ballplayers from Illinois. It was the perfect cover, pitching in towns throughout the Midwest, never staying in one place long enough for the authorities to catch up to him. He adopted a new name—Lefty Wilson. In a Fourth of July game, Wilson won by a score of 5 to 1 against the Lismore

Gophers and John Donaldson, who played outfield and then took the mound as a relief pitcher. The men would have known each other on sight, having played against each other in 1920, 1921, and 1922 when Wilson (then known as Dave Brown) was with the Chicago American Giants and Donaldson played for the Kansas City Monarchs. Nearly five thousand fans witnessed the event at a quaint ballpark just south of the city of Fairmont in southern Minnesota. Donaldson never revealed Lefty Wilson's true identity or that he was a fugitive from justice, but Wilson's four-hit masterpiece could have been a tip-off.[4]

Wilson continued pitching for the Gilkerson club for several games in Minnesota and Iowa through mid-July. He then signed on for a couple of ballgames with the Pipestone Black Sox, a black team based in historic Pipestone, a small town located in the far southwestern corner of Minnesota. The Pipestone Black Sox burst upon the regional baseball scene for only one season, playing an independent schedule in southern Minnesota, Iowa, and South Dakota in 1925 before relocating in Marcus, Iowa, in August 1926. The man behind the team was Frank Whitfield, an African American man from Pipestone (formerly a porter from Sioux Falls), who took over the operation of the Sioux Falls Black Sox.[5]

Wilson was dominant for the Black Sox; his wins included back-to-back shutouts on July 18 and 24. He defeated the Granite Falls ballclub, 10 to 0, and then set down Matlock, Iowa, by a score of 14 to 0.[6]

After the Black Sox moved to Iowa, another team came calling for Lefty, and he signed a deal to pitch for the small town of Ivanhoe. He pitched in three games for Ivanhoe, winning two and losing one, averaging just over fourteen strikeouts in the three games.[7]

A week later Lefty brought his talented pitching arm to the small farming community of Wanda in Redwood County, ninety miles northeast of Pipestone. Wanda was a member of the Redwood-Brown-Watonwan Tri-County League (TCL), a flourishing baseball league. A local sportswriter praised Wilson

The *Pipestone County Star* reported "The famous Wanda baseball club, with 'Lefty' Wilson, great colored pitcher, to meet the fast Tracy team in Pipestone, July 4th." Wilson stood fourth from the left for this picture, perhaps trying not to have his full face photographed.

for his "sharp breaking curve, [his] deceptive change of pace, and his wonderful control" and counted him a "pitcher of the highest class" and "one of the greatest of his race." Wilson helped Wanda win the Tri-County League's second-half championship playoff game against the Comfrey team. He silenced the Comfrey bats by recording eighteen strikeouts en route to the title, allowing Wanda to represent the league in the Minnesota State Amateur Tournament at Lexington Park in St. Paul.[8]

Many fans from Wanda accompanied the team to its first-round game against the St. Paul Armours. Others stayed at home and huddled around their radios to hear the broadcast of the game, along with a dose of static, on WCCO radio. The sounds the people heard were not music to their ears, however. The Wanda bats faded like a radio signal easing into the western ozone as the hometown Armours took their first step on the way to the 1926 State Amateur Championship.[9]

Wilson's success convinced the manager of the Wanda ballclub to make him the team's main pitcher for 1927, and Wilson complied with league rules by taking up residence in the village. He began the year with five straight victories, vaulting Wanda to the first-half championship of the Tri-County League. The team's record of eight wins against one loss edged out the strong Sanborn team by one full game in the standings. The second half proved more difficult for Wanda, largely because Wilson pitched for non-league clubs on a game-by-game basis. One of these appearances was for the Bertha Fishermen in Little Falls and served as a precursor for his 1928 season.[10]

Lefty returned to Wanda for the stretch run and the league championship series against Comfrey. The best-of-three games playoff took only two games as Wilson won both, 8 to 1 and 2 to 1, recording ten and thirteen strikeouts, respectively.[11]

Wanda again qualified for the state tournament in St. Paul but lost to the Franklin Creamery team from Minneapolis, 6–0, in the first round. Despite Wilson's mighty effort, his team failed to score in their 1927 big city appearance, falling 6–0 and closing their season.[12]

In 1928, Wanda applied to play again in the Tri-County League but the league's officials issued a pronouncement directed at Lefty Wilson: "The rules under which the circuit operated last year were approved with the exception that the color line was drawn and the status of home players was defined." The ruling barred Wilson from ever again playing in this small-town Minnesota baseball league. But Wilson's talent was not to be wasted. When John Donaldson left the Bertha ballclub in 1928, manager Ernie Fisher signed Wilson as Donaldson's replacement.[13]

Wilson lived up to Fisher's hopes, winning five of Bertha's first six ballgames. His only loss came at the hands of another black pitcher, Webster McDonald of the strong Little Falls semipro franchise. Wilson finished the season with fourteen wins and eight losses, part of a sixteen-and-nine team campaign. But the team's directors considered the record and attendance figures to be failures. Gross receipts declined from previous years because of the loss of Donaldson and too many nearby teams, like Little Falls and New York Mills, upgrading their ballclubs to compete with Bertha for fan support. The competition for limited sports dollars brought an end to Bertha's dominance in central Minnesota.[14]

The Bertha Baseball Committee decided to downgrade their team, joining eight other towns in the Otter Tail, Todd, and Wadena County League. These teams could use only home talent to fill their rosters, in hopes of developing local players.[15] This move spelled the end of semipro baseball in Bertha, and Lefty Wilson left Bertha for good.

Wilson returned to his life on the road, pitching for traveling ballclubs throughout the Midwest for the next couple of years. In 1929 he played for the Sioux City, Iowa, Auto Kary-Alls, also serving as the team's captain. The next year he was hired to pitch for the Little Falls club while ace pitcher Webster McDonald recovered from an injury.[16]

Little is known of Lefty Wilson's career after he departed from Little Falls after the 1930 baseball season. Perhaps he encountered trouble with the law again, but maybe he matured and left those ways behind him. His historical path appears to have been lost in the turmoil of the Great Depression.

The Bertha Fishermen in 1928: (left to right) Ole Wald, Pete Briere, Sylvester "Hooks" Foreman, Lefty Wilson, Earl Plummer, manager Ernie Fisher, unknown, Carl Gregerson, Al Theis, "Getty" Geithman

Maceo Breedlove: Big Fish in a Small Pond

Kyle McNary

I love baseball. That's the only thing I ever loved. That's the only thing I ever did that my mother told me not to do. Baseball's been my hobby all my life.   Maceo Breedlove

The story has been told before: a pitcher is such a powerful hitter that he's moved to the outfield to get his bat in the lineup every day. The player becomes the most powerful hitter around, and at various ballparks people point to spots well beyond the distant fences and say, "That's where he hit the farthest homer ever in this park!"

The story has been told—just not about the man I'm going to describe. This isn't a story about Babe Ruth, the major leagues' greatest slugger; it's about Maceo Breedlove, the greatest slugger in Twin Cities' segregated baseball history.

Actually, the Babe and Breed were a lot alike in that they both loved baseball, both were outgoing, and both loved the company of women. But their baseball journeys, fortunes, and fame could not have been more different. The Babe made as much as ninety thousand dollars a season, was on the covers of magazines, and was the idol of millions. Breedlove never made more than one hundred dollars a month playing ball, and his name did not appear in a major newspaper until his obituary was printed after his death on May 12, 1993.

Breedlove was born August 7, 1900, in Fayetteville, Alabama. He grew big and strong (six feet two inches, 200 pounds as an adult) and loved the game of baseball as a young child. At the age of fifteen, Breedlove was good enough to be the top pitcher on a Fayetteville team that also featured his brothers Wallace (catcher), Alvin (center field), Albert (third base), and Charles (first base). The Breedlove family moved to the Birmingham area in 1918 where Maceo's father worked in the coal mines. Edgewater, Alabama, had a youth league set up for coal miners and their children, and Maceo played with them for three years before moving to Minneapolis in 1922.

Once in the Twin Cities, Breedlove played for the St. Paul Giants, a black team sponsored by the Johnny Baker Legion Post, and with the Pioneer Limited Railroad team. In 1928 Breedlove was recruited by Harry Crump, the owner of the Original Negro House of David. Crump was a black hotel owner in Minneapolis with a reputation for providing female companionship to guests for the right price. The Negro House of David, like the original white team out of Benton Harbor, Michigan, had their players wear long beards and play pepper to entertain fans.

Former Kansas City Monarch and Chicago American Giant catcher Leland C. "Lee" Davis also played for the Davids. Davis had a reputation as a fine receiver and, according to his son Harry, spent several years traveling the Midwest catching for Negro League legend John Donaldson. Davis, by the way, was not African American—he was a Winnebago-Sioux Indian whose skin was too brown for him to be allowed to play in organized professional baseball.[1]

In 1934 Breedlove and Davis signed with the Twin Cities Colored Giants, which were sponsored by the Stillman brothers who owned Stillman grocery stores. The Colored Giants did not belong to the Negro National League with teams like the Chicago American Giants, Baltimore Black Sox, or Pittsburgh Crawfords. They were, however, a good black traveling team based in the Twin Cities, and they occasionally played Negro League teams

Maceo Breedlove (front row, third from left) and the Twin Cities Colored Giants in 1934

like the Kansas City Monarchs. Mostly, though, the Colored Giants played white semipro town teams. In the 1930s just about every town in the Midwest had a town team made up of local residents, plus a few ringers from the minor leagues now and then. Against these opponents the Colored Giants usually won with ease. Unlike the Negro League teams that played every day from Labor Day through Memorial Day, the Colored Giants scheduled their games mostly on weekends because nearly all of the team's players had regular jobs. Lee Davis worked as a truck driver and would throw benches in the back of his truck bed on weekends to haul the Colored Giants to towns in Wisconsin, Minnesota, and the Dakotas. During the four seasons the Colored Giants existed, the team featured only a few names of notoriety. Bill Freeman, who spent time in the Negro Leagues with the Indianapolis ABC's and Cuban Stars, was the team's best pitcher.

Marcenia "Toni" Stone, "the black Babe Didrickson," was a sixteen-year-old pitcher for the Colored Giants in the 1937 season before going on to fame with the Indianapolis Clowns as one of the few women to play in the Negro Leagues. "She could throw just like a man," remembered Larry Brown, who played with the Colored Giants as a teenager. "She was thin, kind of built like a boy. We never thought of her as a date, she was such a good player." Brown, by the way, remembered being paid an occasional ham sandwich and lemonade in lieu of money. These were Depression times.[2]

The Giants featured men named Chinx Worley, Tom English, Ollie Petiford, Wellington Coleman, Jake Footes, Rubber Arm Johnson, and Bobby "The Grand Old Man" Marshall. There was even an ambidextrous pitcher who had a six-fingered glove. In short, Breedlove was the star player on a good but not great team. It is fair to surmise that, had Breedlove wanted to, he could have played with most of the great Negro League teams of his day.

Harry Davis, tagging along to a Colored Giants game one afternoon in Nicollet Park recalled, "Maceo said to me, 'Little Pops,' he called my dad Pops, 'if I hit a homer today I'm gonna buy you a Baby Ruth candy bar.' He hit one over the fence and off the awning of a store across Lake Street!"[3]

The Colored Giants traveled in a pair of jalopies, one of which towed a homemade enclosed wood trailer in which Ernest "Smokey" Tomlinson, Maceo's nephew, slept. Smokey served as driver, mechanic, cook, and, in a pinch, player. On one road trip that the Colored Giants took, Smokey could not repair one of the cars that broke down so the two cars were tied together at the bumpers to get to a town where they could buy needed auto parts. On another road trip, several games were rained out, and Breedlove had to pawn his watch to buy gas to get home. As expected, the Colored Giants were not always met with open arms in the towns across the Midwest, and they spent many nights sleeping in their cars, at campsites, or even in the dugout of a ballpark.

We probably will never know how good the Twin Cities Colored Giants were. There is not an abundance of box scores from games against teams whose quality can be accurately gauged. In 1934 the Giants beat the Arkansas, Wisconsin, team 23–4 but lost to the Northern Pacific Railroad team 11–9. Davis believed that, when the Giants put their best lineup on the field, they were as good as the teams on the top rungs of the minors. Only in the pitching department, thought Davis, were the Giants not able to compete with the higher-level teams.

> "[The 1935 Bismarck (ND) Churchills baseball team] had a wonderful staff [of four black pitchers]. They were so darn good. Just the color of their skin kept them out of the major leagues. They were men; so powerful and they kept their heads high."
>
> **Ernest Burke, pitcher**

Four games that the Twin Cities Colored Giants played provide some evidence for determining their strength. In 1934 the Colored Giants visited Jamestown, North Dakota, to face the integrated Jamestown Red Sox featuring Negro League stars Double Duty Radcliffe, Steel Arm Davis, Bill Perkins, and Barney Brown. This team, a few months later, would whip a major league all-star in three straight games—the majors featured Jimmie Foxx, Heinie Manush, Doc Cramer, Pinky Higgins, and Ted Lyons.

The Colored Giants were completely outclassed and lost 19–3. Double Duty, an all-star pitcher and catcher, held the Giants to seven hits (one by Breedlove) and collected five hits himself. In fact, the "Colored Quartet" of Radcliffe, Davis, Perkins, and Brown collected two hits each in the fifth inning. Perkins needed a single in his last at-bat to hit for the cycle, but he smacked one in the gap and could not help but take second. The losing pitcher for the Giants was Bill Freeman, the ace of the staff.[4]

The last three games were against the integrated 1935 Bismarck semipro team that Satchel Paige called the greatest team he ever saw. It featured the pitching staff of Paige, Radcliffe, Hilton Smith, and Barney Morris, as well as other Negro League stars Quincy Trouppe, Red Haley, and Art Hancock and white stars Joe Desiderato and Moose Johnson. In the first game, Morris pitched for Bismarck and won, 8–5. Breedlove singled twice against Morris, who pitched in several East-West All-Star games (the Negro Leagues' greatest talent showcase every season). The second game was again won by Bismarck, 9–5, this time behind the hurling of Hilton Smith, a 2001 Hall of Fame inductee. Breedlove singled and homered off Smith, whom many considered the equal of any pitcher of his day, including Paige.

Then came the final game of the series, for which I would like to set the scene. I met Maceo at his home in Minneapolis a few months before he died in 1993. He was lying in bed and hooked up to oxygen. A home nurse was attending to him. I showed him the box score of the game in which he faced Satchel Paige. He gave me a big smile but couldn't talk. The box score confirmed a story he had told for years, a story that he worked into every baseball conversation, a story he could never prove and sounded too good to be true.

"I played against Satchel Paige," he would say, "and I showed him who the baddest man with a bat around these parts was!" Indeed he did. I was going to visit him again, but I got the news of his passing. It was nice to know, though, that he had a happy memory to ease some of the pain of his last days.

Now for the game: On August 12, 1935, Satchel took the mound against the Twin Cities Colored Giants. In the top of the first, Maceo ripped the greatest pitcher of all time, in his prime, over the wall for a two-run homer. "We can beat him!" the Giants might have thought. The feeling did not last long.

Bismarck homered five times in their half of the first inning and eventually rolled to a 21–6 win. Maceo, however, had the day he would never forget. In his next two at-bats he doubled, barely missing homers. Satchel did not appreciate such disrespect, and he set out to show the crowd who the master was. In the Giants' last at-bat, Maceo was scheduled to bat third, and Paige knew it. As Bismarck strolled out to take the field, Satchel stopped his teammates. "A catcher and a first baseman," said Paige, "that's all I want."

So, with no infield or outfield, Satchel struck out the first two batters with ease. Maceo told the story of what followed in a taped interview in the mid-1980s; it matches the account from the *Bismarck Tribune*. He recalled:

At the time, Satchel Paige was the greatest man that was out there. He struck out a man any time he want to. So they had us beat pretty bad and wasn't nobody out there but him [the catcher] and the first baseman. Now he gonna strike me out!

Looked like everybody in North Dakota at that ball game. One boy on the [Bismarck] ball club knew me and he said, "Satchel done picked the baddest boy on the ball club to show up."

I bet I hit 15 foul balls. He was throwing the ball so fast I couldn't get around in time and I fouled 'em off. He couldn't get me out with his fast ball so he threw me his curve ball and I hit it into left field and nobody was out there. I ran around the bases and came back in.

I had one boy playing on the club and when he found out Satchel was pitching he went out sick—he didn't want to play against him. He said to me, "Why didn't you let Satchel strike you out too?"

I said, "I wouldn't let nobody make a fool out of me in front of all these people if I can help it."

In 1938 Maceo formed his own team, the Broadway Clowns, and he barnstormed through Wisconsin, Minnesota, and Manitoba. In 1944 Maceo, a lifelong bachelor, fell in love with Betty Hyatt, got married, and hung up his spikes for good. He coached women's softball teams on which his daughter and nieces played, and he was a popular beer vendor at Metropolitan Stadium in Bloomington, wearing his famous "umbrella hat."

Maceo Breedlove may have been a big fish in a small pond, but in Barney Morris, Hilton Smith, and Satchel Paige, he swam with some pretty big fish.

Maceo Breedlove in four games versus Satchol Poige, Barney Morris, Double Duty Radcliffe, and Hilton Smith, all of whom pitched in multiple East-West All-Star games.

G	AB	R	H	2B	3B	HR	Avg	Slug %
4	17	6	9	2	0	3	.529	1.176

Batting of other Colored Giants players in those four games.

G	AB	R	H	2B	3B	HR	Avg.	Slug %
4	123	13	27	3	1	0	.220	.260

May 23, 1934, at Jamestown

Colored Giants (3)	AB	R	H	Jamestown (19)	AB	R	H
Vicks, 3b	3	1	1	Foster, 2b	6	1	3
Harris, cf	4	1	1	Warden, ss	5	2	2
Coleman, ss	4	0	0	Perkins, c	4	4	3
Foot, 2b	3	0	0	Davis 1b	5	3	3
Breedlove, rf	4	1	1	Radcliffe, p	5	3	5
Jackson, lf	3	0	1	Brown, rf	5	2	4
Oler, 1b	3	0	2	A. Schauer, cf	4	2	1
Freeman, p	2	0	1	F. Schauer, 3b	5	1	2
Davis, c	3	0	0	Deeds, lf	5	1	0
K. Jackson, p	1	0	0	Westby, 3b	0	0	0
Totals	30	3	7	Totals	44	19	23

Twin Cities Colored Giants . . . . 000 001 2 - 3
Jamestown Red Sox . . . . 203 680 X -19

Summary: winning pitcher-Radcliffe, losing pitcher-Freeman

Doubles-Oler, Harris, Perkins 2, Davis, Foster 2, F. Schauer

Triples-A. Schauer, Perkins; Home runs-Perkins

Struck out: by Radcliffe 10, by Freeman 1

*Game ended after the top of the 7th at the request of the Colored Giants.[5]

August 10, 1935, at Bismarck

Colored Giants (5)	AB	R	H	Bismarck (8)	AB	R	H
Coleman, 2b........	4	0	1	Oberholzer, 2b.......	3	3	2
Worley, 1b	5	1	2	Leary, ss...........	3	2	2
Hopwood, cf	4	1	1	Trouppe, c	4	1	1
Hamilton, ss........	4	0	1	Johnson, lf.........	3	1	3
Breedlove, rf	4	1	2	Haley, 1b...........	4	0	0
Carter, 3b	4	1	1	H. Smith, cf.........	4	1	1
McGowan, lf	4	0	0	Desiderato, 3b......	4	0	0
Foote, c............	3	1	0	Paige, rf	4	0	1
Porter, p	4	0	1	Morris, p...........	4	0	0
Totals	36	5	9	Totals	33	8	10

Twin Cities Colored Giants . . . . 030 000 020 - 5
Bismarck . . . . 420 000 20X - 8

Summary: winning pitcher-Morris, losing pitcher-Porter

Home runs-Oberholzer, Leary 2, Smith

Struck out: by Morris 7, by Porter 3

Walks: off Morris 2; off Porter 2

August 11, 1935, at Bismarck

Colored Giants (5)	AB	R	H	Bismarck (9)	AB	R	H
Coleman, 2b........	4	0	0	Oberholzer, 2b......	5	1	4
Worley, 1b	4	0	0	Leary, ss...........	3	1	2
Hopwood, cf	4	0	0	Hancock, cf........	5	2	1
Breedlove, rf	4	1	2	Johnson, lf.........	5	2	4
Hamilton, ss........	4	2	2	Haley, 1b	5	1	2
Carter, 3b	4	2	2	H. Smith, rf.........	5	1	2
McGowan, lf	3	0	0	Desiderato, 3b......	3	1	1
Foote, c	4	0	1	Morris, c...........	4	0	1
Thorpe, p	1	0	1	McCarney, rf	3	0	0
Porter, ph	1	0	0				
Totals	33	5	8	Totals	38	9	17

Twin Cities Colored Giants . . . . 000 000 302 - 5
Bismarck . . . . 200 002 14X - 9

Summary: winning pitcher-Smith, losing pitcher-Thorpe

Doubles-Haley

Triples-Thorpe

Home runs-Breedlove, Johnson 2, Hancock, Haley

Struck out: by Smith 5, by Thorpe 1

Walks: off Smith 0; off Thorpe 1

August 12, 1935, at Bismarck

Colored Giants (6)	AB	R	H	Bismarck (21)	AB	R	H
Coleman, 2b........	4	1	1	Oberholzer, 2b......	6	1	1
Worley, lf, 1b	5	1	2	Leary, ss..........	5	4	3
Hopwood, cf	4	1	1	Hancock, cf........	5	2	2
Breedlove, rf	5	3	4	Johnson, lf.........	6	3	4
Hamilton, ss........	5	0	0	Haley, 1b	6	3	4
Carter, 3b	4	0	1	H. Smith, rf.........	6	1	2
Foote, c	3	0	1	Desiderato, 3b......	5	2	1
Thompson, p	0	0	0	Morris, c..........	5	2	1
McGowan, pr.......	0	0	0	Paige, p	5	3	4
Porter, lf	3	0	1				
Totals	37	6	12	Totals	40	21	22

Twin Cities Colored Giants . . . . 200 101 101 - 6

Bismarck 540 930 00X-21

Summary: winning pitcher-Paige, losing pitcher-Thompson

Doubles-Porter, Breedlove 2, Foote, Haley 2, Paige 2, Johnson, H. Smith, Hancock

Home runs-Breedlove 2, Oberholzer, Leary, Johnson, Desiderato, Hancock

*In the 8th inning the Bismarck players batted from the opposite side of the plate from which they were accustomed.

A Negro League Team in Minnesota, 1942

innesota finally got a franchise in the national Negro Leagues in 1942—the Twin City Gophers. Unfortunately the ballclub did not complete the entire season, most likely because of wartime conditions. Probably for that reason the team does not appear in works on the history of the Negro Leagues.

After the establishment of the Negro League by Rube Foster in 1920, there had been several attempts to include Minneapolis and St. Paul in the all-black circuit. Nothing came of the efforts, primarily because the expenses of traveling to the other league cities by railway and the associated costs of hotels and food appeared to be too great. For the same reason, Minnesota did not gain entry into the white major leagues either.

The year 1942 was a tempestuous one in American history, for the nation had entered World War II after the Japanese attack the previous December. The country cranked up its industrial system for the fight, and the lives of young men became disrupted as they answered the call of military service. All of baseball faced serious changes in personnel and practices due to the war emergency.

The tumult brought an opportunity for Minneapolis and St. Paul to enter the Negro League. A local black newspaper printed the story on its front page in April: "Twin Cities to Have Negro Nat'l League Entry." Details were sketchy at that time, but apparently the ballclub would play its games at St. Paul's Lexington Park when the St. Paul Saints were on the road.[1]

The manager of the team was Jim Brown, a man who was well known in black baseball circles. Brown had gained his reputation on the old Chicago American Giants under Rube Foster. As catcher, Brown helped his team win three pennants from 1920 through 1923, the first in the history of the Negro National League. He became manager of the American Giants in 1929 following Foster's death and played in the league until 1935. Getting a position with the Gophers gave him an opportunity to resurrect his managing career, which had languished.[2]

The big newspapers, the *St. Paul Pioneer Press* and the *Minneapolis Tribune,* were willing to give some (but not extensive) coverage to the local entry in the "Negro major leagues" when the team made its debut on June 21 in a Sunday doubleheader against the Chicago American Giants. The *Pioneer Press* welcomed the "outstanding Negro teams," who could now play league games in St. Paul, rather than making appearances in exhibition games in Lexington Park while on tour. The *Minneapolis Tribune* noted that "more than 1,200 spectators" watched the Gophers sweep the doubleheader against the Giants in a Negro American League matchup.[3]

The star of the team that day was the left fielder, Reece "Goose" Tatum. Better known as a showman in basketball with the Harlem Globetrotters, Tatum was promoted as a "great fielder, hitter and runner" and touted as a "crowd-pleaser with his antics" on the field. In the first game, Tatum "got two hits in three times at bat, one of them a triple," and with the Gophers leading "by one slim run, he made a tremendous throw in from left field to put out the tying run at the plate." In game two, Tatum "collected two more hits and drove in two runs" and "added a couple of sensational catches" to the "prolonged applause" of the spectators. A local reporter referred to Tatum as one of baseball's "rare specimens," a "natural clown who can back his antics up in actual play." He won the crowd's heart with his "amiable, flat-footed, high-stepping" style as an outfielder who "runs bases like Stepin Fetchit but wallops the ball like Babe Ruth."[4]

A three-game set against the Cincinnati Ethiopian Clowns provided a chance for the Gophers to pass the Clowns as "leaders of the Negro major leagues" standings with an "upset triumph." The confrontation turned into a double setback when the Clowns outclassed the Gophers 12–3 in a Wednesday night game and then edged the Gophers 1–0 in a Sunday game, shortened to five innings by rain. The second Sunday game had to be cancelled. The Clowns put on their "white grease-paint makeup" and staged their trademark "series of shadow ball and pepper-game" exhibitions with "showboat practice acrobatics" as a part of the pregame show.[5]

The Gophers played just four home games in June and then left on a road trip to parts unknown on June 28, returning to St. Paul for two games on Sunday, July 12. It was an unusual twin-bill, consisting

Back-Stop

RUFUS HATTON

Catcher For Gophers
Minneapolis-St. Paul Negro
Major League Entrants

The *Minneapolis Spokesman* on July 10, 1942, ran a front-page article about the upcoming games of the Negro League's Gophers.

of a game against the Chicago Brown Bombers first and then a second contest versus the Cincinnati Ethiopian Clowns—the "two top teams of the Negro circuit." The Gophers triumphed in game one, defeating the Chicago Brown Bombers, 3–0, with newly arrived pitcher Gready McKinnis (from the Birmingham Black Barons) pitching a two-hit shutout and hitting a home run. Negro great Ted "Double Duty" Radcliffe had joined the Gophers and was the catcher. Goose Tatum accounted for the other two runs with a single and a triple. The second game was not so good for the Gophers as they lost badly, 12–5, to the Clowns.[6]

At that point in July, the Gophers went off on another road trip, this time for a month, and literally fell off the map. The team was supposed to return on August 12 for games in St. Paul with the Birmingham Barons, Memphis Black Sox, and others, but it apparently dissolved. The last word from the sports pages was that the team "had signed several new men since they left home," which might indicate that players had left the Gophers for other opportunities, perhaps for a more stable team.[7]

A combination of factors no doubt brought on the quick demise of the Twin City Gophers. A military order prohibited night baseball after August 20 in order to comply with blackout rules for civilian defense. All the minor leagues were said to be hurt by the ban. Rationing began for gasoline, and it was more difficult to get enough for a long trip by bus. Additionally, railway rates shot up in wartime (the Minneapolis Millers paid an extra two thousand dollars for players' fares in 1942 compared to 1941). Additional federal taxes for the war effort raised the costs also. Uniforms that had cost twenty dollars each in 1941 went up to twenty-eight dollars. Similarly "sweater coats which formerly cost $15" each rose to nineteen dollars. Baseballs, sold by the dozen for fifteen dollars increased to eighteen dollars per dozen.[8]

The team was sometimes called the "Minneapolis–St. Paul Gophers" and sometimes the "Twin City Gophers," but either way, it did not last very long in the league. Available evidence indicates that the Gophers played only six official home games; total road games are unknown at this point. As for the men, some went on to other playing fields, and some undoubtedly joined the war effort in one capacity or another. Double Duty Radcliffe signed on with the Chicago American Giants the following season. Goose Tatum became a part of the Indianapolis Clowns ballclub in 1943, and his comedic skills served him well in the off-season as he performed with the Harlem Globetrotters.[9]

Roy Campanella and the Breaking of the Color Barrier

Ted Genoways

On May 22, 1948, after the top of the first inning, Roy Campanella strapped on his chest guard and trotted out behind home plate to begin warming up St. Paul Saints pitcher Phil Haugstad. It did not seem like a momentous occasion, but it was the first time an African American had played in baseball's American Association. Unfortunately, it was an inauspicious debut for Campanella. The Columbus Red Birds' rookie pitcher, Harvey Haddix, held him hitless that day—twice striking him out. To make matters worse, in the bottom of the fourth, he tried to pick Mike Natisin off second base. The throw hit the bag and rolled into right field, allowing the runners to advance. An error was charged to Campanella. Years later, he remembered that day in his autobiography, *It's Good to Be Alive*:

If my debut was any indication of my ability, I'd be back in the Negro league real quick.

I wasn't happy with my first game in Triple A baseball, but I wasn't upset either. I'd been around too long to get the shakes because of one bad day. I just hustled and kept my mouth shut.[1]

The pressure of being the first black ballplayer in the league would have been great enough, but, as Campanella remembered, the tension was increased because the "St. Paul papers didn't exactly roll out a red carpet."[2]

Joe Hennessy of the *St. Paul Pioneer Press* was especially critical. When Saints general manager Mel Jones had announced on May 18 that Campanella would be dispatched to St. Paul on twenty-four-hour recall, Hennessy wrote, in an article titled "Saints Get Campanella, Negro Catcher," that the move "came as a complete surprise. No catcher had been expected as Ferrell Anderson has played sensational baseball in every game for the Saints."[3]

If, indeed, Hennessy was surprised by the move, he shouldn't have been. Brooklyn Dodgers' owner Branch Rickey had purchased the Saints during the off-season and had recently been making a concerted effort to integrate not only the major leagues but also the significant minor league affiliates since signing a handful of African American prospects in October 1945. He had grabbed headlines by slotting Jackie Robinson, then Dan Bankhead, into the Dodgers' lineup in 1947, but first he started Robinson with the Montreal Royals in 1946 in order to break the color barrier in the International League. He sent both Campanella and Don Newcombe to the Nashua, New Hampshire, team the following year to break the barrier in the Eastern League. When Robinson was moved into the Dodgers' lineup, Campanella was promoted to Montreal in order to establish integration in the National League, International League, and Eastern League at one time. Any astute observer must have suspected that Rickey acquired the Saints intending to integrate the team. Then, before the beginning of the season, he appointed as their new general manager Mel Jones, the man who had been the GM at Montreal in 1946 and 1947, seeing the Montreal Royals through their first two seasons of integration. Even a casual bystander must have suspected that Jones and Rickey would try out and possibly field African American players.

In fact, while the Royals and Dodgers were holding spring training in the Dominican Republic—whose baseball teams were already desegregated—Rickey tested some of his black prospects out with the Saints in their spring games in Texas. Hennessy reported that Rickey "shattered a precedent or two there by playing a Negro with the Dodgers against both Fort Worth and Dallas—the first time it had been tried in the state of Texas." He went on to observe that, "Had there been any ill feeling between the races it no doubt wou[l]d have been more evident in either Fort Worth or Dallas than in St. Paul. There apparently was none."[4] Thus, Rickey decided that the American Association was ready for integration, and he chose Campanella to do the job.

But there was a problem. Campanella had already proven himself the previous year in Montreal and anyone following the spring games in the Dominican Republic knew that his numbers were good enough to start with the Dodgers. Rickey summoned him to his suite in the Hotel Jaragua to explain his plan. As Campanella remembered it, Rickey told him, "You will be brought up as an outfielder . . . because I don't think you can make it as an outfielder." When Campanella expressed his confusion, Rickey continued:

If I weren't to bring you up to the Dodgers, people would wonder why. . . . If you were brought up as a catcher, you'd make the club. But I don't want you to make the club. I want to send you to St. Paul to lower the barriers in that league. Therefore, you will work out here with Montreal as an outfielder, and shortly before we return to the United States you will join the Dodgers—as an outfielder. You will fail—but your failure will be a glorious success. You will be optioned to St. Paul, and become their catcher. If you do the job there, I will bring you back at the end of the season. But first you will pioneer the Negroes into the American Association. Do you understand?[5]

Campanella told Rickey, "I'm a ballplayer, not a pioneer," but he reluctantly agreed. Dodgers' manager Leo Durocher argued with Rickey over the decision. He had been planning to switch Dodger catcher Gil Hodges to first base so that Campanella could start behind home plate, but he was instructed that his rookie catcher would see only limited action and only as an outfielder. On May 15, when all major league teams had to cut their rosters to twenty-five, Campanella would be sent down to St. Paul.

Campanella walked back to the clubhouse to begin packing for his trip. He later remembered:

> I was getting ready to leave when Jackie Robinson came in from infield practice to change his shirt. He didn't have to be a mind reader to know I'd gotten the ax.
>
> "Where are *you* going?" he asked.
>
> I looked at the man who had broken the color line in baseball and grinned.
>
> "I'm going to St. Paul, man. I'm going to open up a new league."[6]

It should be noted that the purity of Rickey's motives has been questioned from 1945 to the present. When asked about his decision to bring Jackie Robinson to the Dodgers, Rickey once replied, "I couldn't face my God any longer knowing that his black children were held separate and distinct from his white children in a game that has given me all I own."[7] However, he was more cagey at other times. Joe Hennessy reported in the *St. Paul Pioneer Press* that Rickey had explained his decision to field African American players for the Saints by saying that "any baseball man who would not make use of a good player, regardless of his color, was just not showing good business judgment." Hennessy was more apt to accept this explanation; he wrote:

> Dispatch of Roy Campanella, Negro Brooklyn catcher, to St. Paul is only less sensational than the signing by the Dodgers of Jackie Robinson by the difference between the major and minor leagues. . . .
>
> The playing of Robinson in Brooklyn, most baseball men believe did more to boost the Dodger attendance last season than did even the pennant winning club. The Dodgers' road attendance also has been up. The same was true with Montreal, which has played Negroes for two seasons.
>
> The same undoubtedly will be true in St. Paul. The move was aimed at box office results, as the Saints hardly needed a third catcher.[8]

There is no question that the Dodgers had been sagging in the pennant races during World War II and immediately after, and bringing in better players than his crosstown rivals the New York Giants and the New York Yankees was an obvious priority for Rickey. He needed better players to compete, and he also needed revenue from ticket sales to afford increasing salaries. Fielding

African American players suited both purposes; however, this ignores several decisions Rickey made that did not fit his claim that integration was merely good business.

It is often pointed out that New York mayor Fiorello La Guardia was pushing for his Committee on Unity to issue a statement that all baseball in New York would soon be integrated and suggested that Rickey was merely bowing to political pressure. What is less often cited is that Rickey had persuaded the committee's executive director, Dan Dodson, to look into the matter in the first place and had insisted that Larry McPhail, the owner of the New York Yankees, be included on the committee along with Rickey himself.[9] When McPhail began publicly denouncing the signing of black ballplayers in September 1945, Rickey countered by secretly scouting and then signing five players in October. In so doing, he forced the integration of the major leagues before McPhail could gather support from other owners.[10]

At the same time, Rickey was exerting pressure on other teams to integrate. If he really meant to keep the best players to himself, he could easily have signed multiple players to Dodger contracts before competing teams mustered support within their organizations for integration. In fact, the Dodgers already had a binding agreement with Larry Doby when scout Toby Karam reported to Rickey that Cleveland Indians owner Bill Veeck was interested in making Doby the first African American in the American League. Rickey told Mickey McConnell of the farm department, "As much as I would like to have Doby with us, I think it would be a healthy thing for the color line to be broken in the other league."[11] Weeks after Rickey released Doby from his contract, he did the same for Monte Irvin so he could sign with his National League archrivals, the New York Giants.

However, at the start of the 1948 season, Rickey had a more pressing concern for the future of major league integration. After the Dodgers brought up Robinson the previous year, four other African American players had been promoted. Larry Doby was fielded by the Indians in July. Then the St. Louis Browns picked up Willard Brown and Hank Thompson from the Kansas City Monarchs, and Rickey added pitcher Dan Bankhead to the Dodgers' roster in August. Of these additional four players, only Doby was returning to the majors at the start of 1948. Both Brown and Thompson, fed up with bigotry and the Browns' second-rate management, returned to the Monarchs. Dan Bankhead was repeatedly shelled by opposing batters—giving up eight runs in just three innings in his first start and a total of fifteen hits and eight walks over his combined ten innings in 1947. Rickey had been forced to send Bankhead back to the Nashua Class-B affiliate, but the last thing he wanted was for the public to begin to believe that African American players could not compete in the major leagues.[12]

By sending Campanella to St. Paul, Rickey could break the last color barrier among his Dodger affiliates, but he could also further observe how the young catcher handled intensified scrutiny. Shortly after his meeting with Rickey, Campanella hopped a plane for St. Paul. When he arrived with his wife, Ruthe, then almost eight months pregnant, and David, Ruthe's five-year-old son from a previous marriage, Campanella had only a few days to find his family an apartment to rent on Rondo Street before he joined the Saints on the road in Columbus, Ohio.[13]

His first games with the Saints reflected the effects of so many distractions. He recorded just two singles in his first twenty at-bats with only one RBI. Luckily for Campanella, the criticism of the St. Paul media did not reach him, and by the end of the Saints' eastern swing, his bat had begun to come alive. Going four for nine in his last two games with five RBIS, his confidence seemed to jump immediately. He later remembered, "I began to tune up my batting eye," just in time for his arrival in the Twin Cities for a crosstown Memorial Day series against the Minneapolis Millers.[14]

In the first game in Minneapolis's Nicollet Park, Campanella hit two towering home runs over the left-field fence in a 17–9 losing effort. The *Pioneer Press* ran a picture of Campanella rounding third and being congratulated by manager Walt Alston. The next day the Saints hosted the morning game of the holiday doubleheader. Joe Hennessy reported, "Two Saints playing their first 1948 games at Lexington Park contributed mightily toward the Saints' morning 11–6 victory at Lexington. Roy Campanella and Bob Ramazzotti, among other things, each slammed a triple and a homer."[15]

Ferrell Anderson got the start at catcher in the afternoon game in Minneapolis, but Campanella came up later in the game as a pinch hitter. Minneapolis pitcher Mario Picone's first pitch was a fastball high and inside that dropped Campanella to the dirt. Joe Henrickson reported in the *Minneapolis Tribune* that "Campanella picked himself up, looked the other way and never let anyone believe that he didn't enjoy what happened." Campanella told Hendrickson, "I keep one thing in mind. A colored ball player has to be a gentleman. It isn't wrong either that I have to be careful what I do out there. When I'm out, I don't argue. It isn't so difficult. I understand. And I don't let it interfere with my playing."[16]

That much was certain; in fact, the weekend series seemed to be a turning point in Campanella's career with St. Paul. He remembered in his autobiography:

Saints' manager Walt Alston congratulating Campanella following a home run on May 31, 1948, at Minneapolis's Nicollet Park

From then on there was no stopping me. I ran right through the league. It made no difference if the pitcher was right- or left-handed. I tagged them all. In two successive days I drove in eleven runs. Against Louisville I hit a home run, a triple, and a single, and batted in six runs. Next day I got a pair of home runs, a single, and batted in five runs.

Those base knocks stopped the other kind of knocks. The writers and fans treated me swell.[17]

Joe Hennessy was among the converts. He described Campanella's first two weeks of June with awe, writing that he was "ripping loose the Coliseum roof in left field on a home run rampage" and added that he was now "one of the most popular players to join the Saints in many seasons."[18] Indeed, by June 26, Campanella was batting .327 with 13 home runs and 35 RBIS, and his reputation as an excellent catcher was growing as well.

Such numbers could not be ignored for long, especially while the Brooklyn Dodgers had fallen to sixth place and their chances of pennant contention were fading. At the end of June, Rickey called the executives of all his minor league affiliates to Brooklyn for a so-called "council of war."[19] While the executives debated whether Campanella was ready yet for the major leagues, his wife, Ruthe, gave birth to Roy, Jr., in St. Paul on Sunday, June 20—Father's Day. Ruthe's mother took the train from New York to be with her daughter while Campanella went on the Saints' road trip to Toledo. On June 30, Campanella had another remarkable evening, playing outfield in

Campanella showed his powerful swing during his hitting streak in June 1948 for the Saints.

the first game and catching the second, while tallying a single, a double, and a home run.

When the team hit the clubhouse after the game, manager Alston came over to Campanella's locker. He later remembered the exchange, "'I've got news for you, Roy,' he said. 'Bad for me, but good for you. The Dodgers want you back. Right away.'"[20] He was on twenty-four-hour recall, so he was expected to report to Brooklyn in time for the game on July 2. Campanella hurriedly called his wife's doctor to make sure it was not too soon for her and Roy, Jr., to fly cross country. When the doctor gave them the okay, he made arrangements to fly back to meet them in St. Paul. Campanella later wrote:

We cleared out of the apartment in nothing flat and soon Ruthe, the baby and me were on a plane. Ruthe's mother, who had come out just before Roy, Jr., arrived, followed with David on the train.

Flying to New York I had time to think. What a difference compared to that other trip six weeks before, when I'd been flying the other way. In thirty-five games, I had batted .325 and drove in thirty-nine runs. Of my forty base hits, exactly half went for extra bases.[21]

But Campanella wouldn't have long to reflect on his success in St. Paul. When he reported to the Brooklyn clubhouse on July 2, he was informed that he would be starting that night at catcher.

The addition of Campanella to the lineup gave the Dodgers a recognizable surge. They went from last place on July 2 to first place by the first week of August, but the addition was too little too late. The Braves and Cardinals eventually outlasted the Dodgers, who finished third. Jules Tygiel, the noted baseball historian, concluded that "by using Campanella as a pawn in the integration campaign," Branch Rickey had "probably cost the Dodgers the 1948 pennant."[22] The argument is bolstered by the fact that the 1949 season was the beginning of a Dodger dynasty that included five National League pennants and their first World Series victory.

More importantly, Campanella's late-season success in Brooklyn showed that Jackie Robinson's tremendous talent was not an aberration. In late August, Rickey promoted Dan Bankhead from Nashua, where he had become the Eastern League's first twenty-game winner, to St. Paul, where he was to become the American Association's first African American pitcher. This time the local newspapers responded with enthusiasm, especially after Bankhead's debut against the Millers on August 25. Joe Hennessy reported that Bankhead "had a fast ball and he had control. He also had a fooling hook. All told he faced only 35 men, walked four and struck out five."[23] Bankhead recorded a 4–0 record for the Saints and began the next year in Montreal before eventually joining Campanella, Robinson, and Don Newcombe in the Dodger starting lineup.

In 1949, the Minneapolis Millers became the American Association's second team to integrate by signing Ray Dandridge and Dave Barnhill. The Twin Cities teams would eventually play host to six of the first twenty African American major leaguers—Campanella, Bankhead, Willie Mays, Artie Wilson, Hank Thompson, and Monte Irvin, three of whom, along with Dandridge, are now in the Hall of Fame.

The integration of the minor leagues is less well-remembered and less exalted than Jackie Robinson's groundbreaking arrival in the major leagues. However, Campanella's brief six-week stint in St. Paul opened up the last of the northern minor leagues, and his performance both as a player and a person helped pave the way for future players who hoped to follow him in Robinson's footsteps. At the same time, the presence of Robinson and Campanella in the major leagues became a rallying point for more sweeping social justice.

In 1952, on the topic of "The Development of Cooperative Acceptance of Racial Integration," Dean Thompson of Howard University told the assembled crowd:

As a teacher of Negro youth, I would feel that I had not done my real duty as a teacher, if a student of mine would go out to a baseball park and sit in a roped-off, segregated section of the bleachers—or even the grandstand—to see Jackie Robinson and Roy Campanella play, as many Negroes do when the Dodgers start North from their spring training camp. And yet, not only do Negro students subject themselves voluntarily to such indignities, but quite frequently, Negro teachers and principals also.[24]

It was only a matter of time before the effects of racial integration on the field would be felt in the grandstand.

Willie Mays with the Minneapolis Millers, 1951

"We think you'll like Willie," Halsey Hall told the people of Minneapolis in May 1951. Halsey Hall was right. In his first appearance in Minnesota, Willie Mays "won himself a home with Minneapolis fans" in the first inning of his first game at Nicollet Park. The "phenom in center field" made an outstanding catch near the flagpole in deep center for the third out with two men on base and then singled in his first time at bat. Minneapolis fans loved Willie, but they had only a month and a half to catch him in a Millers uniform before the New York Giants yanked him away into the major leagues. He played in just thirty-five games for the Millers, but he put on a show in that span of time. At age twenty, Mays appeared to be a natural athlete, standing five feet, ten and a half inches, weighing 178 pounds, with big, powerful hands and wrists and forearms so thick that a teammate said they looked like Popeye the Sailor's arms.[1]

Willie Mays showed the batting swing that delighted Millers' fans. Within days the stance became an icon in a *Minneapolis Tribune* article headlined, "Such a one is Willie."

His baseball skills were acquired. His father, William Howard Mays, a steel-mill worker in Birmingham, Alabama, had led him to baseball. The elder Mays was a good ballplayer in the city's Industrial League. William Howard Mays, Jr., was born in 1931, and before he was a year old, he learned to walk, and his father had him fetch a baseball. Soon young Willie was hitting a rubber ball with a stick, and by age five, he was playing catch with his father outside their home for hours at a time. Willie took naturally to playing sports.

Mays began playing baseball for pay in 1946, with the nearby semipro Gray Sox. His dad did not want his son to work in the steel mills, and baseball was a way to escape from a dead-end job there. It worked; he signed with the Negro League Birmingham Black Barons at age seventeen. Mays improved his raw talent as an outfielder on the 1948 Black Barons team that made it to the Negro World Series, raising his batting average in three seasons from .262 to .311 to .330 in a portion of a season before moving to the Giants' farm system. Following baseball's recent integration, major league scouts began assessing the Negro Leagues and knew about the talented Mays. The New York Giants offered him a contract in June 1950, buying his rights from the Black Barons. This was just after his high school graduation, the earliest that a major league team could sign him.[2]

Mays did not know what to expect in the minor leagues; in his own words, he was "a wide-eyed black kid entering a white man's world." But the young man excelled in his first minor league stop with the Class B Trenton Giants in New Jersey, batting .353 in 81 games—the best average in the league for the season. He experienced racial slurs in a number of games, but he "had learned how to be thick-skinned" from his time with the Black Barons. His personal highlight in 1950 was a grand slam home run where "the ball hit the top of the fence and bounced over," according to Mays, "that was my big thrill."[3]

The Giants placed the young outfielder in the Minneapolis Millers' spring training camp in Sanford, Florida, in the spring of 1951. The city was still segregated, and Mays had to stay in a boardinghouse with two African American teammates, separated from the white players' hotel facility. He spent much free time watching movies in a segregated theater in the side balcony, reached by a separate entrance.[4]

Leo Durocher watched Willie Mays play in only one game in spring training, and Mays hit a double and a homer, stole a base, and threw out several base runners. Leaving after seven innings, Durocher said nothing to the young player. But Durocher was impressed, as were a host of others.[5]

One of those was Millers' manager Thomas Heath. Heath said, "He's as good, at this stage, as any young prospect I ever saw. In fact, I'll go out on a limb and say he's the best I ever had anything to do with." "What do you look for in a player?" asked Heath, "you look for a good eye, speed, a good arm, baseball sense." About Mays, Heath proclaimed, "He has 'em all."[6]

The high expectations put a "good deal of pressure on Willie Mays," an observer wrote, because he was jumping up two classes, from Class B to Triple A, and had been subjected to "a fantastic build-up." Others had made "big promises for him," and it was "up to him to keep their promises for them." But he "immediately began to field his position brilliantly, hit the ball hard and far and show class and smartness on the bases."[7]

The highlights of his brief tenure with the Millers were numerous. His statistics were fabulous. In a game against the Louisville Colonels on May 7, Willie Mays astounded the fans and the Louisville team when "he literally climbed the right center field wall to pick off Taft Wright's jet drive." The ball was headed for the upper portion of the fence and, according to Mays himself, he got his "spikes in the wall" and "sort of walked up the wall." The putout was "so nearly an impossible catch" that Jimmy Piersall, the runner on second base, raced home and was in the dugout when Mays's throw arrived at second base to complete a double play. Taft Wright cruised into second base with what he knew was a double. Wright "wiped off his hands and did all the other little straightening-out chores a base runner" would do, and as he prepared to take his lead off second base, the umpire told him, "You're out."[8]

Taft replied, "No I'm not. He didn't catch that. He couldn't," and refused to leave the field. Finally, his manager had to lead him off the field, still protesting.[9]

Mays's batting average was .477 for thirty-five games. He hit .563 in seven games against Louisville, getting five hits in five at-bats in one contest, .643 against Milwaukee, and .500 versus Indianapolis. Millers manager Heath said he "just can't believe it even after watching him for weeks, but you can see for yourself."[10]

Twin Cities sportswriters looked for a weakness in Willie Mays; they found none, writing "he does everything well." "He has speed to burn," noted Charles Johnson, and "he has the best throwing arm in the league." Not only that, but "His fielding has been terrific" as he kept on coming up with a "miraculous catch" night after night. Writer Bob Beebe called him "spectacular." Another writer prophesied, "Many veteran observers feel he may well become the greatest player his race has yet produced." Opposing ballclubs were "at a loss as to how to pitch to him" because he could hit to all fields. Even his own manager admitted that he did not "know how he would have his hurlers pitch him if Willie were on the other team."[11]

Mays in the field at Nicollet Park, 1951

Willie Mays's address in Minneapolis was at 3616 Fourth Avenue South, where he rented a room in the home of Mr. and Mrs. William H. Walker. Third-baseman Ray Dandridge and pitcher Dave Barnhill lived just across the street.[12]

Willie Mays did not live in that house very long; he was just too talented to stay in Minneapolis. The New York Giants called him up to the major leagues in late May. Mays was afraid to go, telling Manager Leo Durocher that he was not sure he was "ready for the majors yet" and that he did not think he "could hit big-league pitching." Durocher asked, "What are you hitting now?"[13]

To which Mays answered, "Four seventy-seven."

Durocher, exasperated, asked Willie if he could hit .250 for the Giants, sprinkling his question with a few curse words.[14]

Willie told him, "Sure," because that "didn't seem too hard."

Mays took over in center field for the Giants and won Rookie of the Year honors in the National League for 1951. His team won the pennant when Bobby Thomson hit his dramatic home run—"the shot heard round the world"—with Mays as the on-deck batter. The Giants won the World Series, too.[15]

But Minneapolis mourned the loss of Willie Mays. Without their star, the Millers finished the year in fifth place in the eight-team American Association. Tom Heath said, "I suppose a kid who can play like Willie doesn't belong anywhere but in the big show." Many fans had been waiting for warmer weather to attend a game and to see the star center fielder. They became members of the "I Didn't See Him Club." Those who did witness Mays in action in the early going of 1951 saw a Hall of Famer before he hit the big time.[16]

Mays came back to the Twin Cities to play just three more times, in the All-Star Game at Metropolitan Stadium in 1965 and two exhibitions. He continued his hitting in Minnesota just as he had left off in 1951—belting a 415-foot leadoff home run, walking twice, and then scoring the winning run in a 6–5 National League victory.[17]

For those fortunate enough to have witnessed the play of Willie Mays in his time in Minnesota, they saw the greatest all-around African American player in all of baseball history. The *Sporting News* listed him as number two on its list of Baseball's 100 Greatest Players, behind Babe Ruth. *Total Baseball,* in rating pitching, fielding, batting, and baserunning, included Mays, along with Ruth and Barry Bonds, as the three best players ever. It was fate that brought Mays to Minneapolis in 1951, and it was his good fortune to remain healthy and have a long career. And what a career it was—660 home runs to rate as number four all time, 3,283 hits (seventh all time), first in putouts by an outfielder, and third in runs scored and total bases. A twenty-four-time All-Star, he was named the National League's Most Valuable Player in 1954 and in 1965.[18]

Satchel Paige: Barnstorming in Minnesota

Steven R. Hoffbeck

*L*eroy "Satchel" Paige became a member of the Baseball Hall of Fame in Cooperstown, New York, in 1971. He was a legendary pitcher in the Negro Leagues, a man who could attract large crowds to see him pitch during his prime years from 1926 through 1950.[1]

Paige was tall and skinny, six foot three and a half inches and about 180 pounds (130 when he was young), with long thin legs and long arms. Though slender, he increased his strength by lifting two-hundred-pound blocks of ice while delivering them to families in his hometown of Mobile. He was a big eater; his employer recalled, "That boy et [more] than the hosses."[2]

Paige said that he learned his baseball in an Alabama reform school from age twelve to seventeen. He had gotten in trouble with the law by running with local gangs of toughs where he developed his eye and arm by accurately hurling rocks at rivals' heads. The truth is that his brother Wilson Paige was a ballplayer who played for the semipro Mobile Tigers, and Satchel, no doubt, learned a few things from him. Satchel had been an excellent pitcher since grade school. He had a high leg kick, and he would wing the ball to the plate around his pointed foot. Just for fun, he would sometimes paint the word "fastball" on the bottom of his shoe. Half the time a batter would be swinging at his foot.[3]

When he got a tryout with his brother's team, he threw so fast that the manager, Candy Jim Taylor (formerly a star player with the St. Paul Colored Gophers) asked him, "Do you throw that fast consistently?"

To which Paige answered, "No, I do it all the time."[4]

He developed more as a pitcher when he played for the Birmingham Black Barons of the Negro National League in 1927. Manager Bill Gatewood, who had pitched in Minnesota for the St. Paul Colored Gophers in 1908, instructed Paige and taught him how to throw the hesitation pitch, pausing in the middle of his pitching delivery.[5]

Although his given name was Leroy, he became famous as Satchel. Paige said the name came from his ability to hoist "as many as 10 bags" of luggage and other satchels at a time while he worked as a porter at the Mobile railway station. In the 1940s reporters claimed that his name came from his size twelve shoes, which were as big as satchels, hence he was called "Satchelfoots." One writer said Paige had size fourteen feet; in Pittsburgh, Paige was said to "have size 15 feet." Even his feet were legendary. The core truth appears to be that Paige had stolen suitcases while working as a porter, and an angry victim chased him and caught him and hit him on the head with a satchel, hence the nickname. "He was a bad kid," Ted "Double Duty" Radcliffe commented.[6]

Paige eventually became the best-known Negro Leagues pitcher. Knowledgeable baseball fans learned of his talent through "his celebrated pitching battles with Dizzy Dean, Schoolboy Rowe and others in the 1930s."[7] Word spread and his renown became widespread after *Time* magazine printed a feature story entitled "Satchelfoots." Other magazines got on the Satchel train—the *Saturday Evening Post* in July 1940 and *Life* magazine, first in the summer of 1941 and again in 1948 when he joined the major leagues, a year after Jackie Robinson had integrated white baseball. The media gave another round of coverage to Satchel several years later in his comeback—the *New Yorker* wrote about him in 1952, and *Collier's* did a three-part series on "The Fabulous Satchel Paige" in 1953. His 1961 autobiography resurrected his fame, and *Sports Illustrated* in 1964 found him still worthy of attention. Paige's name resurfaced with his induction into the Baseball Hall of Fame in 1971, and his fame reverberated through the pages of the books, such as *Only the Ball Was White,* that rescued black baseball history from the ash heap of history.

His fastball was like lightning, and in his prime he threw "what was probably the fastest ball ever to leave the hand of man." Hack Wilson, the great National League home-run slugger, once said that Paige's fastball "starts out like a baseball, but when it gets to the plate it looks like a marble." Paige responded by saying, "You must be talking about my slowball, my fastball looks like a fish egg."[8]

Famous black catcher Ted "Double Duty" Radcliffe observed that Paige was fast, so fast that he "threw it harder than Randy Johnson" (today's fastest pitcher) and was "more accurate too." Paige had "fantastic location." Double Duty could throw a fastball about 95 miles per hour, but "Satchel threw over 100." Some said Paige could "throw 105 miles an hour and hit a mosquito flying over the outside corner of the plate." For warm-ups, Paige was said to practice by throwing pitches over a dime. Not just over home plate but over a dime, and he could even put a ball over a corner of the dime. In 1948, he once threw "six strikes out of ten pitches over a chewing gum wrapper."[9]

The great Negro Leagues catcher Biz Mackey commented on Paige's fastball, "A lot of pitchers have a fast ball, but a very, very few—[Bob] Feller, [Lefty] Grove, [Walter] Johnson, a couple of others besides Satchel—have had that little extra juice that makes the difference between the good and the great man. When it's that fast, it will hop a little at the end of the line. Beyond that, it tends to disappear. Yes, disappear. I've heard about Satchel throwing pitches that wasn't hit but that never showed up in the catcher's mitt, nevertheless." Catcher Clint Courtney (St. Louis Browns, 1948) remarked that Paige's fastball had "a hop on the end, and it keeps ticking off the top of my mitt."[10]

The whiplash motion of his pitching arm also fooled the hitters. Paige hired himself out to teams that would pay him his price and helped several Negro League teams to championships in his twenty-five-year career.

In 1935 Paige (along with two of his Negro League colleagues, Quincy Trouppe and Double Duty Radcliffe) agreed to play for the Bismarck semipro

A postcard shows Paige (middle of back row) with the 1935 Bismarck team; Trouppe and Radcliffe are standing, first and second from the right.

team for five hundred dollars a month, a car, and the right to be hired by other teams on off-days. The Bismarck team won the National Baseball Congress championship at the end of the season.[11]

The great hurler pitched in St. Paul in 1941. A June game featured Satchel Paige and the Kansas City Monarchs against the Miami Ethiopian Clowns at Lexington Ball Park. The Clowns performed their legendary "shadow ball and pepper" games for a half-hour as the pregame attraction, but the game itself was outstanding. The Clowns scored a lone run off the Monarchs' pitcher, Bradley, in seven innings. The Monarchs got just one run off of the Clowns' pitcher, protesting all the way that "he was throwing a spitter." Paige came into the game to finish off the Clowns, but he gave up a walk, and the runner scored on an overthrow at second base. In two innings, Satchel Paige struck out five of six batters, but the Clowns prevailed before an excellent crowd of four thousand fans.[12]

In 1950 the legendary Satchel Paige returned to the Upper Midwest to pitch in Moorhead and Austin and in Minot, North Dakota. He pitched "any[where] and everywhere," to earn money and better opportunities. When he came to Moorhead, he arrived in style in his "specially built Cadillac convertible." The pitcher could draw fans who were "all outside the ballpark waiting" for a glimpse of Paige, and one of those fans, Edwin "Sonny" Gulsvig, remembered that it was a pink Cadillac—just as colorful as the pitcher. Paige had the ability to attract sportswriters to write headlines featuring his name and newspaper photographers to splash his image around the daily papers. He was described as being "timeless" and, of his age, would only say, "I'm over 41."[13]

The Moorhead Red Sox hired Paige to throw four innings for the team in a June 3 exhibition game against the Fergus Falls Red Sox. The "ageless colored pitching ace" performed spectacularly, shutting out the Fergus Falls ballclub for the first four innings. He struck out five batters and allowed only two singles. Fans turned out in large numbers, totaling 1,260 at Barnett Field in Fargo. Moorhead eventually lost the game 10 to 4 by giving up too many walks and committing too many errors after Paige left the game.[14]

Before coming to Moorhead, Paige had pitched in three games for the semipro Minot Mallards. The ageless wonder pitched just three innings in each of the three games. He was impressive; in nine total innings, he allowed zero runs, just three hits, and struck out thirteen out of twenty-seven opposing batsmen. One of the games was against the Moorhead Red Sox, and the Moorhead team got only one hit, and an infield hit at that, off Paige.[15]

His performance was memorable. The Minot batboy, Boyd Christenson, age twelve, had been impressed by the kick in Paige's windup. He lifted his "foot higher than the hat on his head," Christenson recalled later, and struck out the side in the first inning. Paige was a true "showman." The Mallards paid Paige five hundred dollars for his nine innings of work. It was the start of his personal barnstorming tour of 1950 in which he reportedly earned more than fifty thousand dollars.[16]

After his performances for Minot and Moorhead, Paige drove to Austin where he again worked three innings of an exhibition game for the Austin Queens versus the Austin Packers. The Packers broke Paige's string of twenty shutout innings by collecting three hits and two runs off the veteran hurler. One run scored due to an outfield error, and the other run came on an inside-the-park home run. Paige struck out six Packers, however, and hit a single in his only trip to the plate. As he always did, he attracted a large crowd and made the game a successful fund raiser for the sponsoring team.[17]

"Until the day you die, that first breath of freedom in so significant. What happened to me in Fargo, North Dakota, changed my whole outlook.... Where I came from, I couldn't eat in a restaurant. But in Fargo, I could. In Fargo, the fans obviously weren't blind to the fact that you were African American, but I think they saw you as a ballplayer trying to follow a dream.... For a young man coming from my situation, that's huge."

Jim "Mudcat" Grant, pitcher

While in Minnesota, Paige spent some time fishing. He and his wife joined Jim Peterson, a Moorhead sports writer, at Charlie Knutson's resort on Big Cormorant Lake just thirty miles east of Moorhead. As always, he garnered much attention, arriving in his Cadillac, driven by a chauffeur. Satchel loved fishing and said, "Man, if I could fish every day, I'd quit playing ball." The walleyes were not biting well that day, and the group got only two. That evening, fishing from shore, his line appeared to be snagged, and he pulled it in by hand and found a turtle on the line. The turtle let go at the last second. Paige and his wife fished again the next day, getting two more walleyes. Paige said, "I could fish, pitch and play ball—fish, pitch and play ball—fish, pitch and play ball—fish; I like variety." The local writer was of the opinion that Paige was "fun to be with and a grand guy." Just before he left Moorhead to drive to Austin, he said, "I'm ready to go [fishing] again" and if he could always go fishing "like he did here" in Minnesota, he would "gladly" give up baseball.[18]

Apparently Paige enjoyed his angling experience in Minnesota lakes country so much that he would take time to fish near Moorhead whenever he toured the region. Legend has it that he would go to a sugar-beet farmer's land "east of Moorhead" and "fish for bullheads and catfish" on occasion. Noted for his ability to exaggerate, he later claimed that he had installed a refrigerator in the trunk of his car. In an interview with *Newsweek* magazine, he said, "I puts fish there. No one believes how big I catch 'em. I puts the biggest ones there and when someone disputes me, I just takes the fish out of the trunk."[19]

Paige came to Minnesota between stints in major-league baseball. He had been the first black pitcher to play for the Cleveland Indians and in the American League in 1948. At age forty-two, he had to try out for the team—and threw fifty pitches, of which forty-six were strikes. He was hired—to help the Indians win a pennant. He was the oldest rookie ever in the major leagues. In his first appearance, he shut out the St. Louis Browns in two innings of relief pitching. A record crowd of 78,382 filled Cleveland's Municipal Stadium for one of his games, and Paige did well against major-league batters because, as he said, "Plate's the same size" (for Negro League batters as well as for American League hitters). He was the first African American pitcher to win a game in the major leagues, even though Dan Bankhead had been the first black pitcher in the majors in 1947. Bankhead had not done well under the intense pressures of being the first black on the mound, pitching in just ten innings in four games with an ERA of 7.20. In contrast, Paige overcame the scrutiny and excelled, winning six timely games in the 1948 season—against just one loss (on an unearned run)—helping the Indians win the pennant in a close race and a World Series triumph over the Boston Braves.[20]

Paige was so good in 1948 that even the umpires marveled at his skill. Veteran umpire Bill Summers remarked, "There are few better pitchers in baseball today. Maybe there aren't any. And there are few with more stuff. He had a slider . . . that cracked like a whip and a curve that exploded. And he was plenty fast." His colleague, Art Passarella, pointed to Paige's pinpoint location: "The old boy's around the plate all the time and calling balls and strikes for him's a breeze." His performance fell off in the 1949 season due to dental and stomach problems, and he won only four games while losing seven. That brought on his barnstorming year of 1950 and his short stints in the Upper Midwest.[21]

Paige rejoined the major leagues with the St. Louis Browns from 1951 to 1953, after getting his teeth fixed. Owner Bill Veeck explained, "Everybody kept telling me he was through, but that was understandable. They thought he was only human." He was marvelous in 1952, appearing in "almost one third of the St. Louis Browns contests, struck out 91 batters, won 12 games,

Paige stopped to chat with Odis ("Oats") LeGrand, baseball coach of the Moorhead Red Sox, outside the office of the *Moorhead Daily News* in June 1950.

lost ten, saved ten" and made the All-Star team. He was perhaps the "most valuable relief hurler" in the American League that season. The year 1953 marked his last full season in the majors. Later, in 1965, he made a three-inning appearance with the Kansas City A's.[22]

Satchel returned to the Upper Midwest for at least one exhibition game in 1959. His team, the barnstorming Havana Cubans, played the Minot ballclub and prevailed over the local team by a score of 10 to 2. Paige worked only two innings, allowing just one hit.[23]

He came again to Minnesota in 1960, pitching with an all-black team in Bagley against an area all-star team. Paige's team reportedly included his son, Leroy Satchel Paige, Jr., who played left field. One of the players on the local team was Robert "Bob" Baab, a medical doctor who was working on the Red Lake Indian reservation. Baab recalled that the younger Paige was "a tall drink of water" like his father and was in his "later twenties." Satchel pitched three innings, and Baab batted against him just one time. Paige threw Baab a "pretty slow pitch" on the inside corner of the plate, and even though the "pitch looked the size of a watermelon," all Baab could do was take a "mighty swing" that resulted in a "dribbler down the third base line." After his short pitching stint, Paige then sat in his rocking chair on the field, watching the remainder of the game.[24]

The fans appreciated Paige's efforts, as did the players who faced him that day. But there was a single exception. The first baseman from Fosston carried on a "disgusting" chatter, calling the black players "every name under the sun." Paige's team exercised "great self control" and did not retaliate. Baab regretted not saying something to the "cracker" from Fosston, to stop his assaultive speech. It was an inhospitable moment in the long history of Minnesota baseball.[25]

The Great Satchel continued his barnstorming ways into the 1960s. In 1963, he traveled through the "northern U.S. and Canada, pitching two or three innings every day for 145 games, still dreaming that he might somehow get back into the majors." In 1967 he toured with the Indianapolis Clowns.[26]

Paige died on June 8, 1982, in Kansas City, Missouri, at age seventy-six. His greatest honor was to become enshrined in the Hall of Fame in 1971, at which he said, "I am the proudest man on earth right today." A black member of the selection committee regarded the action as "baseball's acknowledgement of past sins." As the first Negro League star to gain entrance to Cooperstown, he called upon baseball to recognize the contributions of other Negro Leaguers to the sport, naming his mentor Bill Gatewood as a worthy entrant and also Rube Foster (who had pitched in Minnesota several times).[27]

He left quite a legacy and a few mysteries. Paige estimated that he had pitched in 2,500 games and that he had won 2,000 of them (which would be about four times greater than the major-league record). He pitched in more games than "anybody else in the world." He was such an attraction and had such longevity that he "pulled in more customers than Babe Ruth"; an estimated ten million people saw him play. He would pitch for any team that would pay him enough, and at times he would play as a solo performer; he was a "traveling baseball spectacle." Paige had pitched in "coal mines and penitentiaries"; he said, "I don't believe there's any place I didn't play baseball." A writer quoted Paige, "Bangin' around the way I was, playing for guarantees on one team after another that I never hear of, in towns I had never seen before, with players I didn't know and never saw again, I got lonesome." He knew what people wanted to see, commenting, "People didn't come to see the ball game. They came to see me strike out everybody, all the time. Occasionally, I didn't."[28]

He promoted himself as "Satchel Paige, World's Greatest Pitcher, Guaranteed to Strike Out the First Nine Men." He often lived up to his guarantee, especially in night games in poorly lit ballparks. Sometimes he would deliberately walk the first three batters in an inning and then strike out the next three. Paige said that he had never walked a man with the bases loaded.[29]

Paige was both a showman and a talented ballplayer, a combination like unto Babe Ruth. Both men possessed "charismatic" personalities, being "humorous, colorful, engaging bragger[s]," each with a "child-like personality" and able to "justify his boasts on the field of play." Their similarities are obvious: both had been rescued from delinquency by baseball's redeeming influence, both had prodigious appetites for food and a fondness for feminine company, both were barnstormers who brought throngs of fans to black and white exhibition games. Each was "larger than life," and the "extraordinary was expected as a matter of course."[30]

The great pitcher tended to deflect inquiries into his family life. His father, John, was a gardener, and Satchel said, "He wasn't hardly a part of my life." He was married twice, first to Janet, who was from Pittsburgh and whom he divorced, and then to Lahoma, who was from Kansas City, Missouri. Paige was the father of four children—Pamella, Caroline, Linda, and Leroy, Jr.[31]

Satchel Paige has to be ranked among the greatest pitchers, black or white. Baseball historian Bill James has placed Paige as his seventeenth choice among the one hundred greatest players of all time and second among pitchers only to Walter Johnson. The *Sporting News* lists Paige as nineteenth among Baseball's 100 Greatest Players and as the fifth best pitcher. The SABR (Society for American Baseball Research) organization omitted Paige from its top one hundred list but placed him in a tie for first with Buck Leonard in its 40 Greatest Negro League Figures lineup.[32]

The greatest mystery was his actual age. Satchel claimed that various interested parties had "spent more money researching my age than they did on the atomic bomb." He said that he was born in 1908, but his mother, Tula Paige, said his birth year was 1903. His draft card stated that he had been born in 1906, which is probably correct. Paige was such an old pitcher that he was often accused of "impersonating himself" by people who thought he must have already passed away. On one occasion, he was asked, "How old are you?" Paige responded only with an estimate, "I'd judge between 30 and 70."[33] This was probably appropriate, for his talent was timeless, and his reputation was for the ages.

Paige's last hurrah in Minnesota came long after his death, in 1995, when Twin Cities–based General Mills honored the great Negro League players on an anniversary box of Wheaties cereal. The special-edition package front featured James "Cool Papa" Bell, Josh Gibson, and Leroy "Satchel" Paige on the seventy-fifth anniversary of the founding of the Negro League. It represented a final memorial from the Land of 10,000 Lakes to the man who toured the baseball diamonds of the state and who enjoyed fishing in its sky-tinted waters.[34]

Finally, a poem about Satchel Paige, written by Samuel Allen.[35]

To Satch

Sometimes I feel like I will never stop
Just go on forever
Till one fine mornin'
I'm gonna reach up and grab me a handfulla stars
Throw out my long lean leg
And whip three hot strikes burnin' down the heavens
And look over at God and say
HOW ABOUT THAT!

Jackie Robinson Visits Minnesota, 1955

When baseball great Jackie Robinson visited the Twin Cities on a late January day in 1955, he did not get a hit, steal a base, or throw out a runner at first base. He probably never played a ball game in Minnesota, but the great "Barrier Breaker" was in town to break down other color barriers, giving school talks and speeches. Robinson spoke at seven locations, including Minneapolis Central High School, a luncheon in Minneapolis, and the Macalester College student union,[1] as a part of his nationwide trip sponsored by the National Conference of Christians and Jews.[2]

When asked about his courageous work as the first man to integrate major league baseball, Robinson stated, "I would do it over again, even knowing of the difficulties that would face me." He was the first, and for that reason he believed that he had "taken more heat and abuse than any of the other Negro players that followed him."[3]

Because he had endured more of the bitter struggle to integrate baseball than had other black players, Robinson used his agony as a "driving force behind his dedication to improving human relations"

Robinson autographed a notebook for Don Kolar, left, and Roger Marx on a stop at Central High School in Minneapolis.

in this nation. A local black newspaper editorialized that "of all the Negroes who have gained national prominence in the sports world, Robinson gives more time than any of them to improving race relations."

Jackie Robinson also addressed the issue of the demise of the Negro Leagues: "I like the idea of Negro baseball as such going out of existence, because it means that baseball has become integrated to the extent that it is no longer necessary to have segregated leagues." While black baseball "had played an important part in developing Negroes for the big leagues," he "pointed out that a large number of young Negro players never play in the colored leagues because they are scouted and signed up by scouts in organized baseball, whereas a few years ago most Negro ball players came out of the Negro leagues."

Robinson seemed always to be on the edge of controversy with his outspoken nature and his willingness to combat racism in the United States. At heart he contended, "I only wish to be judged as an individual on what I can or cannot do, not because of the color of my skin." It was a statement that summed up the oft-unspoken aspirations of countless black baseball players in Minnesota from all eras.[4]

Toni Stone: A Tomboy to Remember

Teri Ann Finneman

Leroy "Satchel" Paige (1906–1982) strolled through the Indianapolis Clowns' locker room. Outside, Negro League baseball fans were taking their seats to watch the St. Louis Browns contend with the Clowns. Well known for his pitching and for his mouth, Paige mockingly asked the Clowns how they would like him to pitch—slow, medium, or fast.

"Anyway you like," Toni Stone, the Clowns' second baseman, replied. "Just don't hit me."

As the first woman to play professional baseball regularly, Stone was just a rookie when she shakily stepped up to the plate to face Paige on that legendary day in 1953.

"Hey, T, how do you like it?" Paige called from the pitcher's mound.

"It doesn't matter. Just don't hurt me," Stone answered.

Paige hurled a fastball. SMACK! Stone's bat connected, and the ball soared into center field. Stone was so excited that she barely made it to first base.

It was the only hit off Paige that day. Stone repeatedly described the day as the greatest triumph in her life.[1] Over the years, many of the details of the encounter became shrouded in the mists of memory and entered the realm of legend. Stone stated firmly that the game took place in Omaha on Easter Sunday 1953, but the day and location cannot be confirmed despite extensive research in newspapers.

Marcenia Lyle "Toni" Stone was born July 17, 1921, in West Virginia. Her coal miner father moved the family to St. Paul when Stone was three or four years old, and the Stones lived with relatives for a year or two at 761 Rondo Street.[2] Boykin and Bernice Stone supported their four children by finding work as a barber and beautician and raised their family as Catholics. Neither parent understood their daughter's love of baseball.

"They would have stopped me if they could, but there was nothing they could do about it," Stone said.

Bernice Stone told her daughter, "I just want you to be somebody. Don't you see?"

"I will be somebody," her daughter answered.[3]

Stone's passion for baseball was so strong that she once made her sister eat Wheaties cereal every day until they collected enough box tops for Stone to join a Wheaties-sponsored baseball club. Her sister disliked both baseball and Wheaties. However, the family ate enough cereal for Stone to join the club when she was ten.[4]

Stone was determined to pursue her love of baseball, and this, along with her challenges to boys on the playground, earned her the nickname Tomboy. "She learned to accept labels," Judy Yaeger Jones, a Twin Cities historian, declared. "Besides 'tomboy,' she'd be called 'dyke' and 'fairy.'"[5]

When Stone was fourteen, her family was living at 254 Central Avenue. She was a member of the Catholic parish's diamond ball team and was considered one of the best young girl athletes in St. Paul. But an auto accident almost cut her baseball career short when a hit-and-run driver knocked her off her bicycle. Luckily she only suffered a broken arm.[6]

At this time, Stone began skipping school to play baseball. The only record the St. Paul School District has of Stone's school attendance is for the fifth grade at Hill Elementary School. She joined the Girls Highlex Softball Club, and in 1936, at fifteen, began playing with the St. Paul Colored Giants, a semiprofessional men's team. The team, which toured in Minnesota and Wisconsin in 1937, had a record of 5–3 by July 30. Stone was a pitcher on the roster, and no other team in the Northwest "[could] boast the same." Stone amused the fans with her great skills, and sports reporter Jimmy Lee predicted she would be famous one day.[7]

Stone was interested in playing for the St. Paul Saints but was initially denied the opportunity. After pressuring the team's manager, Gabby Street, a former major-league catcher and manager, Stone was allowed to try out. Although she did not make the team, Street was sufficiently impressed by her skills that he bought her spikes and allowed her to attend his baseball camp.[8]

The myths that surrounded Stone in later years differed as to how much schooling she actually had throughout these early years. To boost public appeal, baseball teams would claim Stone had a master's degree, but she actually did not even graduate from high school. A newspaper article mentioned that she attended West Virginia State University in 1941 and returned to St. Paul for a summer visit. However, neither West Virginia University nor West Virginia State College found any records of her attendance.[9]

After the U.S. entered World War II, Stone moved to San Francisco to find her sister who was a nurse. Stone had less than a dollar when she moved, but she managed to find a place to live, a job, and a baseball team before she found her sister. It was at this time that she gave herself the playing name "Toni Stone" since Toni sounded like Tomboy.[10]

Stone's friendship with Al Love and Lena Morrell, who owned Jack's Tavern, a black social center in San Francisco, aided her quest to join a West Coast baseball team.[11] Love introduced her to the American Legion team, and the five-foot-seven, 146-pound Stone "worked to death" during tryouts.

This determination won her a spot on the San Francisco Sea Lions, a semipro team. "In baseball, I was accepted for who I was and what I could produce," Stone said.[12]

The Sea Lions were one of many black barnstorming teams during this era. Barnstorming was referred to as "baseball on the run," and players received just enough income to make it to the next diamond. The games were unstructured, the fields were rocky, and gate admissions brought in very little money, but Stone was doing what she loved.[13]

"A woman has her dreams, too," Stone said. "When you finish high school, they tell a boy to go out and see the world. What do they tell a girl? They tell her to go next door and marry the boy that their families picked for her. It wasn't right. A woman can do many things."[14]

A turning point in Stone's life came in 1947 when she met and married Aurelious P. Alberga (1884–1988), a World War I veteran. He was nearly forty years her senior. Alberga had graduated from the 17th Provisional Training Regiment at Fort Des Moines in 1917 and was one of the first black officers in the U.S. Army.[15] Like Stone's parents, her husband didn't want her to play ball either.

"He would have stopped me if he could," Stone said.[16]

Nationally 1947 was a memorable year for baseball and, eventually, for Stone. That year Jackie Robinson broke the color barrier of the major leagues, and the Negro Leagues began to decline. Many believe Stone's career would not have taken off if not for these circumstances.[17]

For the first seven years of marriage, Stone spent the off-season with her husband in Oakland, California. In 1949, her spirit for gender equality caused her to quit the Sea Lions when the team barnstormed through New Orleans. Stone was dissatisfied with the broken promises of the Sea Lions' owner, who had said he would raise her pay. She joined the New Orleans Creoles, a team in the Negro League minors, with a contract of $300 per month. Stone played second base, and her publicity rose with her .265 batting average and unassisted double plays. She was knocked down and taken out by base runners, but she loved every minute of it. Stone also played with the New Orleans Black Pelicans before her big break came in

Toni Stone posed with four men from an unidentified Louisiana team. She showed more pleasure when she met the leader of another sport, boxer Joe Louis, about 1949.

1953 when the Indianapolis Clowns signed her to replace second baseman Hank Aaron, who left in 1951 to play for the Boston Braves.[18]

The Clowns were the first professional baseball team to sign a woman. The Clowns' owner Syd Pollock was a sometimes business partner of Abe Saperstein, the owner of the Harlem Globetrotters. Pollock realized that the Negro Leagues were beginning to decline as a result of desegregation and decided he needed something to attract the fans. After World War II, attendance at minor league games had dropped from 42 million to 15.5 million. Basketball and football rose in popularity and drew fans away.[19]

The Clowns were well known for their silly antics as well as their excellent skills. This combination created an acceptance of black baseball players and broke down racial barriers. Clown antics included a "shadow ball routine" during warm-ups. The players went through the motions of the game in exaggerated slow movements with an invisible ball. The team used another invisible ball trick when a ball was hit into the outfield and a runner was on

third. The Clowns let the ball go, and, as the runner slid into home, the catcher pulled a ball out of his uniform and tagged the runner.[20]

The Clowns incorporated Stone into the "show biz" act. Programs listed her as twenty-two when she was thirty-two and claimed she made $12,000 a year. "I never made anything like that," Stone said. "They always made me say I was getting a lot more money than I was. The other players would read that and say, 'If she's getting that much, I deserve more.' But I was really only getting a few hundred dollars. They [also] always made me say . . . I had a master's degree."[21]

A 1953 article in *Ebony* claimed Stone was a graduate of Macalester College and put her in a party dress, when Stone only wore pants. "She knew she was being used," Yaeger Jones said, "but she loved the game."[22]

Stone's teammates were not always accepting of the new addition to their novelty act. "They didn't mean any harm and, in their way, they liked me," Stone said. "Just that I wasn't supposed to be there. They'd tell me to go home and fix my husband some biscuits or any damn thing. Just get the hell away from here."[23]

"It was rough, but I had to prove I could get along," she said. "Some of them could never get a hit and when I got a hit, that would really get to them."[24]

Stone played fifty games and batted .243. Stone said Clowns' manager and Hall of Fame outfielder Oscar Charleston was always supportive of her. "He was the greatest. He'd let me get up there and hit," she said.[25]

One of the greatest disappointments in Stone's life was a false hope that Louisville Slugger would make a special smaller bat and name it after her. "I was all excited. But my manager at the time, he just said, 'The bats we've got are good enough for her,'" Stone said.[26]

During the winter of 1953, Pollack sold Stone's contract to the Kansas City Monarchs. This transition soon ended her career in professional baseball. "[The Monarchs] called me dirty names," Stone said. "They wouldn't let me really play. Maybe an inning or two, that's all. They just were using me." The Monarchs played more serious ball than the Clowns and boasted former players such as Jackie Robinson and Satchel Paige. "They actually hired me as a drawing card and wanted me to wear shorts," Stone said. "I cussed the owner and told him 'No. I came to play ball.'"

Stone's game day routine would begin by dressing in the umpires' room where she would "put on her game face." She would then leave in the seventh or eighth inning to shower before the rest of the team finished the game. She rarely played in league games, mostly exhibition ones, and earned $450 a month. "It was pure hell," Stone said. "I had to keep my composure, never using profanity to respond to critics. I knew that men could drink hard and use lots of profanity, but that if I did I would be criticized."[27]

One Sunday, May 1, 1954, the Monarchs were twelve miles out of Augusta, Georgia, when their bus caught on fire. They had just played an exhibition game against the Clowns and were on their way to Miami. The Clowns' bus had broken down, so the Monarchs' bus was overcrowded with players and equipment. At 2 A.M., the bus driver pulled over and everyone got out. When the luggage compartment was opened, the bus burst into flames and destroyed both teams' possessions.[28]

Stone's baseball career ended at the conclusion of the 1954 season. The desegregation of professional baseball and her inability to receive more playing time were both factors in her decision to quit. Stone returned to Oakland, where she played in men's amateur leagues until she was sixty. She also worked as a nurse until she retired and spent seven years caring for her husband, who died in 1988 at 103. But she felt a void in her life without baseball. "It hurt so bad, I damn near had a heart attack," Stone said.[29]

Even though she was a sensation during her pro ball days, Stone is not included in many reference books, such as *Notable Black American Women* and the *Dictionary of American Negro Biography*. "I just loved the game, but they weren't ready for me," Stone said. "So many of them thought it was a disgrace. But my heart was set and I kept at it."[30]

Stone finally received the recognition she desired. In 1985 she was inducted into the Women's Sports Foundation's International Hall of Fame. On March 6, 1990, the St. Paul mayor and city council honored her by naming the day Toni Stone Day. Stone visited local elementary schools and urged students to fight for their dreams. The day was quite emotional for her.[31] "I wish my mother could see this," Stone said. "She never saw me play. . . . Little girls weren't supposed to play baseball. Part of it was she was afraid I'd get hurt."

Stone died November 2, 1996, in a nursing home in Oakland from heart and respiratory problems. She had no children or other immediate survivors and was buried next to her husband in the Golden Gate National Cemetery.[32] In 1997 playwright Roger Nieboer's *Tomboy Stone* opened in St. Paul to celebrate the life of the first woman who played men's professional baseball. "She was a very vibrant person. You took one look at her and knew she was an athlete," Nieboer said.

On December 19, 1996, city officials renamed Dunning Park Stadium in St. Paul in recognition of her achievements. Toni Stone Field now honors the spunky hometown girl who fought for her dreams. Stone's career may have been short, but her legacy lives on in the city where it all began.[33]

Barnstorming Black Teams: The End of an Era

The last barnstorming black teams toured Minnesota just before major league baseball came to the state in 1961. In 1959, the Baltimore Elites ballclub arrived in Bagley for a pair of Fourth of July games against the local town team—the Bagley Merchants. Fans could pay seventy-five cents to see a great doubleheader and afterward be treated to a free evening fireworks display put on by the Bagley Fire Department.

The Bagley Merchants had a fine team in the 1950s, playing in the Northern Minny League against such towns as Thief River Falls, Fosston, and Cass Lake and challenging bigger towns like Bemidji and Detroit Lakes in non-league games. The team included brothers Jerry and Leroy Riewer (pronounced REE-ver)—Jerry at shortstop and batting leadoff and Leroy in center field. At catcher was Tom Wolhowe, not the usual variety, either, because he stood six feet four inches tall.

The Baltimore Elites (pronounced EE-lights, previously the Elite Giants) were an established Negro League ballclub, now in decline with baseball becoming integrated. The club had embarked upon a 120-game, coast-to-coast and Canadian tour, and they played all the "top semi-pro, independent and league teams, taking on all comers." It was composed of the best players from "Southern schools," and all had "an intense desire to go to the top in baseball circles" now that discrimination had eased. It had once been the team of Roy Campanella, Junior Gilliam, and Joe Black before the major leagues integrated.[1]

The Elites were said to be "one of the finest road clubs in the east" and had played for many years in "their own ball park, the Elites Park, in Baltimore." Publicity for the games included a single photo of Elites first baseman Johney Cherry and stressed the fact that the Elites were "taught to play a fast, colorful brand of ball" in the tradition of the old colored baseball era.[2]

The first game was a victory for the Elites by a score of 8 to 3, and the local newspaper did not have much to say about the game. But the second game had a better result when the home team "turned the tables" and "switched the decision" in another 8 to 3 ballgame. The Merchants' "hitting was good" in the nightcap, and Jerry Riewer won "top honors" for his hitting, going three for four, including two doubles. Bill Lawrence also went three for four, all singles. The Merchants' cause was assisted greatly by the pitching of Dick Palmer, recruited for the game from the Red Lake Falls team, who struck out seventeen, allowing only four hits.[3]

Jerry Riewer remembered few details of the 1959 games in 2002, forty-some years after the event, but his memories provide a mirror of the experience of countless other small-town Minnesotans who played touring black teams at one time or another. Riewer looked at it as "quite an experience for a little white farm boy to play against such fine black players." He thought that "they were probably the first black people" he had ever seen in person. Some of the Elites "hit the ball farther than anyone" he had ever witnessed and had great speed on the base paths. Riewer was most impressed with the "strength of their throwing arms" and "with their baseball abilities." He believed that Bagley gave the team a friendly reception, and he did not "remember any prejudice towards blacks" when he was growing up there, with the "main prejudices at that time" following "along religious lines"—as Lutherans and Catholics. Tom Wolhowe remembered that the Elites had a "junk ball thrower" and a "couple of good long ball hitters and a couple good bunters." Both men reminisced about the Bagley fans enjoying the "humorous chatter" of the Elites on the field and felt "that they put on a good show."[4] Neither man could think of the names of any of the Baltimore players but recalled playing against a Satchel Paige team at some time in the 1950s.

The feeling of the game on July 4, 1959, was much the same as back in 1909 when the St. Paul Colored Gophers played in nearby Bemidji or in 1911 when the Minneapolis Colored Keystones played in Alexandria. The black teams had toured Minnesota since the first years of the twentieth century, but that game in Bagley was among the last efforts of the barnstorming black teams in the state. When the Minnesota Twins came in 1961, the old ways of baseball began to change.

Leroy and Jerry Riewer, about 1955

Earl Battey and the Integration of Spring Training

Kwame McDonald and Steven R. Hoffbeck

arl Battey was said to be slow and stout or maybe short and stout. The truth was that he was a thickset man and slow afoot, but he was not all that short, standing six feet one inch. He was a true athlete, which helped make him a terrific defensive catcher. When the Twins arrived in 1961, Minnesotans welcomed the team with open arms and embraced Battey as one of baseball's best catchers.[1]

Spring training, however, was a different story. The Twins had their headquarters at Tinker Field in Orlando, Florida, and segregation was the norm in that small city, in the days before the 1964 Civil Rights Act and the arrival of Disney World. The white players, including star Harmon Killebrew, stayed in the "high-class" Cherry Plaza Hotel while Battey and four other black teammates were housed in a black-owned motel, said to be "an absolute dump."[2]

Battey, in his second season with the organization, did not speak out publicly about the discrimination that year. However, other outstanding players were willing to protest their treatment as second-class citizens in Florida. Hank Aaron of the Milwaukee Braves criticized the Jim Crow conditions, and Yankee catcher Elston Howard said he would no longer bring his wife and family to Florida due to the poor way they had been treated in previous years. The loudest call for change came from a black Floridian, Dr. Robert Wimbish, chairman of the St. Petersburg NAACP chapter: "Living conditions for the colored players in the Florida camps are not satisfactory." He proclaimed that it was "time the management of the clubs takes a hand" in instituting equality among all players—a condition that was true in spring training facilities in Arizona.[3]

Regarding the spring training segregation, Twins owner Calvin Griffith and club officials "said no change was contemplated" in 1961.[4] But no progress toward equality came in 1962. Or in 1963. Griffith avoided the issue, despite the efforts of a Minnesota civil rights activist named James C. McDonald (later known as Kwame McDonald).

McDonald, director of the Minnesota State Commission Against Discrimination, looked into the Twins training camp situation and his group brought an official complaint against the ballclub's ownership in April 1962, pointing out that the Florida segregation was a violation of the Minnesota laws against discrimination in housing. Conferences began that year involving McDonald and Griffith and Twins road secretary Howard Fox, with McDonald urging that the Twins end their practice of providing separate hotels for the ballplayers.[5]

Two other men were also involved in the effort to make it clear to the Twins president that spring training in Florida should conform to Minnesota's standards for equal housing. One was Rabbi Max Shapiro of Temple Israel in Minneapolis; the other was the legendary Twin Cities sportswriter Sid Hartman. Shapiro asked his close personal friend, Hartman, to arrange a meeting with Griffith to convince him to reverse his policies and then brought Hartman along "for moral support." Shapiro recalled that it was a "nice, pleasant meeting," but Hartman noted that "Shapiro really got on Griffith about the segregation." Still, these kinds of confrontations with the Twins owner from 1962 to 1963 "resulted in no solution to the problem and what appeared to be delaying tactics by the Twins." As Sid Hartman put it, "Calvin did nothing."[6]

Earl Battey signed this photograph for the Hallie Q. Brown Community Center in Minneapolis, about 1970.

Despite the foot-dragging, Griffith tried to establish some rapport with his critics, telling Shapiro, "We've got one of your boys working with us" in the Twins public relations department, pointing to the employee who was present in the meeting. He tried to show that he was not all bad because he had a Jewish man on his staff. The staffer complained, according to McDonald's recollection, "Man, I wish Calvin would shut up, now I'm going to start paying," in that he would have to be more religious and more active in the local Jewish community.[7]

Griffith was stubborn, however, telling McDonald and Shapiro that because spring training was held in Florida, Minnesotans could not tell people in Florida what could or could not be done there. He rationalized that leaving the situation alone was better for everybody. He contended that the southern whites did not need northerners coming down there to interfere with the "Southern customs." Griffith gave "hazy generalizations" about how people were able to get along down there, and the Twins would not be willing to bump up against the Jim Crow laws. It was well known by all, though, that Griffith's adoptive father, Clark, was notorious for his bigotry in his operation of the Washington Senators, and Calvin was much like his father. The elder Griffith refused to break the color line with the Senators, instead signing a black Cuban, Carlos Paula, in 1954. Paula was a token black and not an American citizen.[8]

Calvin Griffith integrated the Senators in a piecemeal manner, only after Clark had died in 1955, by putting pitcher Joe Black on the team in 1957. Black, coincidentally, had helped integrate the St. Paul Saints in 1951 and had been the National League Rookie of the Year for 1952 with the Brooklyn Dodgers. However, his career was on a downhill slide, and he pitched in only twelve innings with the Senators. Center fielder Lenny Green became the first regular black player for Griffith in 1959, and then Battey became the third in 1960. Both Griffiths put Cubans on the team, but they were housed with the colored players in Florida each spring.[9]

News of the spring training segregation dribbled out to the public through the sports columns of Sid Hartman and the local black press. But nothing changed because the anti-discrimination commission "had no teeth" and could only try to bring reform by persuading Griffith to alter his practices and, in the time before the Civil Rights Act of 1964, could not sue the club to compel change in another state.

Earl Battey and the other black Twins players were caught in a difficult situation. Personally they desired equality, but the realities of being cut from the team or being passed over for pay raises for taking a public position on the issue were obvious. Battey did not issue a public statement endorsing integration in 1961 or 1962, for he knew all sides of the issue, but he explained his position to McDonald. Battey reasoned that if "we moved to the white hotel, our good and accommodating friend, who owns the black motel would lose business." He also noted that black youths and other fans would not have the same access to the team members at the ritzier hotel. Furthermore, the arrangement was an economic boon to both the players and the black motel owner. The black players were able to "double dip," that is, they were given a per diem meal allowance, as were all the rest of the players, but the Twins organization also picked up the tab for the meals served to the black players when they ate at the motel's restaurant. There was no scrutiny of the billing by Twins administrators, and many friends in Orlando could get a meal courtesy of the Minnesota Twins. Thus the black businesses in Orlando profited from having Battey and the other black players as part of their clientele. Center-fielder Lenny Green told McDonald to leave the situation as it was, to just "let it alone."

The sad legacy of all this was that the Twins were the last major-league team to integrate their spring training facilities, finally making the change in the spring of 1964. Even then, the progress came only after a public chastisement of the Twins by the press, the state government, and civil rights activists. Minnesota Attorney General Walter Mondale believed that it was "a shame that Minnesota should be the only major league club requiring its Negro players to endure the humiliation of segregation" at that late juncture.[10]

In February, news that the Minneapolis NAACP branch had voted to picket the Twins opening game at Metropolitan Stadium "in protest of the Twins management's continued segregation" in Orlando, followed by a threat of picketing at every major-league regular-season Twins game across the country by the Twin Cities chapter of the Congress of Racial Equality (CORE), led to sustained press coverage of the whole controversy.[11] The picketing would hurt Griffith where he could be hurt the most, namely in the pocketbook. McDonald's commission was ready to ask Attorney General Mondale to conduct public hearings concerning the Twins case, and the State of Minnesota would then "issue orders" to prod the Twins into action. The *Minneapolis Spokesman* headlines screamed for intregation, and the *St. Paul Pioneer Press* and the *Minneapolis Star* and *Minneapolis Tribune* kept pace with the breaking story. After a *Star* editorial issued a clarion call for ending the treatment of black Twins players as "second-class citizens" in Florida and after rapid integration became unavoidable, Griffith finally acceded to their demands. On March 3, 1964, Twins secretary Howard Fox called McDonald long distance to inform him that the Twins were "going to move into integrated facilities at the Downtowner Motel in Orlando, Florida" on the following day. This brought an end to the "festering sore" of being the last spring training camp to integrate.[12]

McDonald and the commission viewed the integration of spring training as a victory, however belated. But this progress must also be viewed as a personal triumph for Earl Battey. Reluctant at first, Battey began to talk to people who were in a position to help bring about the needed changes in Florida. Governor Elmer L. Andersen revealed in 2003 that Battey had telephoned him in the governor's office at some point in the early 1960s and told him that "black and white players were housed in separate, segregated hotels at spring training." Battey asked Andersen to "do something about that" situation. Battey informed Andersen of the realities of segregation in baseball, and Andersen "then leaned on" Griffith to "relocate" to a "hotel that would accommodate both races," with the threat to take the issue "to the press." The pressure from Governor Andersen in 1962 was shunted aside by Griffith, however.

In late 1963 Battey, working in the off-season for General Mills corporation, attended a meeting with Twins official Howard Fox, the Commission Against Segregation's director McDonald and assistant director Viola May Kanatz, and Frank Kent of the public relations department at General Mills. Battey asserted that the "Negro players of the Twins team did not like being segregated and wanted to live with the rest of the team." In January 1964, Battey was the featured speaker at a meeting of the Minnesota Council for Civil and Human Rights, and he repeated his call for integration in Orlando. The council "adopted a resolution" to publicize Battey's statements, and the February news flap about spring training ensued, culminating in the end of racial segregation by the Twins in early March.[13]

Battey's role was not fully known in the 1960s, and his activism has now become a part of Twins history at last. The work of Battey, Governor Andersen, Kwame McDonald and other local civil rights activists, Sid Hartman and the press, and the NAACP and the Congress of Racial Equality must all be taken into account in order to understand how the change came about in 1964.

Battey made history on the field as well as off the field, and that part of his story is well documented. Born on Saturday, January 5, 1935, and raised in Los Angeles, California, Earl Battey, Jr., was a multi-sport athlete. He turned down a basketball scholarship to UCLA to pursue a major-league baseball career. Signed by the Chicago White Sox in 1953, he was too young to put his own signature on the contract; he had to get written permission from his parents. His mother, Esther, signed the document for him, but not until Earl promised her that he would eventually earn a college degree. She recognized that he was gifted—both athletically and mentally.[14]

Battey's first contract with the White Sox called for him to be paid $3,999.99. At that time, the rules stated that if a player signed for $4,000 or more, the club had to keep the player in the majors. Battey started out with Colorado Springs in the Western League and hit just .158 in 26 games. He played in five major league games in 1955, the next year in only four. After playing in 48, 68, and 26 games during the next three years for Chicago, he was traded to the Washington Senators, considered to be the doormats of the league. This was his introduction to Calvin Griffith, the president of the Senators. Battey became a Gold Glove catcher in the 1960 season.[15]

When the Senators moved to Minnesota, Battey again won a Gold Glove, and his batting average was the best he would ever achieve—.302. Being both humble and reasonable, he thought a modest raise in salary of $1,300 would be in order. Calvin Griffith, referring to the Twins last-place finish, responded, "We could've finished last without your .302 batting average and your Gold Glove."

In 1962 and 1963, he was the American League All-Star catcher. In '62 he caught 148 games, oftentimes playing despite injuries that would have caused a lesser person to ride the bench.

He helped the Twins to the American League pennant in their glory year of 1965. According to Jim "Mudcat" Grant, Battey was a great catcher for his

Jim Kaat, Earl Battey, and Vic Power received their 1962 Gold Glove awards in a ceremony at Metropolitan Stadium, April 1963.

Battey being congratulated by Rich Rollins after hitting a homer, one of his 104 lifetime home runs

ability to handle pitchers, saying he was the "best manager of the game I ever threw to" and was "the reason I was a 21-game winner" that year.[16]

The Twins lost the World Series to the Los Angeles Dodgers of Sandy Koufax and Don Drysdale in seven games. Battey was again on the All-Star team and was "generally regarded as the best catcher in the American League" and wanted to use those accolades to get a new contract from Cal Griffith with a "decent raise."[17] Griffith was known to some as a tough negotiator and to others as a tightwad or a cheapskate. Cal's response to Battey's request was "Earl, are you kidding? I would soon go broke."

Earl replied, "I had a better year than Elston Howard" (of the Yankees).

Cal responded, "Well, I will call and find out how much the Yankees are paying Elston Howard this season."

Earl countered, "Oh, you don't have to do that—just pay me what they paid Elston Howard three years ago."

The largest salary Earl Battey, one of the finest catchers in baseball and a consensus pick as the best Twins catcher ever, could realize was $42,000. He played a total of thirteen years in the majors, the last seven with the Twins. He retired from baseball in 1967 after the wear and tear of catching caught up with him.

Plenty has been written about Battey's outstanding baseball career, but little has been known about his accomplishments off the field. After retirement, Battey went to New York and worked as a recreation specialist for twelve years in an institution for disturbed boys. In 1980, the former major-league star all-star, feeling a need to fulfill his promise to his mother, enrolled at Bethune-Cookman University in Daytona Beach, Florida, returning to the region of his spring training drama. He was, perhaps, the first Wildcat student to double as a varsity baseball coach. Remarkably, he sometimes coached players with whom he had classes. He completed his four-year college curriculum in two and a half years by taking thirty-four credits a semester. His academic performance earned him the distinction of being accorded summa cum laude honors—the highest academic level.

Earl then became a high school teacher and baseball coach in his new home, Ocala, Florida. He noted that one of the things he had to adjust to was the continuing informal segregation in the South. Earl responded to the challenge by working harder and proving himself as he had always proved himself on the baseball diamonds of the minor and major leagues. He worked with young people throughout his career.

Earl Battey contracted cancer and passed away on November 15, 2003. His legacy as a catcher will never be forgotten, for he was inducted into the Minnesota Twins Hall of Fame in 2004, becoming the thirteenth member of a select group.

Battey also established a reputation for being among the most articulate, witty, yet thoughtful athletes during the late fifties and sixties. His opinions were often sought on the more heady subjects, such as politics, business, community concerns, and race relations. He often spoke with the wisdom of a seasoned diplomat. Known by all as a connoisseur of the one-liner, his most pungent quote was not found in the news media, nor in one of his many interviews, but on St. Paul's Oxford playground blacktop basketball court back in the 1960s. A group of great athletes, including, at various times, the University of Minnesota's Lou Hudson, Archie Clark, Le Roy Gardner, Bobby Bell, Carl Eller, and Sandy Stephens, played pick-up games there. Others, including high school kids from St. Paul Central and Battey and Kwame McDonald (who both lived in the neighborhood), showed up to play as well. In one of the games, Earl Battey, the stocky major-league catcher who sometimes played at a weight of over 260 pounds, made a quick move to his right. The overmatched defender was heard to challenge, "Shoot, fat man, shoot!" Battey calmly swished a medium range jump shot and replied "Ain't no fat on my eye."

Earl's final legacy came through his family. He married Sonia and was the father of five children. One of his sons, Earl Battey III, played baseball in the San Diego Padres minor-league system. At the induction ceremony for the Twins Hall of Fame at the Hubert H. Humphrey Metrodome in 2004, Sonia Battey thanked the people of Minnesota for helping her husband "to realize the American Dream" of playing in the major leagues.[18]

Only after his death came the realization for the followers of the Minnesota Twins that Battey had been a stout advocate for change in bringing the American Dream of social equality to Florida's spring training just prior to the Civil Rights Act of 1964.

Bobby Darwin: Escape from Watts

Joel A. Rippel

Baseball was Bobby Darwin's avenue out of the ghetto. Watts, in south central Los Angeles, became forever linked with poverty and violence in 1965 when six days of rioting left thirty-four dead and "hundreds of buildings destroyed."[1]

Darwin, born in 1943, lived in Watts prior to its deterioration. "I thought it was a great place to grow up," Darwin recalled. "I didn't realize until I had grown up that I lived in a ghetto." He said the area started to get worse when he was a junior and senior in high school. After he graduated from high school, it got much worse. It was a situation where the concept of survival of the fittest applied to the Darwin family.[2]

"We lived right across the street from a park," Darwin said. "I was about 10 or 11 at the time that I started to play baseball. I asked my dad for a glove and baseball shoes. Gloves back then were $5 or $6 and shoes were about the same. So it would have taken about $10-$15 to get my career started. He told me we couldn't afford it. Money was hard to come by and that was a lot of money.

"But I asked my mom and she sweet-talked my dad and the next day when I got home from school I had my new glove and shoes. Once I started playing and my dad saw how much I enjoyed it, he was very supportive."[3]

In his youth, Darwin was also a batboy for a neighborhood team that included Earl Battey, who later became a major-league catcher with the Twins. "I really admired him," Darwin said. "Everyone knew him and he was a great man. We went to the same high school [Jordan High School], and he was my idol. He really influenced me and motivated me."

Darwin's pitching talent got him a free agent contract with the Los Angeles Angels and the $35,000 bonus allowed him to pay back his parents for his first baseball glove and baseball shoes. "We used some of the money," recalled Darwin, "to get out of debt and pay off the house mortgage."[4]

He made his major-league debut with the Los Angeles Angels as a nineteen-year-old pitcher in 1962, but it was a weak start—he gave up four walks and eight hits in three-and-a-third innings, although he had six strikeouts. After that three serious arm injuries caused him to struggle in the minors for the next seven years.

Finally, in the 1969 season, he got into three games with his new team, the L.A. Dodgers, but had an ERA of 9.84 in a little over three innings pitched. When Darwin finished the season with an 0–6 win-loss record for Spokane, a Dodgers farm team, it appeared Darwin's career might be over.

But on the final day of the season, Spokane manager Tom Lasorda needed an outfielder and put Darwin, a good-hitting pitcher, into the lineup. Darwin wound up hitting a game-winning home run.

"Lasorda told me to go home and forget pitching and come back as an outfielder," Darwin said. "What kept me going those years was my desire to be a major-league ballplayer. I thought if I got healthy I could play in the big leagues. I had confidence in myself. And my family was supportive."

In 1970, Darwin restarted his career when he returned to the low minor leagues (Class A Bakersfield) as a twenty-seven-year-old outfielder. He hit 23 home runs in 86 games for Bakersfield. The next season, he returned to Spokane and hit 17 home runs in 91 games to earn a promotion to the big leagues. In 11 games with the Dodgers that season, he batted .250 and hit his first major-league home run.

That off-season, Darwin's career got a break. He was traded to the Minnesota Twins. During the winter, he hit a Mexican Pacific Coast League-record 27 home runs. When he reported to spring training with the Twins, he picked up where he left off in Mexico. Darwin led the Twins in spring training with six home runs and 18 runs batted in, prompting Twins' president Calvin Griffith to tell the *Minneapolis Tribune* that Darwin was "the hottest thing I can remember in spring training."

Outfielder Bobby Darwin in 1972

Having made the Twins' opening-day roster as their starting center fielder, Darwin had to persevere one more time when the start of the 1972 regular-season was delayed thirteen days by a players' strike.

"I was very disappointed," Darwin said. "I had waited so long and I was ready to go."

The layoff didn't cool off Darwin. He homered in the Twins' first two games. On May 26, he became just the second player (Harmon Killebrew is the other) to hit a home run into the second deck of Metropolitan Stadium. The home run—off Ferguson Jenkins—was measured at 515 feet.

Darwin finished the season with 22 home runs and 80 runs batted in. In the next two seasons with the Twins he hit 43 home runs and drove in 184 runs. But in June of 1975, Darwin was traded to the Milwaukee Brewers in exchange for Johnny Briggs.

"The day I was traded I was heartbroken," said Darwin. "I really had enjoyed the whole experience in Minnesota. I really liked the chemistry our team had; playing with guys like Harmon Killebrew, Tony Oliva, Rod Carew and Jim Kaat was just great. They were great players and quality guys. The fans really treated me well. I have nothing bad to say about Minnesota. I enjoyed everything."

Darwin spent two more seasons in the big leagues, getting traded two more times, before retiring after the 1977 season. After retiring Darwin owned a grocery and liquor store, but he soon realized he wanted to get back into baseball. For the past twenty-one years, Darwin has worked as a scout for the Los Angeles Dodgers.

Dave Winfield: Making a Name for Himself

Kwame McDonald and Steven R. Hoffbeck

While Bobby Marshall was perhaps the best athlete ever to grow up in Minneapolis, the greatest from St. Paul was David Mark Winfield. Because Winfield came of age in an era when African Americans were no longer barred from organized baseball, he had no artificial limits placed upon him. He was free to rise to the heights, and he went all the way from the playgrounds of St. Paul to the Baseball Hall of Fame in Cooperstown, bringing the story of black baseball in Minnesota full circle, since Cooperstown was the home of Bud Fowler. How many Minnesotans are there in the Hall of Fame? Only three—Albert "Chief" Bender, a Native American born in Brainerd; Dave Winfield; and, in 2004, Paul Molitor, also a St. Paulite.

Dave Winfield was born in St. Paul in 1951, four years after Jackie Robinson broke the color line in baseball. It was the year that Willie Mays played for the Minneapolis Millers, batting .477 in thirty-five games and then joined the New York Giants. Maybe Dave was fated to be a baseball player, for on that day, October 3, Bobby Thomson hit a home run to win the National League pennant for the New York Giants, probably the most famous homer in the history of baseball.[1]

Then again, maybe he was destined to become a disadvantaged child. His Rondo neighborhood was mostly black and ranked among St. Paul's poorest areas. Rondo was soon to be targeted for destruction to make way for the construction of Interstate 94 in the 1960s. It was not a ghetto, nor was it a "bad" neighborhood; it was old houses lived in by poor people.[2]

Winfield was not born into the best family situation, however. His father, Frank Charles Winfield, was a native of Duluth where his father operated a shoeshine parlor. Frank served in World War II and, upon his return from the war, settled in St. Paul where he worked as a porter for the Great Northern Railway. Frank was away from home for five-day stretches of time, traveling from St. Paul to Chicago, to Seattle, and back to St. Paul. Dave's mother, Arline Vivian Allison Winfield, had grown up in St. Paul, where she met and then married Frank in 1949. Dave was the second son; the first was named Stephen (Steve), born in 1950, a year and a half before Dave. Arline, disappointed by the fact that her husband was not "very interested in father-hood or responsibility," obtained a divorce in 1953.[3]

Frank Winfield departed from the family and from Minnesota, moving to the West Coast. He had failed in his marriage promises and in providing child support payments also, leaving Arline and his two sons in a broken home and in poverty. His failure reflected a growing problem in the black community; the percentage of fatherless homes grew with the passing decades so that by the year 2000, "roughly half of 11.4 million black children" lived in homes without a father to help raise the kids.[4]

As a single parent, Arline took a job in the audio-visual department of the St. Paul public school system. The Winfields "didn't have much money," as Dave later recalled, and didn't have "many clothes or material things—no family car, no summer cabin or even magazine subscriptions." Significantly, Dave Winfield said: "My father didn't do anything for me."[5]

But his mother and his brother did. Arline Winfield was the "pillar," the support, the soul, and the conscience for her sons, leading and guiding them. Brother Steve was Dave's "best friend in life" and his "baseball playing buddy." The Winfields may have been poor in regard to money, but they were rich in family. Grandmother Jessie Allison, who lived just a block away, "took the kids to her house all the time" when Arline first started working for the school.[6]

The Rondo neighborhood had a richness and diversity, too. Steve and Dave "had neighbors and families in the community where we could spend time in their homes," and "very importantly, all of our friends were of different colors and backgrounds, and we all played together."[7]

Much of the activity took place at the Oxford playground, less than a block from the Winfields' home. The brothers spent their summers "rounding up the neighborhood kids for impromptu" baseball games. Dave later recalled that "he had no problems with race that prevented [him] from participating in activities with other kids" in the 1950s and 1960s. Friend Ronnie Reed remembered the days as part of a "beautiful childhood" and that "we didn't see ourselves as second-class citizens."[8]

Dave Winfield found father figures in his youth. A key man was Bill Peterson, a St. Paul Central High School grad who returned to the Oxford neighborhood after graduation from the University of Minnesota and a stint in the Marines. Dave Winfield began playing baseball at age eight, and his coach was Mr. Peterson, a man who could look into the soul of a child and make that kid feel as though he were the most important person in the world. In PeeWees, he was a third baseman, in the Midget Leagues, he played shortstop and pitched. Peterson insisted that baseball be played properly. "I learned how to play the game right at Oxford Playground," recalled Winfield, "Bill drilled it into me every day: You hustle on the field *all* the time."[9]

The Minnesota Twins arrived in the Twin Cities in 1961, and the ten-year-old Dave Winfield adopted some of the players as his "heroes and idols." His first baseball glove was a Zoilo Versailles model, and Twins catcher Earl Battey was a worthy example for black youngsters. But Harmon Killebrew also ranked high in Winfield's estimation. Dave listened to Twins games on the radio and joined his elementary school friends at Metropolitan Stadium to see the games live with free tickets provided for youth league Knothole

Steve and Dave Winfield, about 1980. Steve's informal clothes matched his open manner; Dave was more formal.

Steve Winfield, Bill Peterson, Steve Baldwin, and Dave Winfield taught fundamentals to inner-city kids at the Dave Winfield baseball clinic, about 1980.

Days. He decided that he wanted to be a ballplayer when he first saw "professional baseball players when I was 8 or 9 years old."[10]

National television coverage brought these other heroes to Winfield's home. The boys watched games on a "black-and-white TV," said Steve Winfield later, "and you had to jiggle the coat hanger [antenna]" to get a good picture. Dave put posters on his wall of such greats as "Willie McCovey, because of his strength and dominance yet gentlemanly demeanor." He admired Bob Gibson and Hank Aaron and Willie Mays.[11]

The real heroes for Dave were nearby—coach Bill Peterson and other neighborhood kids' fathers who helped him learn how to play ball. The Winfield brothers became integral parts of Bill Peterson–coached teams at the Little League level and on into American Legion summer ball. In 1964, their Oxford playground team won the St. Paul City Midget League championship, and Dave Winfield was not even the tallest player on the team. Year after year, Coach Peterson led his players to other championships; as Peterson said, "We were city champions in just about every level." Dave Winfield started out as a "skinny and gangly and, at times, uncoordinated" player, but he played with "older, more experienced players," such as brother Steve. As Dave matured, he became "one of the key players" on the Attucks-Brooks American Legion team from St. Paul.[12]

The Attucks-Brooks team became synonymous with "victory" in 1967, when Bill Peterson coached it to the Minnesota State Legion championship. Dave Winfield was the main cog in the team's repeat state championship in 1968, and he experienced a wonderful accomplishment in the midst of a turbulent year. That April, Martin Luther King, Jr., was assassinated, and violence broke out in many cities. In June, Bobby Kennedy was also gunned down. The summer erupted in inner-city rioting, with one person being killed in Minneapolis. In St. Cloud that August, at a ballpark located sixty miles northwest of St. Paul, Dave Winfield was named Most Valuable Player in the American Legion state tournament for his play at shortstop and pitcher as the Attucks-Brooks team won the championship.[13]

Winfield had talent, and as a teenager, he admitted, he could be "free, cocky, egotistical, loud, and just a bit overbearing." According to teammate John Hughes, Winfield asked a player on the Ely team, "Did you ever hear of a cat named Dave Winfield?" The answer was, "No." Winfield told him, "Well, you will." After Winfield batted better than .500, the Ely player approached him and said, "I won't forget you now."[14]

After graduating from St. Paul Central High School in 1969 and a prep career in which he was a starter on both the baseball and basketball teams, Dave faced a crossroads. Drafted by the Baltimore Orioles in the fortieth round, he could have attempted to play professional ball for $30,000, starting in the minor leagues. Following consultations with his family, coaches, and friends, he turned down the Orioles, feeling that he would have to endure the travails of life in the minors, probably in redneck towns in the southern states. Instead, he accepted a half-scholarship offer from the University of Minnesota to gain an education and to play baseball.[15]

Winfield became a legend on the Minneapolis campus of the U of M, but not right away. Under the tutelage of Dick Siebert, nicknamed the "Chief," Dave became a starting pitcher by his sophomore season but found the coach to be "aloof" and "gruff." Siebert had played for Hall of Fame manager Connie Mack, known as a dignified, quiet leader who wore a business suit on the field. Mack had been Chief Bender's manager with the Philadelphia A's.[16]

But in 1971, in his second year of college, Dave Winfield made a monumental mistake in judgment and almost became a loser rather than the winner he had always been. His brother, Steve, also at the U of M, had gotten involved in civil rights activism and could not always watch over his younger sibling. In his freshman year, Dave "became friends with and began running around with a couple of the wrong kind of guys." Money was short for a half-scholarship student like Dave, and his friends led him to help them steal tires. In his sophomore year, Winfield moved out of his mother's house and into an apartment in Minneapolis. With the rent payment due, Winfield and one of his pals stole a snow blower from a warehouse, and the police caught them. He pleaded guilty to a felony, and the judge sentenced him to three years in prison in the St. Cloud Reformatory. St. Cloud was the same city where Winfield and his Legion baseball team had won the state championship just four years before. The judge, mercifully, put Winfield on three years' probation and suspended the sentence.[17]

Dave Winfield had come close to losing his way. While the theft of a snowblower seems like a north-woods crime and like an offense against the soul of a Minnesotan, it was no different from the theft of a wallet, television, or tape player; it was wrong. He had let down his mother and his brother, and he regretted what he had done. "I feel bad about what my mother had to go through," he said a year after the incident. "She'd given me a lot of encouragement and tried to help me in every way. She's so proud when I do well, and now I'm trying to prove that I'm not a bad dude. But every time you go to fill out an application for a job or something you have to put down that you've been in jail." But his family and sports put him back on the right path. Winfield said he came to realize that "if it wasn't for sports" he would be "on the streets." One of his old Rondo friends, Fred Price, got hooked on drugs in the 1970s and ended up dead. Dave admitted that he got "some grief from some of the guys on the streets," but he resolved to carve a future for himself by "playing ball for Minnesota."[18]

Dave became legendary the following year as the athlete who was picked from an intramural basketball league at the university and became a starter on the varsity squad. He had begun playing basketball on the St. Paul Central varsity team only in his senior year. He admitted that he "couldn't do much except jump" and that he "couldn't shoot very well or handle the ball." But he had shot a few hoops on the Oxford playground after baseball practice. "Once I started playing," Winfield recalled, "I liked it." The Central team won the city championship, and Dave was named to the All-City team.[19]

His intramural team carried the title of the Soulful Strutters, wearing Afro-style hair in keeping with the "Black is Beautiful" influence of the late sixties. Typically, the Strutters, with Steve and Dave Winfield, won the intramural championship and became a practice team for the junior varsity. Gopher assistant coach Jim Williams heard of Winfield's great talent, watched him play, and informed new head coach Bill Musselman that maybe Winfield "could help the Gophers."[20]

Winfield came out for the team because, as he said, "I thought maybe I'd get a little playing time." It turned out to be a lot of playing time, after an infamous brawl between the Gophers and Ohio State on January 25, 1972. The Buckeyes center, Luke Witte, had dished out an elbow to Gophers' center Jim Brewer in the first half and then punched Gopher guard Bobby Nix in his face on his way to the locker room at halftime. Later, in the very "close and rough game," Witte got knocked down at the end of a fast break after the Buckeyes stole the ball with an obvious foul. Witte hit the back of his head on the floor when he went down. As Gopher Corky Taylor was helping him up, Witte spat in Taylor's face (according to Taylor's account), and Taylor then "kneed him in the groin." Ron Behagen, who had fouled out, went from the bench and attempted to "stomp on Witte's head." Winfield joined the fracas, getting in "some great punches right in front of press row, but he didn't get caught," according to sportswriter Sid Hartman. The Big Ten suspended Behagen and Taylor, while Witte received no penalties, some said because Witte was white. Dave Winfield became the starting forward for the Gophers. Known popularly as Musselman's "Iron Five," they played almost every minute of every game as they won the Big Ten title for the first time in thirty-seven years. Again, Winfield was on a championship team.[21]

In baseball, Winfield pitched for the freshman team, gaining four wins against no losses. During his sophomore season, his first on the varsity, he compiled a record of 8 and 3, with an ERA of 1.48, the lowest ERA in the Big Ten. The next year, Dave hurt his pitching arm and lost his junior season.[22]

But he found his future that summer, when he played in Alaska for the Fairbanks Goldpanners, and it was as a hitter, rather than as a pitcher. Coach Jim Dietz viewed Winfield as a complete ballplayer, and Winfield responded to the challenge, leading the team in batting average (.315). In recognition of his record for scoring runs and driving in runs, the team chose him as their Most Valuable Player.[23]

The year 1973 was one of athletic glory for Dave Winfield. With him as a power forward for the Gophers basketball team, they almost repeated as Big Ten champions and played in the National Invitational Tournament. The Gophers did win the conference title in baseball that spring; Dave played left field and became the ace of the pitching staff. The success was unexpected, for when Winfield pitched the first game of the season against the Texas Longhorns, the Gophers lost. Dave was the only "black guy on either team," and the Longhorns, as Winfield said, "called me just about everything you can and can't imagine." But it turned out to be his only regular-season loss, and the Gophers "turned the season around," according to Siebert, in a May 4 game against Northwestern. Trailing by five runs, the Gophers won the game on Winfield's two-run homer. Siebert said, "Our men refused to believe they could be beaten" after that. Winfield went 13 and 1, with a 2.74 ERA, and he hit .385 with 8 home runs and 53 RBIs in 43 games. The Gophers were ranked No. 3 in the final national regular-season poll.[24]

The Gophers gained entry into the College World Series, with Winfield pitching a masterful game against Southern Illinois in the District 4 playoffs, striking out 13 in a 2–0 shutout. In the opening game of the tourney versus Oklahoma, Winfield turned in a "magnificent pitching performance," registering 14 strikeouts, the last two with the bases loaded in the ninth inning. Dave "simply challenged" the opposition, blowing fastballs past the Sooner batters for the first five innings and then mixing in "fast curves" in the late-afternoon shadows of the final innings of a tight 1–0 game.[25]

The Gophers defeated Georgia Southern, 6–2, with Winfield going 2-for-4 at the plate and clubbing a home run over the left-field wall. They beat Arizona State next and gained the semifinals against the University of Southern California. Coach Siebert told the press, "I'm as proud of them as I can be — a bunch of Minnesota kids holding their own in this caliber of play."[26]

The matchup with USC turned out to be one of the most memorable games in College World Series history. USC had won three straight CWS championships, but Dave Winfield turned in a "superb performance," shutting out the Trojans on one hit going into the ninth inning and striking out 15. This was against a team that featured future major league stars in Fred Lynn, Rich Dauer, and Roy Smalley and football great and slugger Anthony Davis. Dauer said, "In my whole career, even facing the big boys in the majors, I have never seen anything like [the six-foot-six Winfield]—when Dave let go of the ball, it was three feet in front of your face and it seemed like it was going 110 miles an hour."[27]

But Winfield got tired in the ninth inning. He had started the game with only three days' rest, and when he reached a count of 165 pitches, with the team leading 7–0, he needed relief. The Big Ten had been playing seven-inning games in their double-header schedule, and Winfield had not previously gone nine innings except in the district and CSW games. USC began to choke up on the bat and punch the ball and rallied to win 8–7 when two relief pitchers surrendered the lead.[28]

Years later, Winfield's catcher, Tom Buettner, blamed the home-plate umpire for the loss. Winfield had to throw so many pitches, according to Buettner, because the umpire was so short that he could not see low-pitch strikes over Buettner's head, calling them balls. The "midget umpire" kept telling Buettner to "Get down, get down, I can't see the outside corner" of the plate. Buettner was already down as low as he could get. Winfield was charged with nine walks that game, and Buettner claimed that "it would have been a couple of walks and 20-some strikeouts if the umpire had been able to see the pitches." The game would have been won before Winfield ever got to 160-plus pitches. USC went on to win the College World Series championship, but Winfield's talent was evident as he won the Most Valuable Player award for the series and became a member of the All-America college baseball team.[29]

In his last two years at the U of M, Winfield was "very responsible," according to one of his coaches, and was a student-athlete who "went to class, worked hard," and made the dean's list. He majored in political science and took courses in Afro-American studies.[30]

Dave Winfield had been drafted by several sports teams during the college baseball season of 1973—the NBA's Atlanta Hawks selected him in the fifth round and the Utah Stars of the ABA made him the team's sixth round choice. The Minnesota Vikings spent a low draft choice (the seventeenth round) on Winfield in case he wanted to try out as a tight end, even though he had never played organized football. But his future was in baseball, not in being signed as a low-draft choice, and the San Diego Padres chose Winfield as the fourth overall pick in the first round of the amateur draft. The St. Paulite was the only man drafted by four pro teams in three different sports. It is unlikely that anyone will ever match that feat.[31]

Winfield went directly to the major leagues after the College World Series and played his first game on June 19. He never played in the minor leagues, a rare accomplishment. He signed with San Diego for a $50,000 bonus plus a first-year salary of $15,000, which was the major-league minimum. Wisely, he insisted that the contract stipulate that he would join the Padres directly and not start out in the minor leagues. Having begun operations as an expansion team in 1969, the Padres needed some talent, and Winfield held great promise as a hitter. Signed as an outfielder, Winfield said at the time, "If I don't make it as an outfielder, I assume they'll try me as a pitcher."[32]

Winfield got a hit in his first game, and he got a hit in each of his next five games. He didn't quit hitting until he collected over 3,000 career hits. But his first season was not easy. He played in 56 games, getting 39 hits in 141 at-bats for a .277 batting average with three home runs. He felt alone. As Winfield recalled later, "I didn't know anything about the National League. I was seeing pitches I'd never seen before. I was playing in a ball park the size of an airport.

I'd get my legs all tangled up in the outfield. I was holding my hands too low on the bat. I was hitching my swing, overstriding, overswinging. I'd been a pitcher. Now I was an outfielder. I was thrown into a sink-or-swim situation. I learned to swim the hard way." The Padres had not had much success, and the management allowed him to learn on the job.[33]

Winfield became a big-league player, accustomed to travel, adulation, life on the road, and the grueling pace of the 162-game season. He gained skills and honed his talent so that he was a five-way player—he could hit for average, hit for power, throw out runners, run the bases, and play defense. But San Diego, as with other West Coast teams, was far from the limelight. In eight seasons with the Padres, he led the club in home runs five times (1976–80) and in RBIS six times (1974–75, 1977–80). He was named to the National League All-Star team four times (1977–1979) and batted .364 in the four games. He was voted as the Most Valuable Player on the Padres in 1978 and 1979. In his time in San Diego, Winfield hit 154 home runs, batted .284, gathered 626 RBIS, and stole 133 bases.[34]

Willie McCovey became Winfield's mentor with the Padres from 1974 to 1976 and, as Winfield later wrote, "took me under his wing." Dave needed a father figure and got guidance from the man who had been the NL Rookie of the Year back in 1959 and MVP in 1969. McCovey, in turn, had been a longtime teammate of Willie Mays, and Mays had been his mentor. Winfield "wanted to be like" McCovey.[35]

Another powerful influence came from Al Frohman, who became Winfield's agent. It was an unusual relationship, but necessary, it seemed, for Winfield, who stated that Frohman meant "so much more to me than my real father." Indeed, Frohman would exclaim about Winfield, "What can I say—he's my son." The matching of the six-foot-six black St. Paulite with the five-foot-seven Jewish businessman transplanted to California from New York seemed ludicrous, but it was a real and deep relationship. Winfield met Frohman, the retired former kosher caterer, in 1973 and "mutual admiration blossomed" quickly. Frohman negotiated Winfield's contracts and advised him on business investments, and Winfield paid Frohman, not by percentage, but out of gratitude.[36]

Upon becoming an adult, Dave Winfield had some contact with his biological father, but they were not close. They "talked every few months or so, but it was always strained," according to Winfield. His mother Arline was still the most important person in his life.[37]

Winfield wanted to become a positive role model for young people. Early in his career, he made a commitment to provide service to the greater society, donating $2,000 of his $15,000 first-year salary to charities. As his income grew, Dave could give away more money, and he established the David M. Winfield Foundation for Children in 1977. That year he founded a scholarship program for minority youth and donated $1,000 to the Martin Luther King Recreational Center in his native St. Paul. He also initiated a program to spend $25,000 on baseball tickets for needy children in San Diego. "I'm not doing it for publicity," he said, "I was born poor myself. I didn't have a father in my home after I was 2 years old."[38]

The public did not know much about the personal life of Dave Winfield during his eight years with the Padres. Fans of Winfield in Minnesota followed his career as he rose in stature in the game, becoming an All-Star and the mainstay of the Padres. When he started out, he had "nowhere to go, no car, no friends." But as a professional ballplayer, Winfield soon found plenty of people who wanted to be with him. He was a single professional athlete, and opportunities to meet women were numerous in the big-league cities. Winfield acknowledged in his autobiography, *Winfield: A Player's Life*, that his relationships were "free and easy" in his college years and early pro baseball career, but he contended that he was not "boisterous." The temptations and relationships were the same for traveling players in all eras, but the prospects for casual or serious relationships alike for black ballplayers changed over the course of time. While Bobby Marshall was said to be the "pet of the lady fans" in 1909, his personal relationships were limited by the current social conventions. No such restrictions applied in the 1980s and later for Winfield or for other stars like Kirby Puckett.[39]

The 1970s propelled Dave Winfield onto the national scene as an All-Star, but the 1980s brought free agency and millionaire status to the young man from St. Paul. Al Frohman helped precipitate Winfield's entry into the free-agent market when he became eligible in 1980. The New York Yankees and owner George Steinbrenner considered Winfield to be "a premier player" who could "run, throw and hit with power" and had the potential to help the Yanks regain the American League pennant.[40]

Steinbrenner negotiated with Frohman and signed Winfield to a ten-year contract, the largest one for 1980. They called the newest Yankee the "Twenty-four-million-dollar man," as one of the few in baseball to be paid a salary of over a million dollars per season. Fans and owners alike watched to see if Winfield would earn his pay. The *Minneapolis Tribune* printed an editorial that spoke of the joy of seeing a "local person make good," that his "hard work" was rewarded with the "good luck" of signing one of the "most lucrative" contracts in sports history. While praising Dave for using a portion of his earnings to finance his health foundation for children, the editorial panned the "silly and skewed" system that would pay a ballplayer that much.[41]

Winfield had delayed signing with the Yankees for a time due to his "concern that he could not operate" well under the control of Steinbrenner. Finally he decided that he "wanted to play for a contender," and he "wanted to wear the pinstripes."[42]

In his first season with the Yankees, in 1981, Dave Winfield got to play in his home state again. In his homecoming at Metropolitan Stadium, he got three hits, and the Yankees beat the Twins 7 to 0. Winfield did what he was supposed to do that night and during the rest of the season. The Yanks won the American League pennant for the thirty-third time in team history—the first title since 1978. Dave led the ballclub in hits, total bases, and game-winning RBIS. He ranked fifth in the league in RBIS. In his first postseason series ever, against the Milwaukee Brewers, Winfield hit .350, but in the World Series against the Los Angeles Dodgers, he batted just 1-for-24.[43]

Steinbrenner was not happy with the World Series loss. His team had benefited from the slugging of Reggie Jackson, celebrated as "Mr. October" for his World Series home runs, and Steinbrenner referred to Winfield as "Mr. May," known for hot starts and cold September finishes.[44]

Throughout the 1980s, Winfield became a more complete player, noted for his ability to hit runners home. In 1982, he began a string of five straight 100-RBI seasons. In 1987 he drove in 97, but in 1988 he again topped the century mark, knocking in 107 RBIS. Dave earned the Gold Glove for fielding five out of his eight years there. Despite his consistency, the Yankees did not win another pennant. Steinbrenner contributed to the difficulties of the decade because his management never put enough strong pitching on the field. Relief pitcher Rich "Goose" Gossage was a star, starter Ron Guidry was really good, but the pitching staff was not of championship caliber, with Dave Righetti, Tommy John, and others being sometimes great, sometimes not.[45]

The decade of the eighties was a tempestuous time for Winfield. As sportswriter Tim Kurkjian reported, Steinbrenner "signed him, spied on him, sued him and savaged him." And those were just some of the bad things that happened that started with the letter "s." There was shouting also. Winfield said that Steinbrenner was trying to "slime" him by destroying his reputation. The strife often became focused on the Winfield Foundation. Winfield had to sue Steinbrenner three times in the 1980s "to force him to make contractually required payments" to the foundation. The Yankee owner often tried "to diminish Winfield's reputation" by resorting to such "petty" acts as keeping the right fielder's "photo off the cover of programs and yearbooks" and making countercharges that the foundation was "mismanaged" and that Winfield had not kept up on his own contributions to the fund. Ultimately, both Steinbrenner and Winfield had to make further payments.[46]

Steinbrenner complained in mid-1982 that Winfield was not "a winner, the way Reggie Jackson was" and that Winfield could not "carry a team." The Yanks owner did not know enough about Winfield's early years in Minnesota.[47]

Winfield expressed how he felt in his autobiography, and it stirred the controversies in New York even more. He told the public that teammate Willie Randolph had informed him upon his arrival that "as a black man, you're never going to be a 'true' Yankee" even though you "can be a 'good' Yankee and a well-respected one." Randolph believed that "something subtle and unspoken" would work to "keep it that way." The Yankees had a long tradition of playing "without black athletes" and was "tradition bound." Randolph, presumably pressured by his owner, denied he had made the statement. The second baseman, formerly one of Winfield's best friends on the team, stopped talking to Winfield after the book came out.[48]

Wearing the Yankee uniform may have been a point of pride for Dave Winfield, but the reality of playing in New York took the fun out of the game. To Winfield, New York was a great city that had the "best and worst of everything. And I saw it all." Reggie Jackson echoed Winfield's comments about the Big Apple, "It's the greatest place to play and it's the toughest; it can be Disneyland or it can be hell." Well, for Winfield, it was not Disneyland; that came when he was traded to the California Angels in 1990.[49]

Winfield's heart did not give out in New York, but his back did. In an operation that could have ended his playing career, leaving him short of his career goals and without a World Series championship, doctors surgically repaired a herniated disc in 1989. Due to his excellent conditioning, he bounced back after a year away from baseball. The Angels wanted Winfield "more for his leadership than for his bat." And when Winfield agreed to the trade to California, he found that the management and owners of the ballclub granted him "respect," and he felt appreciated. His back did not fail him, nor did his bat, and he was the Comeback Player of the Year.[50]

After the second of two fine years in California, Winfield signed with the Toronto Blue Jays as a free agent and joined the Canadian team for the 1992 season. The ballplayer was a "short-term addition to a team with veteran talent," and they wanted him to "bring discipline to the pregame clubhouse and class to the organization." The veteran was hired to be the team's designated hitter and to "lead them to the World Series." He did those things and more. At age forty, he set records, becoming the oldest player to get 100 RBIs, gaining a total of 108 for the year. Winfield teamed up with slugger Joe Carter, who had 119 RBIS. Dave also led his team in doubles with 33 and hit 26 homers.[51]

The Blue Jays had a great team with Jack Morris (of St. Paul) as the ace of a deep pitching staff and a young Roberto Alomar as an offensive catalyst. Under the direction of manager Cito Gaston, a former teammate and friend of Winfield's from his San Diego days, Toronto put all the right pieces together and reached the World Series against the Atlanta Braves. Dave Winfield became a World Series hero. Although he had often "stung the ball" in games one through six in the series, he had only 4 hits in 21 trips to the plate. Some of the hits really counted, however, as he drove in a run in game two in a comeback Jays' victory, his lone RBI, and his bunt in the ninth inning of game three helped set up the winning run.[52]

In game six, Winfield saved the day. In the eleventh inning, with two runners on base and two out, Dave admitted that he "said a couple of extra prayers going up there" to bat. His hits had not been falling in, and he felt he "had to look above for some extra help." But on a 3-ball, 2-strike pitch, the veteran hit a ground ball "just inside the third-base line for a two-run double," providing the winning margin for the Blue Jays over the Braves. Winfield knew that that double, just "one stinking hit" as he termed it, had erased a decade of heartache over never winning the big game and that he had "silenced once and for all the haunting mantra," as sportswriter Claire Smith put it, "of '1 for 22' which [had] played from the lips of the Yankees' owner George Steinbrenner, ever since Winfield had suffered through" the 1981 World Series with the Yankees. Winfield appeared "grateful and relieved" but also overwhelmed by the "sweet" hit that made his "bitter story" with the Yankees "obsolete."[53]

His winning hit was the "favorite thing" he had done in baseball because it brought him back to his youth in St. Paul when he was "playing in the sandlots" with his brother, Steve. "Every practice we would always say, 'you're the man up, men on base, two outs, last game of the World Series—here's the pitch.'" The brothers "always tried to get that hit to win the game for our team, and finally, I was that man—that key man—up at bat at the right time, and I got the hit, so it was beautiful."[54]

Joe Carter said about the hit, "That was awesome." Jays' general manager Pat Gillick summed it all up when he said, "Dave's a great human being who hasn't been treated in his career as well as he should have been. It was probably a little bit of redemption that his hit won the championship for us." Winfield was once more a "winning player" on a "winning team," just as he had been in his schoolboy days in St. Paul. And the dramatic World Series triumph assured Winfield of a place in baseball's Hall of Fame. He had made history as the "oldest every-day player" on a World Series winning team. He had been in pro baseball longer than the Toronto team had existed—it started in 1977, Winfield had started playing in 1973.[55]

The following year brought Winfield home to Minnesota, where he played for the hometown Twins for two seasons. Dave had been replaced as designated hitter in Toronto by fellow Minnesotan Paul Molitor, who had also played on the Attucks-Brooks Legion team. In the indoor Metrodome, Winfield provided some veteran leadership for the struggling Twins. Another moment

Winfield posed with Carl Pohlad after signing with the Twins in December 1992.

Winfield's bat connects with the ball for his historic 3,000th hit.

of glory came for Winfield when he got his 3,000th hit off the great reliever Dennis Eckersley, becoming just the nineteenth player in baseball history to reach the milestone. Winfield had garnered "hits during the terms of six presidents" and off 681 pitchers. He had homered off Hall of Famers Bob Gibson and Tom Seaver and plenty of others. He said of his accomplishment, "This is history." His combination of "talent and determination," longevity and consistency, saw him through to 3,000 hits. At age forty-one, he knew baseball from the inside out, "from last place, the hospital, the wrong side of a World Series, and . . . from the winner's circle."[56]

Winfield played two seasons in Minnesota. Sadly, his mother, Arline, never got to see her son play in a Twins uniform, for she had passed away in 1988 on Dave's thirty-seventh birthday. In that same year, Winfield married Tonya Turner, and he was able to enjoy close ties with her family in Houston. It was Tonya who witnessed his run at baseball history as he garnered hit number 3,000, and she helped him endure the media hype surrounding the event.[57]

The 1995 season proved to be the last one for Dave Winfield. He had been traded to the Cleveland Indians during the players' strike of 1994. It was not a memorable finish to his career as he played in only 46 games, getting just 115 at-bats, with 2 home runs, a total of 22 hits, and 4 RBIs (all career lows). The Indians won the AL championship and went to the World Series but without Winfield on the roster because he was no longer a regular player. He retired from pro ball in February 1996, after twenty-three seasons. Late in his career, he had hoped to match the longevity of Satchel Paige, saying, "If he could play until he was 50, I can too."[58]

The final year of his baseball career also marked a beginning for Winfield. His wife, Tonya, gave birth to twins, David and Arielle. Technically, they were not Minnesota twins, for the family was living in California at the time. His role as a father proved to be a learning experience for the forty-five-year-old Winfield.

His personal life during his career had been rocky at times. As a Yankee, the highly paid outfielder became a celebrity, and such magazines as *Jet* and *People* often chronicled his off-the-field activities. He was included in *People's* list of eleven men who were "prime catches" in 1986—appearing along with such hunks as John F. Kennedy, Jr. One who tried to catch him was flight attendant Sandra Renfro, who had a longtime, on-again, off-again relationship with him, beginning in 1972. In 1982, the two journeyed to Brazil, spending a week in Rio, where Sandra became pregnant. Their daughter, Lauren, was born in Houston, and Winfield "acknowledged that [he] was the father." While he stated that "he was never the type of guy who would want to father children outside of marriage," he was not ready to start his family at that juncture in his life. He believed that he was caught in a dilemma, that he was "repeating the pattern" of his own life in which his "mother and father had separated" when he "was a little boy," that "Sandra herself was brought up by foster parents," and that both of them had had incomplete home lives. The pair parted company in 1985, but Winfield paid child support. Eventually because of circumstances, the relationship ended up in court, with the ensuing publicity surrounding a celebrity's life.[59]

Winfield came to understand that as a ballplayer he was "expected to be a role model" as part of a "demand that goes along with the money and the fame." He realized that he could do well in certain areas of life, especially by using his foundation to help children with health-care issues and to deliver an antidrug message, but that he might not be able to live up to all expectations. With the strengths of his own family, particularly his mother, Arline, and the shortcomings of his own background, centered in his father, he ranked parents as the most important role model for children, followed by teachers, and then by athletes.[60]

Other weaknesses were apparent in his life. When controversy dogged him during his tenure with the Yankees, he thought that he could shut it out. He believed he was strong enough to endure the abuse, using "his many layers of protective coating" to keep his inner peace. His coaches, too, assumed that he was "immune to nerves" and pressure. But no one is that strong, and this giant of a man got an ulcer in 1984 from his Yankee experience, and it flared up again in 1987. To Winfield, professional baseball was "rarely fun."[61]

As a nationally known sports figure, Winfield gained glory and notoriety. But the glamor came with the scrutiny of the media, which was happy to reveal his flaws and miscues. Winfield had human weaknesses, magnified by the curse of celebrity. He may have been touched by a problem called "acquired situational narcissism." Defined by Robert B. Millman, professor of psychiatry and medical adviser to Major League Baseball, the malady strikes movie stars and rock singers, pro athletes and famous politicians, and pulls them into "tantrums, affairs, [or] addictions." Some celebrities have difficulties with marriage, parenthood, or chemicals, as could anyone, but greater difficulties can develop when "once-ordinary people achieve extraordinary success." Only time and maturity allowed Winfield to avoid the excesses of his stardom. He was in the forefront of the era of "equal-opportunity" superstars in sports; a man did not have to be white to be a famous athlete.[62]

Winfield made a name for himself in baseball. He was elected to the Baseball Hall of Fame in Cooperstown in his first year of eligibility, a benchmark of greatness. Although he had played for six different teams, he chose a Padre hat for his bronze plaque, and he was the first San Diego Padre to be admitted to Cooperstown. He was also the tallest baseball player ever to make the Hall of Fame (along with six-foot-six Don Drysdale). He was a rare sort of player, one who could "combine power and consistency." The Minnesotan had hit more home runs than Joe DiMaggio, who was known as "one of the truest Yankees of them all"; he had more career RBIs than Reggie Jackson or Mickey Mantle; he had more hits than Babe Ruth, Mickey Mantle, or Ted Williams.[63]

Many terms have been used to describe Dave Winfield: "Bright. Sensitive. Articulate. Generous." He was a "durable strongman," who would sometimes "intimidate opposing pitchers by swinging a sledgehammer in the on-deck circle." He was a "wicked mix of power and speed," who once hit a "bullet" line drive at shortstop Greg Gagne at the Metrodome, and the ball "tore his glove off." Manager Mike Hargrove called him "a class guy" who "plays the game hard." Others commented that he played the game of baseball "with style, effort, and effortlessness" due to his great athletic ability. He appeared at first to be just an athlete, maybe "one of the best pure athletes ever to play major league baseball."[64] Winfield decried such talk, which seemed most often pointed toward black ballplayers. He put hours of his time into physical conditioning and becoming a student of the game.

Some said Winfield was "slick" or aloof or a "self-promoter."[65] In the era when baseball players became millionaires and celebrities, he needed protection from the hangers-on who would be happy to siphon away his fortune. Whatever advocates or detractors called him, he was a part of baseball history, for his mammoth contract with the Yankees in 1980 became a milestone in the era of big-money baseball of the 1980s and 1990s.

Dave Winfield's life in baseball was marked by the bigger-than-life accomplishments of a magnificent athlete. He personified power and gracefulness on the playing field. But his success would not have been possible without a foundation found within the brotherhood of baseball. His baseball odyssey began with the pure joy of playing ball at the Oxford Playground with his blood brother Steve Winfield. He learned about the essence of the pro game in San Diego from veteran Willie McCovey. Winfield formed bonds with other players in other places—with Willie Randolph in New York, with Joe Carter in Toronto, and with Kirby Puckett in Minnesota.

By the end of Winfield's career, all Minnesotans, white or black or otherwise, were able to embrace this African American man as a hometown hero in a way that earlier black ballplayers would never have dreamed possible. The *Minneapolis Star Tribune* and the *St. Paul Pioneer Press* newspapers published special sections dedicated to Winfield upon his entrance into the National Baseball Hall of Fame in 2001. At the same time, Winfield gained a place alongside Walter Ball, Bobby Marshall, and John Donaldson in the pantheon of great African American athletes who played ball in Minnesota. He had become deeply aware of the debt he owed to the Negro League players who had created a level playing field for him and other black players. In his Hall of Fame induction speech, he paid homage to Satchel Paige, Cool Papa Bell, and Jackie Robinson for overcoming "all kinds of obstacles and problems along the way" and making it possible for him to rise to the heights of major-league baseball as an equal-opportunity superstar. These oldtimers had paid him a deep compliment, saying, "Man, you could have played with us." In fact, Dave Winfield could outplay just about anybody, black or white.[66]

Lyman Bostock, Jr.: Death of an Outfielder

The tale of Lyman Bostock, Jr., is just about the saddest in Minnesota's baseball history. His story could have been a delightful epic journey as he went from rags to riches, overcoming all obstacles in his basepaths. But his life ended too soon in a senseless murder on the mean streets of a grimy city.

Bostock's life contained echoes of Negro League baseball with all of its unfulfilled hopes. His father, Lyman Bostock, Sr., gained fame as an All-Star first baseman with the Birmingham Black Barons, batting over .400 several times. He had a dream to play in the integrated major leagues. After all, his teammate Willie Mays had been signed by the New York Giants. But he never made it, playing in the Negro Leagues from 1938 until 1949. In 1950, Lyman Bostock left Alabama and the Negro Leagues to play baseball in Canada and abandoned his wife, Annie Pearl, pregnant with their first and only child, a boy who would be named Lyman, Jr. Annie struggled to earn a living as a single parent, separated permanently from her baseball-playing spouse. He created a bitter legacy by deserting his wife and son. "My father helped teach Willie," recalled Lyman Bostock, Jr., "but he never taught me."[1]

Annie Pearl Bostock and her son moved in with her parents and siblings, the Turner family, in Birmingham. Little Lyman loved baseball and learned the game without any real equipment or his father's help by throwing "rocks in the air" and hitting "them with a broom handle."[2]

Annie eventually moved to Los Angeles with young Lyman, arriving in the city in 1958 with just seven dollars in her purse. She got a job working in a hospital, and he began to excel in baseball at Manual Arts High School and at California State University, Northridge. The Twins drafted him in the twenty-sixth round and brought him to the majors in 1975 after three years in the minor leagues.[3]

Lyman Bostock, Jr., had an "effervescent" personality—a man filled with joy and humor, a player who loved the jostle and bustle of the clubhouse. A man of many words, his teammates called him "Gibber-Jabber." Bostock "would talk to anybody, anytime, about anything," according to teammate Roy Smalley.[4]

And he could really play ball. In his first season with the Twins, he got 104 hits in 98 games (.282 BA). In 1976, the young outfielder batted at a .323 clip (fourth-best in the American League) and hit for the cycle (single, double, triple, and homer) in July against the White Sox. In just his third season in the big leagues, he was the third-best hitter in all of baseball with a .336 batting average (teammate Rod Carew hit .388). Nolan Ryan, the all-time great pitcher, referred to Bostock as "one of the few natural hitters" in the American League.[5]

Bostock's closest friend in the Twins ballclub was fellow outfielder Larry Hisle. The two ballplayers were "roommates and constant companions" when the team played games on the road. They were also fishing buddies, spending time on Minnesota lakes early in the morning in the off-time between games. As Hisle noted, "I've never had a friend as close as Lyman." Bostock said that Hisle was "my main man" and that "we were each other's shadow."[6]

But the brotherly bond would be broken due to the legendary penny-pinching by Twins owner

The slugger and the natural hitter, friends Larry Hisle (left) and Lyman Bostock, 1976

Calvin Griffith. Bostock's salary was low; he earned $25,000 in 1976. The more-experienced Hisle got just $46,000 that year. Both players were eligible for free agency after the 1977 season. Bostock asked for $250,000, and Griffith showed his contempt for the new rules of baseball contracts by cutting the young star's salary by 20 percent, the maximum allowable, to a paltry $20,000. The money was just above the major-league minimum. As a result, both Bostock and Hisle left the Twins and entered the free-agent draft where they became "millionaires-in-waiting." Sportswriters called Bostock the "leading light" and "star of the free-agent draft" because he had "become one of baseball's best hitters."[7]

Bostock signed a five-year contract with the California Angels for an estimated $2.5 million. He chose the Angels for family reasons; the Los Angeles metro area was home for him and his wife, Youvene, and both of their mothers. Bostock considered an offer from the New York Yankees, but he did not want the "controversy" that came with life in the Big Apple.[8]

Larry Hisle garnered a multi-year, $3.1 million deal with the Milwaukee Brewers and the friends parted ways. Hisle played until 1982, concluding a fourteen-year major-league career.

Bostock did not make it through the 1978 season. After the Angels played a game in Chicago, he went to nearby Gary, Indiana, to visit his uncles on his mother's side, Edward and Thomas Turner. Lyman often stayed at Edward's house when he played a game in Chicago. On the night of September 23, Thomas Turner and Bostock visited Joan Hawkins and her sister Barbara Smith (age twenty-six), whom Turner had supposedly helped raise to adulthood as their godfather. Bostock had previously met Joan Hawkins during a visit to his uncle's home in 1957. After Bostock signed autographs for Joan's family, Turner and Bostock agreed to give the two women a ride to another house. As they were driving in downtown Gary, Barbara Smith's estranged husband drove alongside their car and shot Lyman Bostock in the head with a shotgun at point-blank range. The shooter, Leonard Smith, might have been aiming at his wife, Barbara, but more likely he was gunning down a man he thought was his wife's boyfriend. Police at the scene believed that Bostock "just happened to be in the wrong place at the wrong time" and that Barbara Smith was only a "recent acquaintance" of Bostock's. Whatever the truth may have been, Bostock's big mistake was being in the back seat of a car with another man's wife at 10:40 P.M., "driving through one of the grimy steel town's worst sections." Bostock died shortly after being shot.[9]

When Larry Hisle heard the news the next day, he became "too upset to play" and "asked if he could sit out" of that day's game "because of the death of his friend." His eyes were red and "his voice [was] choking" when he left the Brewers' ballpark to grieve at home.[10]

Youvene and Annie Pearl Bostock and all of his California teammates were among the fifteen hundred mourners who attended the dead Angel's funeral in Los Angeles. Lyman Bostock, Sr., was there, too.[11]

Lyman, Jr., had lived out his father's dream of playing in the major leagues. He had told his relatives at one point, "Somebody in this family's got to become somebody [and] I guess I'm the one." The difference in salary alone pointed to the disparity in the paths their lives had taken. The elder Bostock had been paid $5,000 per season in his prime years in the Negro Leagues, while the younger was making that much per game.[12]

Father and son saw each other "once in a while" after Lyman, Jr., made the Twins roster in 1975. The Twins included Lyman, Sr., in an Old-Timers game in 1976, partly in recognition of the father-son relationship as well as of the senior Bostock's career in baseball. The younger Bostock reportedly said to his father, "I've never met you. How do I know who you are?"[13]

Kirby Puckett: All Player All the Time

Jay Weiner

From the moment Kirby Puckett burst onto the Minnesota scene, he was more than likeable. He was positively embraceable. Besides his obvious skills of hitting, running, and throwing, this roundish man knew how to adjust to his surroundings, how to invite smiles, and how to stir emotions.

Puckett's trek one May day in 1984 from the minor leagues to the majors was instantly the stuff of legend: an adventurous taxi ride, an unpaid bill, a four-hit debut. But soon, his longer, larger, more arduous, and socially significant journey to the very top of American baseball was known, and it was impressive: ninth of nine children living the first twelve years of his life on the fourteenth floor of a sixteen-story housing project on the gritty, violent, nearly all-black South Side of Chicago.

Kirby Puckett, cute as a button, always had a flare for the dramatic. As a free-swinging, leg-lifting, self-described "hacker" at the plate, he giveth home runs. As a leaping, fearless, wide-ranging center fielder, he taketh them away, too. With his fleet feet, he could steal a base. With his strong

Kirby Puckett, the joyful face of Twins baseball

arm, he could shoot down a base runner trying to advance. With his short—five foot eight inch and rotund—more than two hundred pounds at the peak of his career—presence, he was physically understandable, even a bit like us. This was no Adonis-like specimen. This was our neighbor, a guy we might know and look straight in the eye.

Except he was a black, major-league baseball player in Minnesota in the 1980s and '90s and a star. And he would become a millionaire, the state's highest paid athlete of his day. He was different from just about everyone around him, but, somehow, he more than fit in, even when traveling on

Twins off-season marketing caravans from Bemidji to Worthington. "And I was treated as if I went into a black neighborhood," he said of his forays into Minnesota's predominantly white hinterlands.[1] He became the most popular sports figure in the state's history, up there with the likes of Bronko Nagurski, George Mikan, Harmon Killebrew, and Fran Tarkenton. In an end-of-the-century review by the *Minneapolis Star Tribune,* Puckett was named as Minnesota's most important sports figure of the twentieth century.[2]

That's why the sad and sudden end to his career in 1996, and then his tragic fall from grace seven years later, hit Minnesota and Twins fans so hard. When his playing days ended, when his devil-may-care persona was shattered, his stage and his shining public image melted away. Local newspapers reported on his divorce from his wife, Tonya, who had become a public figure in Minnesota, the de facto First Lady of Twin Cities baseball. But on March 17, 2003, Kirby Puckett's post-career tawdry tumble was splashed on the cover of *Sports Illustrated.* His overweight face, punctuated by his drooping and blind right eye, stared out at us, juxtaposed with a photo of him as we remember him: svelte, angelic, youthful. "The Secret Life of Kirby Puckett," screamed the *Sports Illustrated* cover headline. Inside were the gory details of his years of purported philandering, his alleged abuse of Tonya, and the accusations that he assaulted a woman in a Twin Cities area nightclub.[3]

Across the nation, Puckett's reputation was besmirched. Later that month, his trial in Hennepin County Court in Minneapolis would be covered as if it were Minnesota's version of the legendary O. J. Simpson trial, a local analog for the sports star who forgets where the playing field begins and ends. Sadly, through the week-long trial, he was repeatedly identified by witnesses as that "big, fat black guy." Puckett, in size fifty-two suits, sat Buddha-like in the courtroom. This was no game. This was real life.

Eventually, on April 3, 2003, he was acquitted of all charges, even as jurors stated they suspected he did something wrong, if not criminal. Twelve years after his World Series achievements, twelve years after Kirby Puckett could have said anything and been believed, a panel of twelve jurors had difficulty believing his story about his encounter with that woman in that suburban night spot. Gone was the mythic image of a happy-go-lucky athlete, putting his arm around little kids or joshing with the news media or high-fiving with a teammate. Gone was the glow, tarnished was the legacy.

In the so-called "good old days," when an African American baseball player performed admirably on and off the field, he was paternalistically praised for being "a credit to his race." Thankfully, Puckett played in an era when the national pastime had evolved beyond such nonsense. By 2003, barely two years after his induction into baseball's Hall of Fame, Puckett reflected a newer major-league sports cliché, a more modern role for the athlete; even memories of his aggressive swing and diving catches could not shroud his clay feet and his shattered image. According to *Sports Illustrated,* "The media and fans in Minnesota turned the Twins star into a paragon of virtue—which made his human flaws all the more shocking."[4]

If equality means that any athlete—no matter his race, stature, or popularity—can tumble from his pedestal with the same degree of disgrace and ignominy as any other human being, then, as Minnesota baseball moved into the twenty-first century, there was a sad state of equality. The state's greatest player of all time was an example of decline.

How long it was since Puckett joined the Twins nineteen years earlier. How much had happened during which Puckett, more than any other local athlete, symbolized a sporting joie de vivre and a longed-for racial harmony in a state not known for its diversity. Through years of demographic transition in Minnesota, Puckett was the state's crossover dream.

His 1984 entrance onto the scene of the lowly Twins had Hollywood-like comedy and warmth attached to it. His departure from the playing field had heartfelt pathos. His forced retirement was an episode that triggered a collective cry from Minnesota and the baseball world. Puckett's exit from the game was no commercial melodrama. It was harsh, painful reality—blindness in a man who relied on pinpoint eyesight to hit a speeding white ball.

Kirby Puckett had a way of flattening out differences, of minimizing tensions. He was one of baseball's most respected stars during a period of tectonic change in U.S. professional sports and in Minnesota demographics. When Puckett broke into the major leagues, players rarely wore earrings and never sported tattoos. When he was promoted from the Twins' Class AAA Toledo team to the big leagues on May 7, 1984, the highest salary in the game was $1.3 million and the average salary was $329,408.[5] By the turn of the twenty-first century, the top salary was $15 million and the average was $1,895,630.[6]

Puckett became the game's first $3 million player in 1989 and six years later one of the first $6-million-a-year players. Economically, he was a key player. He was also a modern rarity and among the last of a dying breed in an age of peripatetic free agents. He spent his entire career with one team—the Twins.

As Puckett played, America's sports world was in flux. In 1984, the National Basketball Association, which would go on to become the premier league for African American athletes, was emerging from its economic malaise and attempting to gain a firm place at the table for the nation's sports fans; a

North Carolina basketball player named Michael Jordan had not yet made his debut with the Chicago Bulls.

In 1984, despite a series of labor struggles between its players and owners, baseball could still cling, however tenuously, to its claim to be the national pastime, even as pro football was firmly elbowing the sport of Albert Spalding, Josh Gibson, Babe Ruth, Jackie Robinson, and Mickey Mantle out of the way.

By the time Puckett was forced to retire in 1996, baseball had begun to lose its hold on a nation of young fans and certainly on the nation's black population. No longer did the boys in the Robert Taylor Homes, where Puckett grew up, play stickball against a wall. By the time he left the game, Puckett was playing under the terms of one of the game's biggest contracts. It was a remarkable feat for a player from one of the game's smallest markets, Minneapolis–St. Paul. Of course, he had helped to deliver two World Series for the Twins. But the game among young people of his background and skill was a fading experience. Inner-city baseball was a rarity, and he regretted that. And the sport and his franchise were set to be contentious issues because of stadium construction politics in the state that once embraced him and his team.

Still, examining his role against a racial backdrop, Puckett alone could not aid the Twins in engaging a growing black consumer base that, for years, turned its back on the local team. For reasons both understandable and inexplicable, Puckett's wild popularity did not seem to increase the number of African Americans who pushed their way through the Metrodome turnstiles. This, even as the state's minority population grew faster than in the nation as a whole during his years of competition.[7]

To be sure, Minnesota's black population was miniscule compared to larger, urbanized states. But from 1980 to 2000 the black population in Minnesota— almost all in the Minneapolis–St. Paul metropolitan area—increased by more than 200 percent. African Americans still made up only 3.5 percent of the state's population, but even when the Twins were winning, nary a black face was seen in the Dome's blue seats.[8]

Puckett's fame did not seem to translate into a direct connection to the state's black population. Much of that likely had to do with a long-standing tension between Minnesota's minority populations and the franchise. It was a friction created by the public pronouncements and actions of one-time owner Calvin Griffith, even though it was Griffith who first signed and promoted Puckett to the big leagues.

But Puckett was embraced by a state of white people in a way that no other black athlete ever had been. Perhaps it was his non-threatening manner.

Perhaps it was his palpable lack of anger at a time when young, black males were characterized as especially angry and unemployed. Perhaps it was his pure joy of playing the game and his ability to block out distractions. "Who would I get mad at?" Puckett asked me in an interview as we discussed why he was so mellow on issues of race in baseball. "I think we know if you're a black man growing up in this society there's racism everywhere. It's there. Even for me. It's alive and well. I think it's one of those things that if you don't talk about it or say much about it, it'll kind of go away, just blow in the wind."[9]

Upon his arrival in 1984, Puckett literally integrated into relatively lily-white Minnesota and a very white team, with only two other black players, Ron Washington and Darrell Brown, and Puckett replaced the latter in the Twins' starting lineup. As with many teams, there was a sense of brotherhood, a cross-racial, cross-demographic acceptance of people because of the jobs that they performed to keep the group moving in the right direction. In this unit, Puckett saw racial progress. "I know that my great, great, great, great ancestors were hung and killed. They were slaves, I know that. Have I made it better? From a baseball aspect, I was able to do that as a team. I think I've made great strides as far as being a black person," Puckett told me.[10]

But we must be careful not to place too many sociological demands on Puckett's contributions to baseball and Minnesota. We must not, in retrospect, scold him for being something he never was. He was smart, but not deep. He was cuddly, but it would be learned after his playing days that he was a carouser of Ruthian proportions. For better or for worse, Puckett was, simply, a baseball player and a friendly fellow, but really nothing more. He preferred it that way. He knew his limitations. He seemed happy with himself.

Perhaps, no one could have fairly expected him to be anything more than the sort of "Human Mascot" he became. Teammates rubbed his bald head for mystical good luck. Children seemd attracted to him as if to Santa Claus. Normally level-headed NBC broadcaster Bob Costas was so enamored with Puckett's smile and style that he gave his son the middle name Kirby.[11]

Puckett was no natural social activist, no politician, no philosophical figure of any weight or substance. He was, simply, a man with spectacular athletic skills who transformed a compact body into a force able to create some of the most breathtaking statistics in the history of the game, statistics that stand the test of time despite the unexpected brevity of his career.

And, yet, given his unique people skills, his statewide, even national, fame, one wonders just how much social good Puckett could have delivered beyond his marvelous baseball performances. He and his wife, Tonya, did start a foundation at the University of Minnesota. Puckett did sponsor an annual billiards tournament that raised a reported $4 million over the years for children's health issues.[12] And late in his career, with the aid of the Twins, he and St. Paul native Dave Winfield, who played one season with the Twins, "sponsored" a Little League program in the housing projects of Minneapolis and St. Paul. But Puckett never rose to the level of community leader, not like former Vikings star Alan Page, for instance, even though a platform would have existed for Puckett had he wanted it.

But Puckett was not a value-neutral or blank slate. He brought a certain working-class soul to an otherwise suburban white-guy franchise. He did challenge, in a way that went largely unnoticed, the financial tightness of an ownership long considered cheap. He did become the focus of a community's deeply felt affection, and that was extremely meaningful for a state eager to remain close to its teams at a time when pro sports and Minnesotans were growing farther apart as its NHL hockey team moved, its NBA basketball team threatened to relocate, and all its teams sought controversial public subsidies for stadiums and arenas.

Puckett's was an image and a bond borne of spectacular results on the baseball field. He had a .318 lifetime batting average. He finished with 2,304 hits, and baseball historian Bill James projected that he would have had a 62 percent chance to hit 3,000 had his career not been cut short.[13] James, whose analysis of players' skills is unquestioned, rated Puckett—shortened career and all—as the eighth greatest center fielder of all time, behind only Willie Mays, Ty Cobb, Mickey Mantle, Tris Speaker, Joe DiMaggio, Duke Snider, and Ken Griffey, Jr. (and Griffey's injury-prone nature in the prime of his career likely drops him below Puckett, who was incredibly durable). James also ranked Puckett as the ninety-eighth-best player ever at any position.

Puckett led his team to World Series victories in 1987 and 1991. He picked up a half-dozen Gold Glove awards for his aggressive defense. In game six of the 1991 World Series, he produced what some have considered one of the great postseason performances in history. He drove in a run with a triple in the first inning; he robbed Atlanta's Ron Gant of a home run in the third inning, leaping high off the Metrodome Plexiglas in left-center field to grab it; he hit a sacrifice fly in the fifth; he singled and stole a base in the eighth; and he blasted the game-winning home run in the eleventh.

All the glory and high spirits turned violently ugly on September 28, 1995. Puckett was accidentally hit in the face by a fastball from Baltimore's Dennis Martinez. His jaw was shattered. His season ended. The next spring, Puckett appeared to be his old self. He posted a .360 batting average during the pre-season in Florida. Then, on March 28, 1996, his right eye stopped working. He could not see anything on the sides. It was glaucoma, and surgery could not fix it. By July 12, 1996, Puckett retired. He was thirty-six years old. Five years later, on his first ballot, Puckett was voted into the Baseball Hall of Fame, the third youngest player so honored, older only than Lou Gehrig and Sandy Koufax.[14]

Rather than mourn the end or shake our heads at the off-field aftermath of a so-called "sports hero," let us return to the beginning. On that very first day he put on a Twins uniform, he was instantly accessible, down-to-earth, and a creator of grins. It was as if the Minnesota Twins, in need of a superstar, nay, in need of a *black* superstar to move into the modern era, had invented Puckett in a laboratory somewhere.

On Monday, May 7, 1984, Puckett, then twenty-three, needed to travel swiftly from Portland, Maine, where the Mud Hens were playing an away game, to the Twins road game in Orange County, California, against the Angels, who played in the shadow of Disneyland in Anaheim. Puckett survived the following: the airplane he was on needed repairs; the taxi he was in traveled longer than he expected; and the bill was eye-popping for a minor leaguer.

Imagine Puckett. See him rushing frantically into the Anaheim Stadium clubhouse less than ninety minutes before the Twins and Angels were to play. Hear Billy Gardner, the wise-cracking, mispronouncing Twins manager, asking in his New England accent, "Where's Punkett?"[15]

Before Puckett became the most widely known Twins player in history, he was "Punkett," he was broke, and he was a little bit lost.

"He didn't go to Dodger Stadium, did he?" Gardner asked.

No, he was headed in the right direction and thankfully so because he was sorely needed. The Twins possessed fresh-faced first baseman Kent Hrbek, gritty third baseman Gary Gaetti, and temperamental left-handed pitcher Frank Viola as the core of what would become a World Series champion. But, three years before their first unlikely World Series victory, the Twins were relying on the likes of "Downtown" Darrell Brown (one career home run, forty-four career RBIs) to hold down center field. That was not good.

Puckett was hitting only .270 with the Mud Hens, but he was being compared with former Houston Astros star Jimmy ("Toy Cannon") Wynn—compact, powerful, fast. Gardner was in need of speed, solid defense, and some pop at the front of his lineup. Anxious and excited, Gardner had "Punkett," penciled into the starting lineup, batting first, that Monday night.

The young Twins brotherhood in the dugout: Gary Gaetti, Tom Brunansky, Kirby Puckett, Kent Hrbek, and Roy Smalley, Jr., 1986

"When they draft you into the Army they put you in the front line, right, pal?" Gardner told a reporter hours before the game. But it was already six o'clock, the Twins were due for batting practice, and still no Puckett. Twins traveling secretary Mike Robertson was getting worried. Puckett's plane was due at Los Angeles International Airport at 1 P.M. He should have arrived in Anaheim.

At 6:10 P.M., Puckett, carrying his Toledo equipment bag, raced through the swinging doors of the visiting clubhouse. "I got to get some money, man," he said breathlessly to Robertson. "I got to pay the cab." Okay, no problem, Robertson replied. "Eighty-three dollars," Puckett said.

It is not a whole lot today by major-league standards, but it was a ton to a minor leaguer who had just taken the long route to his major-league arrival. That morning, at 5:30 eastern time, Puckett boarded a flight from Maine to Atlanta. All seemed fine. But when he changed planes at Atlanta's busy Hartsfield International, the aircraft needed a new windshield.

"Twice," Puckett said. He was delayed for four hours.

When he arrived in Los Angeles just before 5 P.M., he was in a big hurry. He hopped in a cab, told the driver, "Anaheim Hyatt," and prepared for the big leagues. The cabbie told him the fare would be eighty-three dollars.

"I was stunned," Puckett said that night. But when he realized how late he was, he told the taxi driver to forget the Hyatt and go directly to Anaheim Stadium. "He said, 'Since you're not going right to the Hyatt, I'll have to charge you more,'" Puckett reported.

Eighty-three bucks. Robertson dipped into his pants pocket and ran out to pay the driver. No-necked Puckett quickly put on his No. 34 for the first time. But Gardner altered the lineup and told him to sit on the bench for the night. "I think the kid needs a rest," Gardner said.

But just for twenty-four hours. The next day Puckett slashed out four singles in five at-bats and stole a base. He became only the ninth player in history to pound out four hits in his debut. That first game triggered a memorable quote from Darrell Brown. Brown was hitting .274 but fielding like a high schooler and was in the throes of a domestic dispute over alimony payments. Gardner instantly decided Puckett was the Twins center fielder of the future. Said the unsuspecting Brown of Puckett's arrival, "They're entitled to play whoever they want. I'm just here coming to the yard every day. There ain't nothing to panic about. I've been in worse positions." Not true. Brown was bound for extended exile; his major-league career ended when the 1984 season did.

Puckett parachuted into a marvelous situation: a young Twins team eager to get better, a young team with no egos, a young team open to anyone willing to have fun and play hard. But Puckett also walked into an uncertain, even unkind, racial situation. After all, this was a young man who grew up in Chicago's meanest public housing project—indeed, the nation's. Here he was buttoning up the shirt of a uniform representing a franchise known for its paucity of African American players, and its owner, Calvin Griffith, was remembered for saying he moved his team to Minnesota from Washington, D.C., to avoid the capital's large black community. Griffith was an owner who, in letting future Hall of Famer Rod Carew go to the California Angels and in trading rising star Larry Hisle to the Milwaukee Brewers, seemed to be unloading his most talented and thoughtful black players. In so doing, he was an owner who had totally alienated himself from the Twin Cities' black population and, for that matter, its progressive-thinking white populace.

When Kirby Puckett broke into the major leagues with the Twins, there were about 54,000 African Americans living in the state of Minnesota, fewer than there were seats in the Metrodome.[16] By comparison, in the housing project where he grew up, Puckett was one of 20,000 black children who lived within a few city blocks.[17] In moving to Minnesota, the color of Kirby Puckett's world changed drastically. But like any good hitter, he adjusted.

Puckett joined the Twins four years after Griffith had delivered his infamous "Waseca speech." On September 28, 1978, in addressing the Waseca Lions Club, Griffith provided his ugliest public relations moment and his most lasting. In what he thought was a private, unmonitored environment, he made fun of players' sexual activities and revealed himself in racist comments. Little did he know that Nick Coleman, a *Minneapolis Tribune* reporter, was in the audience.[18] "I'll tell you why we came to Minnesota. It was when we found out you only had 15,000 blacks here," Griffith was quoted as saying. "Black people don't go to ballgames, but they'll fill up a rassling ring and put up such a chant it'll scare you to death. . . . We came here because you've got good, hardworking white people here."

Griffith's comments came months after two of the Twins top black stars, Hisle and Lyman Bostock, had bolted for Milwaukee and Anaheim, respectively, as free agents in baseball's new era of player emancipation. His comments came months before Carew haggled over money with Griffith and then signed with the Angels as a free agent. He left saying of Griffith, "I'm not going to be another nigger on his plantation."[19] To this day, Minnesota's black baseball fans refer to that period as the breaking point in relations between the community and the team.

Money, race, deep resentment—they shrouded the Twins and Griffith's ownership. Amid the aftershocks of the loss of a tremendous talent pool, the Twins were rebuilding. Enter Puckett, who was the anti-Carew. If Carew, the great Twins hitter, was seemingly aloof, sometimes surly, and surely introspective, Puckett was effusive, friendly, and blessed with a melodic name. It was not that Minnesotans were "colorblind" or had collectively raised their racial consciousness because of the arrival of Puckett. At the same time many African Americans from the Chicago area were migrating to Minnesota to take advantage of the state's welfare system and strong economy. It was causing concern in a state comfortable with its long-standing monochromatic character. But Puckettt, as star and celebrity, was stunningly non-threatening. He was virtually apolitical, never causing a fuss. He was easy to like because it was evident he liked us, the fans, too. This was a gift he had. Unlike many modern athletes, he did not pop off, even when the opportunity lay there like a big, fat, hanging curveball.

That chance to express his views came less than two years after he arrived in the big leagues. He was developing as a star. In April 1986—thirty-nine years after Jackie Robinson broke the color barrier—Puckett was the lone African American player on the Twins twenty-five-man roster. It was left for Angels' superstar and slugger Reggie Jackson to point it out and make a case of it. On Sunday, April 27, 1986, during batting practice, on the day after the Metrodome's roof happened to be torn by a violent storm, Jackson caused a verbal tornado of his own.[20]

"The real story isn't the roof," Jackson told reporters lingering around the batting cage. "The real story is why aren't there colored boys on this team [the Twins]. . . . It's a shame, an absolute shame. . . . You got players [on the Twins] who can't even play and there are colored boys who need work. . . . You have Kirby Puckett and that's it," Jackson said. "There's [Alex] Sanchez, but he doesn't count. He's a foreigner. . . . No colored boys on a team playing on a concrete field," he said, referring to the hard and artificially turfed Dome diamond. Jackson went on, "Minnesota is a great place and this is an embarrassment for this great place. There aren't prejudiced people here. It's a wonderful place to play. It's a beautiful place. There are more interracial marriages here than anyplace in the country. . . . I always liked coming here. I like the people. These people are probably too nice to notice [the absence of blacks on the Twins roster]."

Puckett's response? Silence.

Sixteen years later, sitting in his Dome office, a team vice president after his forced retirement as a player, Puckett said, "Reggie stirred up all that mess about race, and then he left town. Like I told Reggie, 'I'm the only black man on this team but my teammates never treated me any differently.' I was just here to play baseball."[21]

Still, to watch him play was to understand that he did play with a certain ethnicity. Black scholars and sports observers in the Twin Cities, who spoke to me on the condition of anonymity because they did not want to criticize Puckett publicly, acknowledged that the way he could elevate his roly-poly body to prevent home runs from clearing a fence and the passion of his game were clearly identified as being part of the African American culture.

And yet, given the historical context—Griffith's words, the Hisle and Bostock trades, Carew's seething—Puckett almost inadvertently fell into a slot that needed to be filled: the role of the engaging, going-along-to-get-along black employee. It is not as if he consciously decided to play that role. He was simply a perfect fit for a state that has always had difficulty facing its racism.

Puckett, with his winning smile, his integration into a predominantly white, suburban team, and his ability to love and be loved, was the antithesis of the emerging black athlete of the '80s and '90s. Other great outfielders, such as Curt Flood, who stood tall for economic freedom, and Henry Aaron, who fought hate mail as he broke Babe Ruth's career home-run record, were symbols of black athletes' deep anger and pain. But Puckett came across as a teddy-bear figure. He stood for nothing but athleticism and entertainment. He made black players palatable for a lot of Minnesotans, these scholars told me.

He also represented the best of the sport and the spirit of the game. For Kirby Puckett always kept his eyes on the baseball prize. There was no need to trash the owner or offend the customers. He was just happy to be here. And, frankly, he had arrived at a very good time. Between his 1984 arrival and Jackson's pointed comments, Griffith sold the Twins to billionaire banker Carl Pohlad. Change was nigh and so was Puckett's ability to make the kind of money that Griffith never would have granted him. It was riches that he never could have dreamed of as a boy. It was a situation that called for playing the game, not rocking the boat. And Puckett never saw any reason to shake things up. Only in 1993, when it looked as if he might jump ship and join the Boston Red Sox as a free agent, was there ever any evidence of an independent streak. Kirby Puckett was, more or less, a company man.

Kirby Puckett, born on March 14, 1960, learned to play baseball where there was no grass, no real baseballs, and brick strike zones. "Where I grew up you had to take your beatings," Puckett once told an interviewer. "I always considered myself a survivor."[22]

The best description of his childhood comes in his surprisingly frank and well-written autobiography, *I Love This Game!* published in 1993 and ghost-written by Mike Bryan.[23] In it, Puckett calls the Robert Taylor Homes in Chicago "the place where hope dies. . . . The standard line they give is that you may very well come out of the Robert Taylor Homes wearing a uniform with a number, but it's more likely to be issued by the state prison, not by a baseball or basketball or football team. That reads great, but I resent it."[24]

His childhood was no field of dreams. It was a concrete jungle. In apartment No. 1410 at the corner of Forty-third and State, fantasy and creativity flourished. This little boy became fascinated with baseball. He made aluminum foil balls. He rolled up socks and wrapped them with tape to create baseballs. He painted squares on the brick wall of his apartment building, and that was his strike zone. Home runs were achieved by hitting the other apartment building across the way. He broke windows and got spanked. This was Kirby Puckett's Little League because there was no organized baseball in the projects.

On the other hand, it was not the drug-infested, gang-dominated landscape of the inner cities of the 1980s either. According to Puckett's sister, Fran Hunter, "Even though we were reared in the Robert Taylor development, we were not there because we couldn't afford anything else." She added, "We were there because we needed a home with many [three] bedrooms. Actually, when we moved in, we didn't know what it was like. And at the time we moved in, it wasn't like it is now. At that time there were mothers and fathers, there were role models. It wasn't to be a place to stay forever; you were there to move on and better yourself."[25]

Puckett's father, William, was hard at work at two jobs to feed his nine children. His day job was at a department store and his night one was with the U.S. Post Office. His mother, Catherine, was fully employed at home with enough kids to field a baseball team. And that started early for her; Puckett's oldest brother, Charles, was born twenty-two years before Kirby, when Catherine Puckett was only fifteen years old. William was thirty at the time.

Although Kirby Puckett writes in his autobiography that his father was once a left-handed pitcher in the Negro Leagues, research by a newspaper reporter in 1996 questioned that; there is no record at the Negro League Hall of Fame of a William Puckett ever pitching in the pre–Jackie Robinson black leagues.[26] And there is no mention in Puckett's book or other tales of father and son playing catch together. The family lore alone may hold the truth that he pitched for a black team at some point in time.

When Puckett turned twelve and after his father apparently received a promotion, the family moved from public housing to a house at Seventy-ninth and Walcott, still on Chicago's South Side but, as Puckett told me in an interview, "in a nice mixed neighborhood." He waited three more years to play organized baseball, in high school and with semipro teams in the area, starting as young as fifteen to play against men twice his age. "I was holding my own with these guys," he said of the independent brand of baseball he played.

Baseball did not seem to be in his future when high school ended in 1979. He went to work in a Ford plant, installing carpets in Thunderbirds, and also took a job with the U.S. Census Bureau. Before long, he was attending a tryout camp for the Kansas City Royals. He was noticed by the coach at Bradley University, where he was offered a sports scholarship, but his experience at Bradley was soured by a lack of playing time. He was promised he would play third base, his best position, but instead he did not play at all. Ultimately, he was placed in the outfield, his first outfield experience, but his Bradley tenure was cut short when his father died.

Soon after, Puckett enrolled at Triton Community College, known for its baseball program. There, Twins scout Jim Rantz spotted him. Puckett was drafted in 1982, signed to a minor league contract, and given a twenty-thousand-dollar bonus. The Twins and this kid from Chicago had a thing going.

In his first minor-league season, he hit an impressive .382, followed by a strong .314 his second year. He was stealing bases with abandon and driving in runs. Meanwhile, the Twins were indescribably putrid. The club was 130–194 in the two years before his arrival. He walked into a situation where a bunch of young players—first baseman Hrbek, twenty-three, right fielder Tom Brunansky, also twenty-three, third baseman Gaetti, twenty-five, pitcher Viola, twenty-four—were poised to mature. They needed a leader, a glue for their developing unit. That was Puckett.

At first, he hit singles. In 1984 he hit no home runs. In 1985, a grand total of four. But during spring training in 1986, he came under the tutelage of Twins' hitting great Tony Oliva. Things changed. As Puckett's compact frame began to carry more pounds and power—he jumped from 185 to 210 in a few years—so did his batting stance and style. In an interview after his career, Puckett said his transformation from a no-homer guy to a slugger "happened overnight."[27] Indeed, he is the only player in baseball history to, in one season, get more than 500 at-bats and not hit one homer and then in a later season to hit more than thirty homers. But overnight? Not exactly.

During the winter of 1985–86, Puckett explained in his book, he began lifting weights. Then, in spring training in 1986, he and Oliva developed a new high leg kick of Puckett's left, front leg before he swung. It was reminiscent of the New York Giants' home-run-hitting great Mel Ott. It cranked up Puckett's power significantly, although his thirty-one dingers in 1986 were to be the most he ever hit in a season.

Puckett's offensive statistics speak for themselves. He registered more than 2,000 hits in his first ten major-league seasons, the only major leaguer to do so in the twentieth century and only the second in history behind Wee Willie Keeler, who played at the turn of the twentieth century. In 1987, in the greatest display of hitting in any one 48-hour period, he lashed out ten hits in eleven at-bats against the Milwaukee Brewers.

"I was unconscious," Puckett told a reporter years later. "Before the game, me and Tony [Oliva] came out and sat on the tarp, and I said, 'You know, Tony, I feel great. I feel like something's going to happen.'

"I went 6-for-6 [in the second game]. I was 5-for-5 and on deck with one out left in the game and Gags [shortstop Greg Gagne] struck out, but the ball got past the catcher and he's so fast, he made it to first. So I come up and there's a shadow and I'm facing [Dan] Plesac—geez, he could bring it then—and he threw me a fastball away and I hit it and it was a line drive six rows up in the stands."[28]

Defensively, he was also a game saver and a game winner. Statistician Bill James analyzed Puckett's value to the Twins in 1992, when he recorded 394 putouts in one season in center field. That same year Oakland's Dennis Eckersley won the Cy Young Award for saving 51 games. But James points out that Eckersley pitched only 80 innings, getting 240 hitters out. By comparison, Puckett could be credited with retiring 394 hitters, which amounts to more than 131 innings of outs."[29]

Through it all, Puckett won a special place in the hearts and minds of his teammates, who were impressed by his work ethic—he took extra batting practice almost every day—and were enamored of his good spirit. As the team matured from a bunch of inexperienced big leaguers to a two-time World Series champion juggernaut, one symbol of the Twins' brotherly love was Puckett's oft-times shaved head. Whenever Puckett felt he was not hitting well, he would shave the hair from his round head. He would be as bald as a cue ball at one of his annual billiards benefits.

For good luck, his teammates would rub his head. It became a team tradition, but it raised the eyebrows of older black men in the Twin Cities who viewed rubbing an African American's head as a racist act. In an earlier time, it was considered an act of good luck on the part of a white person to "rub a darkie's head." This procedure, often in public, by white Twins players with Puckett was common. But Puckett said it was never tinged with racial motivations. In an interview, he told me, "I didn't think it was racism. If I would have thought it was racist, I wouldn't have let them do it. I didn't walk on the streets and allow that to happen. You'd be amazed how many people would walk up to me on the street and ask me if they can rub my head. And I said, 'Of course not.' This was just in-house. It was something that was personal with my teammates."[30]

There was nothing more personal with his teammates than Puckett's ability to put them on his back and carry them to victory. While his red-hot hitting streak in Milwaukee in 1987 might have been his most awesome offensive display, his performance in game six of the 1991 World Series was likely the one shining moment that embedded him in the memory of America's fans and probably won him his place in Cooperstown.

What Puckett refers to as The Catch in his autobiography is still the stuff of highlight films, his five-foot-eight body reaching as high as possible, his leaping and timing perfect as he robbed Gant of at least a triple. That was immediately followed by his tremendous throw that almost doubled-off Terry Pendleton at first base. It was a classic play that saved runs early in a game the Twins had to win. At that point, they were trailing in the World Series three games to two.

After producing the defensive gem of the series, Puckett delivered the game-winning home run in the bottom of the eleventh inning to push the series into a seventh game. The story about that dramatic homer to left center field is certainly entertaining, but is also astonishing. With the score tied, and Puckett leading off the inning and ready to face lefty Charlie Liebrandt, No. 34 chatted with teammate Chili Davis, who was in the on-deck circle. "I said to him, 'I can just bunt. [Third baseman Terry] Pendleton is playing deep. If I get this down where I want it, I can get on base and you can drive me in," Puckett told me in an interview.

Davis, a veteran, was incredulous. "Puck, you see 60-some thousand people in here?" Davis asked Puckett. "You think they came to see Chili Davis hit the game-winning hit. They came to see Kirby Puckett do that."

Puckett added, "He said to me, 'Bunt, my ass. Get one of those change-ups, hit a damn home run and let's go home.'"[31]

And so it was. Puckett hit the homer. The Metrodome went bonkers. The Twins took game seven the next day. Kirby Puckett was never more popular.

By 1993, Kirby Puckett was the most respected player in all of major-league baseball, the pure, hard-working champion of two World Series. Anchored in one of the smallest markets in the big leagues, Puckett's skills were known far and wide, and he was already being paid handsomely. He was long represented by one of the top agents in the game, Ron Shapiro of Baltimore. During the winter of 1993, Puckett was a free agent, able to shop his talents to the highest bidder.

The memory is that, in the end, he stayed. At a time when so many players were leaving small towns for the bright lights of New York or Los Angeles or the boom-and-bust markets of Dallas or Atlanta, Puckett's decision to remain in Minnesota was hailed as a symbol of his deep integration into this community. But the real story is that he was "this close" to leaving, Puckett said, holding his left thumb and index finger a centimeter apart during a 2002 interview. Puckett was deeply serious about taking his skills elsewhere, most likely to Boston. The Red Sox offered between six and eight million dollars more to him than did the Twins. While Twins fans assumed it was a fait accompli that he would remain in Minnesota, Puckett said, "Oh, no, oh, no," in retrospect.

Kirby makes The Catch as Dan Gladden backs him up.

In those negotiations for what would become Puckett's final contract, Twins fans, as well as Puckett, saw the negotiating style of team owner Carl Pohlad. His three techniques of business negotiations were as follows: wait, wait, and wait. During the 1992 season, Pohlad could have signed Puckett for $27.5 million for five years. But Pohlad believed he could get Puckett for less money.[32] Such was the mentality and approach of Pohlad. As Pohlad waited, Kirby began to prepare to move. He visited Philadelphia and Boston. Ideally, he did not want to switch to the National League Phillies because he would have to learn a whole new set of pitchers and umpires. Puckett worried about Boston, interestingly enough, because of the Red Sox poor record on race relations through the franchise's history; the Red Sox were the last team in the major leagues to integrate, finally doing so in 1959, twelve years after Jackie Robinson joined the Brooklyn Dodgers.[33]

Ultimately, it was Tonya Puckett, Kirby's Minnesota-born wife, who confronted Pohlad at a last-gasp dinner as a decision on his contract was nigh. There, at Pohlad's Edina home, Tonya Puckett told the team owner that she was open to change, implying that Kirby was poised to move. The next morning, Kirby Puckett was offered a five-year, $30 million contract, which he accepted. He would remain a Twin forever, which was, unfortunately, for just three more seasons.

He never blamed it on Martinez. To the contrary, Puckett thought he was in the best shape of his career during spring training of 1996, just months after getting beaned. And all was well until the morning of March 28, 1996. He looked at his wife, and he could not see her face, just her hair and her shoulders. "I thought maybe I slept on my eye wrong," he said.[34] No, it was more than that. He was, essentially, blind in his right eye.

Suddenly, instantly, inexplicably, his career was over. Surgeries and hope attempted to bring back the sight of man who knew no strike zone, only that if the ball was in reach he would hack at it. By July 1996, he announced his retirement in a conference room at the Metrodome, his teammates and former teammates in tears. Martinez was in attendance, his team coincidentally visiting Minnesota on the day Puckett said he was through.

Puckett's demise came at a particularly inopportune time for the Twins' franchise. Not only was its greatest player never to swing a bat again, but Pohlad was about to embark on an expensive and prolonged political campaign to seek public funding for a new stadium. The absence of Puckett on the field hurt the product, although team public relations and lobbying consultants managed to toss Puckett into the fray as he was used in television commercials and even at the Minnesota state legislature to gather support.

Kirby was named MVP of the All-Star game in Baltimore, July 13, 1993. Interviewing him is sportscaster and former Twins' pitcher Jim Kaat.

On this front, he was not able to hit a political home run. Puckett's ability or willingness to master the ins and outs of stadium economics and politics was lacking.

For all of his simplicity, the sudden end to Puckett's career was remarkably complex. It was as if the Twins had lost all of their energy on-field and off-field and their rock of corporate constancy when Puckett could no longer play. The drive for a stadium was undercut. The hopes of a franchise were removed. The end was legitimately tragic. The state seemed to weep in unison.

The *Star Tribune*, the state's largest newspaper, editorialized:

Can there be a Minnesotan, or a baseball fan anywhere, who is not affected by the shattering news that Kirby Puckett will play no more? . . . In an era when sports stars too often behave like overpaid spoiled brats, Puckett has been that rare commodity: a player awestruck by his own success, ebullient, open, friendly and—yes—well-paid and well-worth every penny of it. With major league baseball seemingly intent on doing everything possible to antagonize its fans, Puckett has been a happy reminder of the joy and satisfaction that the game can provide.

Thanks in large part to Puckett, the storied era that Twins fans now look back on is not that of the 1960s and early '70s but of the late-'80s and early '90s—the era of Hrbek, Gaetti, Brunansky, Viola, [Jack] Morris, Gagne and [Dan] Gladden. What thrills and inspirations that gang provided Twins fans, especially the young ones. Puckett was the last of those '87 champs to wear a Twins uniform. And now he too is gone from the team—well before what should have been his time. . . . Thanks, Kirby, . . . you will always occupy a place in the hearts of Minnesotans.[35]

Still, for those in the African American community who look back at Puckett's contributions, they mention his on-field charisma, not his off-field social service. History records that he never fully reached out to do hands-on community work; not until 1993 did he associate his name with a youth baseball program in the Twin Cities. But, from a distance, when his playing days were over, Puckett seemed to have the state in the palm of his pudgy hands. Athletically, he had earned it. He never cheated the game the way he was cheated out of at least three more good seasons.

When his career ended, without a college degree, his sight hampered, with no other marketable skills than merely being Kirby Puckett, all he could do was work for the team. He was handsomely compensated for some public relations tasks and for spending time with younger players in the minor leagues. He was steadfastly portrayed as a loving husband and father. He slowly gained weight. Six years after his forced retirement, he became involved in an ugly and highly publicized divorce case wrapped in allegations that he physically assaulted his wife, which he denied. Soon after, other women came forward, alleging sexual harassment and, ultimately, fifth-degree sexual assault, or groping in the men's bathroom of a suburban nightclub.

While not directly addressing his personal problems, Puckett told me in an interview weeks after revelations of his marital separation that one of the messages he likes to tell schoolchildren is that major-league baseball stars are plain old human beings. "When I speak to kids at schools I tell them I put one [pants'] leg on at a time," he said. "I put soap on when I take a shower, too. I go to the bathroom like you do, if you're a boy. People think I'm super-natural, that normal things don't exist for you."[36]

Alas, "normal things" did exist for him after the cheering faded. His trial in March and April 2003 was a pathetic story of a "hero" fallen. It was not the Kirby we knew. It was not the Kirby we wanted to know about. For a while, he went into a self-imposed shell, dropping out of public events and discontinuing his trademark pool tournament.[37]

Perhaps, some local pundits whispered, the alleged physical threats to his wife revealed an anger within him that he had long restrained, an anger from a tough childhood, or the manifestation of a certain delayed-stress syndrome, an understandable pent-up explosion from his career-ending disability, an injury that imposed a tragic darkness where once this special hitter saw the tiniest seams on a horsehide ball traveling at ninety-five miles per hour. Perhaps.

In the end, what did he stand for? He stood for baseball, nothing more, nothing less. And when challenged about any civil role he might have played more noticeably, Puckett said,

All I ever wanted to do when I was a kid was grow up to be a baseball player. How do I deal with all the responsibility and everything that goes with it? You don't know. It's just thrust upon you. Once you're here, you can't separate the two.

It's part of the job, but I wish it wasn't that way. I wish kids didn't idolize me. I wish they idolized their teachers and professors and parents, and these people that go out to war and fight. To me, those are the heroes.[38]

In a touching, down-to-earth speech that was Puckett through and through, his Hall of Fame induction remarks on August 5, 2001, were remarkably sociological and political for a fellow who denies such tendencies.

There may be a few people out there who remember a time when the word on Kirby Puckett was that he was too short or didn't have enough power to make it to the big leagues. . . . Well, despite the fact that I didn't get to play all the years I wanted to, I did it. And to any young person out there, if anyone tells you that you can't do what you want to do and be what you want to be. I wanted to play baseball ever since I was five years old. And I want you to remember the guiding principles of my life: You can be what you want to be. If you believe in yourself, and you work hard because anything, and I'm telling you anything is possible. . . . And don't feel sorry for yourself if obstacles get in your way. Our great Twins World Series teams faced odds and we beat 'em. Jackie Robinson faced odds and made this game truly the national game. We call it the national game because of its great and unique history. And it doesn't matter where you came from. From the projects like me, in Chicago, or the gated communities of Beverly Hills. And because it doesn't matter what race, creed or national origin you are: black, white, Hispanic, Japanese, or whatever. It just matters how you play the game. And I played it with all my heart, with all my soul, and with all my might.[39]

Other modern black athletes, such as basketball's Michael Jordan and golf's Tiger Woods, have been criticized for not taking stands on social issues. Puckett defends himself for being a baseball player and not a spokesman for off-the-field political causes.

If there is something that concerns him about the future of baseball among African Americans it is that there are few young people playing and few black fans. "Even in the white neighborhood, the kids are playing everything else but baseball," he said. "I'm afraid to say, it's [baseball] going away."

But beyond his fears for what's next for his game, Puckett was never a philosopher, never a politician. "In order for me to take a stand on something, it has to be something significant," he said. "On politics, the guys making the laws don't give a damn how I feel personally. . . . I'm proud to be a black man. I've never run away from that. I know that I'm black. I've been black since the day I was born and I'll be black when I leave this world."[40]

It is a comment, simple, obvious, yet poignant. It could very well apply to all of the great black baseball players who have blessed Minnesota, then, now, and into the future. We may have wanted them to be outspoken advocates for justice. We may have wanted them to transform this game into some sort of social theater or this state into a bastion of racial harmony. But the culture these men were a part of was simply about bats and balls. All they longed for was acceptance and justice.

On May 31, 2003, two months after his acquittal in Hennepin County District Court, Puckett made his first post-trial public appearance at the Metrodome. He showed up to pay tribute to the Twins longtime public address announcer Bob Casey, who was being inducted into the Twins Hall of Fame. Puckett honored Casey because the announcer was among the first people to welcome Puckett warmly to Minnesota in 1984, helping him find a hotel and local restaurants.

"He brought me into his family and treated me like I was family," Puckett said. "It didn't matter that I was a black man or not."[41]

Highlights of Kirby Puckett's Career

1984 *May 8* Singled off California's Jim Slaton in major-league debut and went on to become ninth player in history to get four hits in first big-league nine-inning game / Finished third in AL Rookie of the Year voting

1985 *April 22* Hit first major-league home run, off Seattle's Matt Young at the Metrodome *July 31* Suffered only career ejection when thrown out of game by umpire Drew Coble at Seattle

1986 *July 15* Voted starting center fielder for AL All-Star team and played entire game at Houston *August 1* Hit for cycle against Oakland / Became only player with no home runs in 500 at-bat-season ever to come back with 30 or more homers in a subsequent season / Won first Gold Glove for top defense

1987 *August 29–30* Set AL record and tied modern major-league record for hits (10) in two consecutive games, at Milwaukee *August 30* Tied AL record for hits (six) in a nine-inning game, set team record of 14 total bases, and tied team mark of four extra-base hits, at Milwaukee *October 24* Tied World Series record for most times reaching base in one game (five) and most runs scored (four) in game six against St. Louis / Tied for league lead in hits (207), third in total bases (333), and fourth in batting and led majors with 65 multi-hit games / Third in AL MVP balloting

1988 *September 15* Became only the fourth player ever to get 1,000 hits in his first five seasons when he doubled off Chicago's Shawn Hillegas / Tied Rod Carew's Twins' record of eight four-hit games / Led majors in at-bats, hits, singles (163), total bases (358), multi-hit games (73), runs produced (206), outfield putouts (450), and total chances (465) / His .356 average was the highest by a Twin since Rod Carew hit .388 in 1977 / Second in majors in batting with league's highest average for a right-handed batter since Joe DiMaggio (.357) in 1941

1989 *May 13* Tied major-league record of four doubles and tied team mark of four extra-base hits, against Toronto / Became first right-handed hitter to win full-season AL batting title since California's Alex Johnson (1970) / Also was first right-handed batter to lead the majors in hits in two consecutive seasons / Posted baseball's third-highest batting average of 1980s, .3233 (Wade Boggs .352, Tony Gwynn .332, Don Mattingly .3232) / Became fourth player in century to have four straight 200-hit seasons / Joined Ty Cobb and Tony Oliva as only American Leaguers to lead league in hits three straight years / Had 1,064 hits in first five seasons, two shy of Joe Medwick's major league record / Named baseball's best player by *USA Today*

1990 *May 12* Hit 100th career home run, off Milwaukee's Mark Knudson *August 16* Started in right field and also played shortstop, third base, and second base in eighth inning at Cleveland *July 10* Singled as pinch hitter in All-Star Game at Chicago's Wrigley Field

1991 *May 23* Had second career six-hit game (6-for-7 in 12-inning game), against Texas *June 29* Doubles off Chicago's Greg Hibbard for 1,500th career hit *September 24* Steals 100th career base, against Chicago / Started out 1-for-8 in AL Championship Series, then went 8-for-13 with two homers and five RBIS to earn ALCS MVP honors *October 26* Became ninth player to end a World Series game with a homer on final pitch, off Atlanta's Charlie Leibrandt in the eleventh inning of game six

1992 *May 29* Hit first career grand slam, off Detroit's Les Lancaster, in 5,219th career at-bat (after 131 homers) *June 3* Hit second career grand slam (five days and 29 at-bats after first), off Toronto's Juan Guzman *August 14* Hit third grand slam of season, tying club record, and eighth career two-homer game, connecting off Seattle's Brian Fisher in first two at-bats *September 26* Became first Twin and 18th player in major-league history to collect 200 hits five times in career *September 28* Became first Twin to score 100 runs three times in career and gather 300 total bases four times, first Twin to hit .300, get 200 hits, score 100 runs, and drive in 100 runs twice in career (1988) / Led majors in hits (210) and grand slams (3) / Did not go more than two consecutive games without a hit *December 4* Signed five-year, $30 million contract

1993 *June 6* Hit 150th career homer, off Cleveland's Dennis Cook *June 12* Hit fourth career grand slam, off Oakland's Bobby Witt *July 13* Made eighth straight All-Star game appearance and fourth start and became first Twin to earn MVP honors with a homer and RBI double at Baltimore *July 28* Became Twins' all-time doubles leader

1994 *April 8* Reached 2,000-hit mark and went 5-for-6 with four RBIs in a 10–9 loss to Oakland and got sixth five-hit game of career

1995 *May 17* Scored 1,000th run of career *May 26* Drove in 1,000th career run against Texas *August 20* Hit 200th career home run against Detroit *September 28* In what was to become the final game of his career, Puckett is hit on the left side of the face by a pitch from Cleveland's Dennis Martinez, suffering a fractured upper maxillary sinus, lacerations on inside of mouth, and two loosened teeth.[42]

Appendix: Rosters of All-Black Teams, 1920s and 1930s

1922

Mill City Buffaloes, Minneapolis, played Little Falls, Minn.

Joe Davis, p

Source: *Minneapolis Messenger*, July 8, 1922, p. 1.

Askin and Marine Colored Red Sox Ball Club, won 14 out of 21 games

Harry Lewis, lf.
Ike Bradley, 1b
Harrold Lewis, ss
Joe Davis, p
Bob Ramsey, cf
Speed Coleman, 2b
Lee Davis, c
E. Jackson, rf
Harry Davis, 2b
Will Brooks, utility, captain, manager

Source: *Minnesota Messenger* [Minneapolis], September 23, 1922, p. 1.

St. Paul Uptown Sanitary [Uptowns]

Coleman
Dennis Ware
Frank Ware
West
Mosely, 1b
Du Love, cf
Rudolph
Roach, p
Harry Davis

Sources: *Northwestern Bulletin* [St. Paul], April 19, 1922, p. 4, July 29, 1922, p. 4.

1923

Minneapolis Askin & Marine Colored Red Sox

Lineup in team photo, June 1923	Game vs. Moorhead, June 1923
Bert Jones	Jones, 1b
Bert Tucker	
Geo. Howard	Howard, 3b
Coop Longly	Longly, p, cf
Joe Davis	J. Davis, cf, p
Bill Brooks	
Roy Jackson	Jackson, lf
Geo. Coleman	Coleman, 2b
Lefty Wilson	Wilson, rf
Lee Davis	L. Davis, c
Harold Lewis	Lewis, ss
Eddie Blackman	Blackburn, rf*
W. R. McKinnon, promoter and financial backer of the team (a white man)	

Source: *Fargo Forum*, June 5, 1923, p. 10.
          **Fargo Forum*, June 4, 1923, p. 10.

[Note: This Lefty Wilson was not also known as Dave Brown.]

Actual lineup	Pre-season lineup
W. A. Smith, manager	Will Brooks, Manager, rf
Charles L. Gooch, president	
Isaac Bradley	
Eddie Blackman	
Lefty Williams (south paw)	
Joe Davis	Joe Davis, p
Bob Ramsey	
Lee Davis	Lee Davis, c
Harold Lewis	Harold Lewis, ss
Joe Williams (All formerly of the Askin Marine Red Sox)	
Gilbert Rice	
John Craig	
Otto Mitchell of Indiana, formerly of the Southern League	
M. Richards	
Art Jones	
Jesse Reed	

Lefty Wilson, p
Coot Longley, p, x
Bobby Marshall, 1b
Coleman, 2b
George C. Howard, 3b, x
Roy Jackson, lf, x
Harry Lewis, cf
Edgar Jackson, rf, x
Will Brooks, rf
Sonny Lucas, utility, x
Tommy Young, utility, x

x= Coming from
Southern League

Identified as Askin & Marine Red Sox of Minneapolis in
Northwestern Bulletin [St. Paul], May 12, 1923, p. 4. Pre-season
lineup in *Minnesota Messenger*, March 10, 1923, p. 1.

Uptown Sanitary Baseball Team, St. Paul

Johnny Davis, former International Harvesters twirler, p, 2b, business manager
Joe Davis, p
H. Davis, p [perhaps this was Johnny Davis]
E. Roach, p
Williams, p
Bobby Marshall, 3b [and c]
White
Dennis Ware, ss
Howard, c
Moseley, 1b
Coleman, 2b
Dolove, manager and cf
James West, rf
George White, lf
Hogan
Tucker
Maybe Stephens, p, later
Owen Howell, president
Luck, c (in a late September game)
Lee Davis, c (in a late September game)

Sources: *Northwestern Bulletin* [St. Paul], May 26, 1923, p. 4, May 12, 1923, p. 4.

There may have been another Minneapolis team, called the Minneapolis Browns. Source: *Northwestern Bulletin*, January 27, 1923, p. 4.

1925

Uptown Sanitary Baseball Team, St. Paul ("The club is five years old.")

League: Golden Valley League, the only colored team in the league

Johnny Davis, manager (formerly with Daddy Reid's Old St. Paul Gophers)

Dennis Ware, assistant coach

Johnie Doris, coach

Lionel West, 1b

Harold Roach, p

Eugene Jackson, lf

James West, rf

Timothy Howard, c

Ottis Woodard, cf

George White, lf

Savannah Fields, ss

Johnnie Williams, utility

Lawrence Tucker, 3b

L. Loyd Hoggatt, 2b

O. Howell, president, sponsor

Lucille Howell, mascot

Sources: *Northwestern-Bulletin-Appeal* [St. Paul–Minneapolis], July 4, 1925, p. 3 (photo and caption), June 6, 1925, p. 1 (Davis).

Potts Motor Company baseball team

Bill Brooks, manager

Eddie Boyd, ss and relief pitcher

B. Suggs, 3b, from Ft. Wayne, Ind.

H. Rice, 2b, from Des Moines, Ia.

Bobby Marshall, 1b

Luck, c

Cooper, c

E. Ja[c]kson, of

D. Blackman, of

A. Freeman, of

Bill Freeman, p

Roberts, p

Source: *Northwestern Bulletin*, May 30, 1925, p. 4, May 23, 1925, p. 3 (lineup).

1927

St. Paul Colored Gophers

Singleton, ss

P. Jones, lf

A. Jones, 2b

Scottie, 1b

West, rf

Bowen, cf

Saleman, 3b

Wingfield, p

Davis, c

Source: *Tracy Herald*, June 10, 1927, p. 10 (box score).

Colored All Stars (formerly the Uptown Sanitary team of St. Paul)

John Davis, manager

Source: *St. Paul Echo*, May 28, 1927, p. 1, June 4, 1927, p. 1.

1930–1932

St. Paul Monarchs ("organized two years ago")

Gerhart Dunlap, c

Earl Thompson, p

George Earl Roach

Bobby Marshall, 1b

"Bill" Coleman, 3b ("another veteran")

"Bill" Johnson, ss

Jimmy Lee, 2b

Thomas English, of

Victor McLowan, of

"Rubber-Arm" Johnson, of, c

Frank Boyce, organizer

Source: *Twin City Herald* [Minneapolis], July 23, 1932, p. 4.

1934

Minneapolis Colored Giants

Vick

Coleman

Ollie

English

Big Bill Freeman, p

Source: *Twin City Herald*, May 19, 1934, p. 1.

1935

St. Paul Gophers

Jake Footes, 1b, manager

Tom English, ss

Charles Hilton, 2b

Wellington Coleman, 3b

[Maceo] Breedlove, rf

Hopwood, cf

John Van, c

Chinx Worley, lf

Ollie Pettiford, 1b

Jean Thomas

"Lefty" Porter

Bill Freeman, 1b

Dennis Ware, c

New Faces Who will be seen:

Gean Tucker

E. N. Smith

Robert Wethers

Victor McGowan, umpire

Source: *Minneapolis Spokesman*, May 10, 1935, p. 1, March 29, 1935, p. 1 (lineup).

1936

St. Paul [Colored] Gopher Baseball Team

White, cf

Worley, 2b

Oler, 1b

Foots, c

Flash, ss

Roach, lf

Taylor, 3b

Johnson, rf

Thompson, p

Wakeoff, p

Source: *Twin City Herald* [Minneapolis–St. Paul], August 15, 1936, p. 1.

1937

St. Paul Colored Giants

Worley, 3b

Lefty Oller, lf, p

T. Porter, 1b, p

J. Feets, c

J. Johnson, rf

Jimmy Lee, 2b

G. White, cf

F. Johnson, ss

G. Roach, p

Wakoff, p

Guyden, utility

Martin, utility

George White, manager

Tom English, captain

Marcenia "Toni" Stone, p

Source: *Minneapolis Spokesman*, April 16, 1937, p. 1, July 30, 1937, p. 6 (English and Stone).

Notes

They Didn't Want to Play with Fisher

1. *Winona Weekly Republican*, Oct. 27, 1875, p. 3.

2. Minnesota, *Census, 1875*, Winona.

3. *Winona Weekly Republican*, Oct. 6, p. 3, June 25, p. 3, July 14, p. 4, July 28, p. 2, Aug. 18, p. 3—all 1875; *Winona Weekly Herald*, Aug. 20, 1875, p. 3.

4. *Winona Daily Republican*, Aug. 14, 1875, p. 3; *Winona Weekly Republican*, Oct. 6, 1875, p. 3.

5. *Winona Daily Republican*, Sept. 13, 1875, p. 3.

6. *Winona Daily Republican*, Sept. 13, 1875, p. 3.

7. *Winona Daily Republican*, Sept. 13, 1875, p. 3; *Chatfield Democrat*, Sept. 18, 1875, p. 3.

8. *Winona Daily Republican*, Sept. 13, 1875, p. 3.

9. *Winona Weekly Herald*, Sept. 24, 1875, p. 3; *Winona Weekly Republican*, Sept. 29, 1875, p. 3.

10. *Winona Daily Republican*, Sept. 15, 1875, p. 3; *Winona Weekly Herald*, Sept. 19, 1875, p. 3.

11. *Winona Daily Republican*, Sept. 15, 1875, p. 3.

12. *Winona Daily Republican*, Sept. 16, 1875, p. 3.

13. *Winona Daily Republican*, Sept. 20, 1875, p. 3.

14. *Winona Weekly Republican*, June 25, 1875, p. 3, Sept. 15, 1875, p. 4.

15. *Winona Daily Republican*, Sept. 20, 1875, p. 3; *Winona Weekly Republican*, Sept. 15, 1875, p. 4.

16. *Northfield Standard*, Sept. 23, 1875, p. 2 (Note: the bannerhead of the newspaper erroneously listed the date as Sept. 24, 1875, but all subsequent pages use the Sept. 23, 1875, date.)

17. *Winona Daily Republican*, Sept. 16, 1875, p. 3; *Winona Weekly Republican*, Sept. 29, 1875, p. 3, Oct. 6, 1875, p. 3; *Winona Weekly Herald*, Sept. 24, 1875, p. 3.

18. *Winona Weekly Republican*, Oct. 6, 1875, p. 3; *Winona Weekly Herald*, Oct. 15, 1875, p. 3.

19. *Winona Weekly Herald*, Oct. 15, 1875, p. 3.

20. *Winona Weekly Republican*, Oct. 20, 1875, p. 3.

21. *Winona Weekly Republican*, Oct. 20, 1875, p. 3; *St. Paul Pioneer Press*, June 1, 1896, p. 5.

22. *St. Paul Pioneer Press*, June 1, 1896, p. 5.

23. *Winona Weekly Republican*, Oct. 20, 1875, p. 3, Oct. 27, 1875, p. 3.

24. *Winona Weekly Republican*, Oct. 27, 1875, p. 3.

25. *Winona Weekly Herald*, Oct. 22, 1875, p. 3; *Winona Weekly Republican*, Oct. 27, 1875, p. 3.

Prince Honeycutt and the Fergus Falls Musculars

1. *Fergus Falls Daily Journal*, January 1924; *Fergus Falls Tribune*, Jan. 31, 1924, *Fergus Falls Advocate*, May 28, 1873—all in Honeycutt file, Otter Tail County Historical Society, Fergus Falls.

2. *Fergus Falls Daily Journal*, Feb. 19, 1996, p. 1, 3, Honeycutt file.

3. *Fergus Falls Advocate*, June 18, 1873, p. 1.

4. *Fergus Falls Weekly Journal*, June 24, 1875, p. 4, June 10, 1875, p. 4, Honeycutt file.

5. *Fergus Falls Journal*, July 8, 1875, Honeycutt file.

6. *Fergus Falls Advocate*, July 26, 1878; *Fergus Falls Weekly Journal*, July 19, 1878; Village of Fergus Falls, *1880 Federal Census*, Otter Tail County, and Fergus Falls City, *1900 Federal Census*, Otter Tail County—all Honeycutt file.

7. *Fergus Falls Daily Journal*, Feb.12, 2000, p. 6 B, Apr. 8, 1896, Apr. 7, 1896, January 1924; *Fergus Falls Tribune*, Jan. 31, 1924—all Honeycutt file.

8. *Fergus Falls Daily Journal*, January 1924, and *Fergus Falls Tribune*, Jan. 31, 1924, Honeycutt file.

9. *Minneapolis Tribune*, Aug. 31, 1876.

10. *Minneapolis Tribune*, Sept. 21, 1876.

Bud Fowler and the Stillwater Nine, 1884

1. *Stillwater Daily Sun*, Mar. 27, 1884.

2. L. Robert Davids, "Bud Fowler," in *Nineteenth Century Stars*, ed. Robert L. Tiemann and Mark Rucker (Cleveland: Society for American Baseball Research, 1989), 48; *Cincinnati Enquirer*, Apr. 12, 1895.

3. Davids, "Bud Fowler," 48; *Boston Globe*, May 18, 1878.

4. Robert Peterson, *Only the Ball Was White: A History of Legendary Black Players and All-Black Professional Teams* (New York: Oxford University Press, 1970), 18–19.

5. *Stillwater Gazette*, Jan. 2, 1884.

6. *Stillwater Daily Sun*, Apr. 10, 1884.

7. *Stillwater Daily Sun*, Mar. 27, 1884.

8. *St. Paul Daily Globe*, June 2, 3, 1884.

9. Box score, *Sporting Life*, May 6, 1884; Box score, *Peoria Daily Telegraph*, May 4, 1884; Box score, *Stillwater Daily Sun*, May 6, 1884; *Peoria Transcript*, May 6, 1884.

The Northwestern League did not publish official statistics for the 1884 season because their documents were burned in a fire at the league headquarters at Chicago in November of that year. The author is indebted to the efforts of Brent Peterson of the Washington County Historical Society for the season and game statistics compiled from several newspapers. Unfortunately there are differences in game statistics in many cases among newspapers as each one often had its own reporter score the game the way he himself saw it.

10. *Stillwater Daily Sun*, May 8, 1884; *St. Paul Daily Globe*, May 8, 1884.

11. Box score, *Sporting Life*, May 10, 1884.

12. *Stillwater Gazette*, May 14, 1884.

13. *Fort Wayne Daily Journal*, May 27, 1884.

14. Box score, *Sporting Life*, May 28, 1884; *Terre Haute Evening Gazette*, May 30, 1884; *Stillwater Daily Sun*, June 3, 1884.

15. Lloyd Johnson and Miles Wolff, eds., *The Encyclopedia of Minor League Baseball*, 2nd ed. (Durham: Baseball America, Inc., 1997), 109.

16. *Muskegon Daily Chronicle*, June 3, 1884.

17. *Reach's Official American Association Base Ball Guide, 1884* (Philadelphia: A. J. Reach and Co., 1884), 160.

18. *Spalding's Official Base Ball Guide, 1885* (Chicago: A. G. Spalding and Brothers, 1885), 88.

19. *Muskegon Daily Chronicle*, June 4, 1884; *Stillwater Gazette*, June 11, 1884.

20. *St. Paul Daily Globe*, June 14, 1884.

21. *Stillwater Messenger*, June 14, 1884.

22. *Fort Wayne Daily Journal*, May 24, 1884.

23. Box score, *St. Paul Pioneer Press*, July 3, 1884; Box score, *St. Paul Daily Globe*, July 4, 1884.

24. *Sporting Life*, July 9, 1884; *Stillwater Gazette*, July 16, 1884.

25. *St. Paul Daily Globe*, July 18, 1884.

26. *St. Paul Pioneer Press*, July 27, 1884.

27. *Sporting Life*, Aug. 6, 1884.

28. *Stillwater Messenger*, June 28, July 12, July 26, Aug. 9—all 1884.

29. *Stillwater Daily Sun*, Apr. 9, 1884.

30. Here and below, Johnson and Wolff, eds., *Encyclopedia of Minor League Baseball*, 108–9.

31. *Stillwater Daily Gazette*, Dec. 29, 1884.

32. *Sporting Life*, July 15, 1885, Aug. 26, 1885.

33. *Reach's Official American Association Base Ball Guide, 1887* (Philadelphia: A. J. Reach and Co., 1887), 61.

34. *Rochester Chronicle*, July 5, 1877.

35. *Newark Daily Journal*, Aug. 8, 1887; *Reach's Official American Association Base Ball Guide, 1888* (Philadelphia: A. J. Reach and Co., 1888), 75.

36. *Rutland Herald*, Aug. 24, 1887.

37. John Holway, *The Complete Book of Baseball's Negro Leagues: The Other Half of Baseball History*, ed. Lloyd Johnson and Rachel Borst (Fern Park Fla.: Hastings House Publishers, 2001), 25.

38. *Grand Rapids Democrat*, June 9, 1889; Holway, *Complete Book of Baseball's Negro Leagues*, 26.

39. L. Robert Davids, "Memorial Observance for John (Bud) Fowler: Black Baseball Pioneer," published by the Society for American Baseball Research (SABR) for the ceremony at Oak View Cemetery, Frankfort, N.Y., July 25, 1987; *Dubuque Daily Times*, July 28, 1890.

40. *New York Age*, Nov. 19, 1904.

41. Sol White, *Sol White's History of Colored Base Ball: With Other Documents on the Early Black Game, 1886–1936*, ed. Jerry Malloy (Lincoln: University of Nebraska Press, 1995), 24.

42. *St. Paul Pioneer Press*, Apr. 23, 1895.

43. *St. Paul Pioneer Press*, Apr. 25, 26, 1895.

44. White, *History of Colored Base Ball*, 24.

45. Davids, "Bud Fowler," 48.

46. *New York Age*, Nov. 19, 1904.

The Quicksteps Duel the Brown Stockings, 1887

1. Stew Thornley, "Minneapolis Millers" and "Minnesota Baseball History," http://www.stewthornley.net/minnesotabaseball.html (accessed Aug. 23, 2004). Thornley is author of *On to Nicollet: The Glory and Fame of the Minneapolis Millers*. David Anderson, ed., *Before the Dome: Baseball In Minnesota When the Grass Was Real* (Minneapolis: Nodin Press, 1993), 22, 28–31.

2. *Western Appeal* [St. Paul], July 30, 1887, p. 1, July 23, 1887, p. 4.

3. *Western Appeal*, Aug. 13, 1887, p. 4.

4. *Western Appeal*, Aug. 20, 1887, p. 4.

Drawing the Color Line on Walter Ball, 1890–1908

1. *St. Paul Pioneer Press*, June 5, 1898, p. 20; Frank Leland, *Frank Leland's Chicago Giants Baseball Club* (Chicago: Fraternal Printing Co., 1910), 7.

2. James A. Riley, *The Biographical Encyclopedia of the Negro Baseball Leagues* (New York: Carroll and Graf Publishers, 1994), 47.

3. Minnesota, *Census, 1895*, Ramsey County, St. Paul, Ward 8, Precinct 8, roll 89, p. 10–12, Minnesota Historical Society (hereafter MHS); *St. Paul City Directory 1890* (St. Paul: R. L. Polk Co., 1890), 242; *St. Paul City Directory 1894* (St. Paul: R. L. Polk Co., 1894), 275; *St. Paul City Directory 1898* (St. Paul: R. L. Polk Co., 1898), 252.

4. *St. Paul Pioneer Press*, Aug. 4, 1896, p. 6, June 5, 1898, p. 20.

5. *St. Paul Pioneer Press*, May 15, 1897, p. 6.

6. *St. Paul Pioneer Press*, May 30, 1897, June 6, 1897.

7. *St. Paul Pioneer Press*, Aug. 12, 1897, p. 6.

8. *St. Paul Pioneer Press*, Oct. 3, 1897, p. 7.

9. *St. Paul Pioneer Press*, Apr. 21, 1898, p. 6, July 25, 1898, p. 6, Aug. 5, 1898, p. 6, June 5, 1898, p. 20.

10. *St. Paul Pioneer Press*, June 27, 1899, p. 6, Aug. 7, 1899, p. 2.

11. *St. Paul Pioneer Press*, Aug. 12, 1899, p. 3.

12. *St. Paul Pioneer Press*, Aug. 19, 1899, p. 6.

13. *Devils Lake Inter-Ocean,* June 22, 1900.

14. *Polk County Journal* [Crookston], Nov. 30, 1899, p. 7; *Grand Forks Daily Herald*, Nov. 28, 1899, p. 1.

15. *Crookston Daily Times*, Nov. 29, 1899, p. 4; *Grand Forks Daily Herald*, Oct. 25, 1882, p. 1.

16. *Grand Forks Daily Herald*, Jan. 17, 1900, p. 1. Dorsey served time in Stillwater until 1912 when his sentence was commuted due to poor health; "Bish Dorsey," *Polk County Criminal Cases*, Book C, file 977, Minnesota State Archives, MHS.

17. *Grand Forks Daily Herald*, July 28, 1900, p. 5, Aug. 3, 1900, p. 6.

18. *Grand Forks Daily Herald*, Aug. 30, 1900, p. 4; *Grand Forks–East Grand Forks City Directory, 1900–1901* (St. Paul: R. L. Polk Co.,1901), 24.

19. *Grand Forks Daily Herald*, Apr. 9, 1901, p. 5; *St. Cloud Daily Times,* Dec. 19, 1902, p. 7. Ball was listed as a porter in the 1900 census; see Thomas P. Newgard, William C. Sherman, and John Guerrero, *African-Americans in North Dakota: Sources and Assessments* (Bismarck: University of Mary Press, 1994), 195, appendixes.

20. *Daily Plaindealer* [Grand Forks], Apr. 14, 1901, p. 1.

21. *Daily Plaindealer,* May 24, 1901, p.1.

22. *Daily Plaindealer,* June 1, 1901, p. 1; *Grand Forks Daily Herald*, July 16, 1901, p. 3.

23. Leland, *Frank Leland's Chicago Giants Baseball Club*, 7.

24. *Grand Forks Daily Herald*, May 3, 1902, p. 6.

25. *Grand Forks Daily Herald*, May 3, 1902, p. 6.

26. *St. Cloud Daily Times*, May 10, 1902, p. 3, Feb. 6, 1902, p. 3, June 24, 1901, p. 3.

27. *St. Cloud Daily Times*, May 6, 1902, p. 3; *St. Paul Pioneer Press*, Aug. 12, 1898, p. 6; *Minnesota Messenger* [Minneapolis], June 16, 1923, p. 1; *Northwestern Bulletin* [St. Paul], Apr. 28, 1923, p. 1; *Appeal* [St. Paul], Aug. 3, 1907, p. 3.

28. *Daily Journal Press* [St. Cloud], July 2, 1902, p. 3; *St. Cloud Daily Times*, July 3, 1902, p. 3.

29. *St. Cloud Daily Times*, May 8, 1902, p. 3.

30. *Daily Journal Press,* May 12, 1902, p. 3, May 31, 1902, p. 5; *St. Cloud Daily Times*, May 19, 1902, p. 3.

31. *St. Cloud Daily Times*, June 2, 1902, p. 3.

32. *Daily Journal Press,* June 4, 1902, p. 3, June 5, 1902, p. 2; *St. Cloud Daily Times*, June 4, 1902, p. 3.

33. *Daily Journal Press,* June 11, 1902, p. 2, June 16, 1902, p. 3; *St. Cloud Daily Times*, June 11, 1902, p. 2.

34. *St. Cloud Daily Times*, June 10, 1902, p. 3.

35. *St. Cloud Daily Times*, June 17, 1902, p. 3, June 18, 1902, p. 2; *Little Falls Daily Transcript,* June 19, 1902, p. 3.

36. *Daily Journal Press,* June 27, 1902, p. 1, June 30, 1902, p. 3; *St. Cloud Daily Times*, June 30, 1902, p. 3; *Daily Plaindealer,* June 30, 1902, p. 8.

37. *Daily Journal Press,* July 3, 1902, p. 1, July 5, 1902, p. 1.

38. *St. Cloud Daily Times*, July 7, 1902, p. 3, July 8, 1902, p. 3; *Daily Journal Press,* July 7, 1902, p. 1, July 8, 1902, p. 2.

39. Henry Metcalfe, *A Game for All Races* (New York: Metro Books, 2000), 23–24.

40. Riley, *Biographical Encyclopedia of the Negro Baseball Leagues*, 387–88, 286.

41. *St. Cloud Daily Times*, July 10, 1902, p. 2, July 14, 1902, p. 5; *Daily Journal Press,* July 14, 1902, p. 2, July 16, 1902, p. 2.

42. *Daily Journal Press,* July 19, 1902, p. 2.

43. Metcalfe, *Game for All Races,* 31.

44. *Daily Journal Press,* July 11, 1902, p. 3, June 14, 1902, p. 3; *St. Cloud Daily Times,* Aug. 15, 1902, p. 3.

45. *St. Cloud Daily Times,* July 28, 1902, p. 3.

46. *Daily Journal Press,* July 29, 1902, p. 3; *St. Cloud Daily Times,* July 31, 1902, p. 3.

47. *St. Cloud Daily Times,* Sept. 6, 1902, p. 3, Oct. 28, 1902, p. 3.

48. *St. Cloud Daily Times,* Sept. 8, 1902, p. 3, Nov. 25, 1902, p. 2.

49. *St. Cloud Daily Times,* Nov. 20, 1902, p. 3; *Daily Journal Press,* Nov. 20, 1902, p. 3.

50. *Daily Journal Press,* Nov. 1, 1902, p. 3, Dec. 19, 1902, p. 6, Dec. 3, 1902, p. 5.

51. *St. Cloud Daily Times,* Mar. 2, 1903, p. 3.

52. *Crookston Daily Times,* Mar. 18, 1903, p. 7; *Grand Forks Daily Herald,* Apr. 30, 1903, p. 6.

53. *Grand Forks Daily Herald,* Apr. 14, 1903, p. 6.

54. *St. Cloud Daily Times,* Apr. 16, 1903, p. 3.

55. *Grand Forks Daily Herald,* Apr. 18, 1903, p. 6.

56. Leland, *Frank Leland's Chicago Giants Baseball Club,* 7; *Daily Plaindealer,* Apr. 29, 1903, p. 5; *Grand Forks Daily Herald,* Apr. 30, 1903, p. 6.

57. *Daily Plaindealer,* May 15, 1903, p. 4; *Grand Forks Daily Herald,* May 19, 1903, p. 8; *St. Cloud Daily Times,* May 20, 1903, p. 3.

58. *St. Cloud Daily Times,* May 6, 1903, p. 3. ERA (Earned Run Average) is computed for pitchers on total runs allowed that they are responsible for. Since St. Cloud did not keep this statistic and the newspaper also did not record it, Ball's ERA for 1902 is based on the total runs that scored when he pitched. This caused his ERA to be higher than it would be with proper statistics.

59. Riley, *Biographical Encyclopedia of the Negro Baseball Leagues,* 889; *St. Cloud Daily Times,* Sept. 21, 1903, p. 3.

60. Metcalfe, *Game for All Races,* 31; Dick Clark and Larry Lester, eds., *The Negro Leagues Book* (Cleveland: Society for American Baseball Research, 1994), 57.

61. Metcalfe, *Game for All Races,* 32; Holway, *Complete Book of Baseball's Negro Leagues,* 48, 50; Clark and Lester, eds., *Negro Leagues Book,* 57–58; Leland, *Frank Leland's Chicago Giants Baseball Club,* 7.

62. *St. Paul Pioneer Press,* May 6, 1907, p. 3; *St. Paul Dispatch,* May 18, 1907, Sports sec., p. 4; *Grand Forks Herald,* June 21, 1907, p. 2.

63. *St. Paul Pioneer Press,* May 7, 1907, p. 4; Leland, *Frank Leland's Chicago Giants Baseball Club,* 7; Albert Spalding, *Spalding Official Baseball Guide for 1908, Chicago Supplement, Leland Giants–All Star Series* (New York: American Sports Pub. Co., 1908), 5.

64. *Minneapolis Tribune,* May 3, 1908, Sports sec., p. 4, Apr. 19, 1908, Sports sec., p. 1, June 14, 1908, Sports sec., p. 4, July 19, 1908, Sports sec., p. 4; Leland, *Frank Leland's Chicago Giants Baseball Club,* 7; Holway, *Complete Book of Baseball's Negro Leagues,* 57, 58; Clark and Lester, eds., *Negro Leagues Book,* 59.

65. Larry Lester, Sammy J. Miller, and Dick Clark, *Black Baseball in Chicago* (Chicago: Arcadia Publishing, 2000), 24; Clark and Lester, eds., *Negro Leagues Book,* 60.

66. Bill James, *The New Bill James Historical Abstract of Baseball* (New York: Free Press, 2001), 176; Holway, *Complete Book of Baseball's Negro Leagues,* 62, 64; *Twin City Star,* July 21, 1910, p. 1.

67. Holway, *Complete Book of Baseball's Negro Leagues,* 74, 82, 88 (Holway lists Ball with the Giants in 1910 and the Leland Giants in 1911); Roberto Gonzalez Echevarria, *The Pride of Havana: A History of Cuban Baseball* (New York: Oxford University Press, 1999), 128, 137; Riley, *Biographical Encyclopedia of the Negro Baseball Leagues,* 48; Clark and Lester, eds., *Negro Leagues Book,* 63; Philip Dixon, *The Negro Baseball Leagues: A Photo History* (New York: Amereon Ltd., 1992), 171.

68. *Chicago Defender,* Dec. 21, 1946, p. 10; Holway, *Complete Book of Baseball's Negro Leagues,* 94; Clark and Lester, eds., *Negro Leagues Book,* 64–65.

69. Clark and Lester, eds., *Negro Leagues Book,* 67–79; 1923 date in Peterson, *Only the Ball Was White,* 313.

70. *St. Cloud Daily Times,* June 10, 1930, p. 14.

71. Dixon, *Negro Baseball Leagues,* 157.

72. White, *Sol White's History of Colored Baseball,* 118; Riley, *Biographical Encyclopedia of the Negro Baseball Leagues,* 47.

Opposing the Color Line in Minnesota, 1899

1. *Revised Laws of Minnesota, 1905* (St. Paul: West Publishing Co., 1905), 540; *Bemidji Weekly Pioneer,* Feb. 20, 1902, p. 1. The Wisconsin civil rights bill passed in 1899 after a failed attempt in 1891; *The Appeal* [St. Paul and Minneapolis], Feb. 18, 1899, p. 4.

2. *Afro-American Advance* [Minneapolis], June 17, 1899, p. 2; *The Appeal* [St. Paul], Aug. 24, 1901, p. 3.

3. *The Appeal*, Jan. 3, 1891, p. 3, Nov. 21, 1891, p. 1

4. *The Appeal*, Aug. 24, 1901, p. 3.

5. *Bemidji Weekly Pioneer*, Sept. 5, 1907, p. 1, 8; *East Grand Forks Courier*, Sept. 29, 1899, p. 1; "Minnesota vs. James A. Godettes," *Register, Criminal Actions, Polk County, MN*, Vol. C, Dec. 12, 1899, p. 976.

9. *Grand Forks Daily Herald*, Oct. 24, 1882, p. 1 (3 articles), Oct. 25, 1882, p. 1 (3 articles).

Bobby Marshall, the Legendary First Baseman

1. *Long Prairie Leader*, June 29, 1909, p. 1; *Fargo Forum*, July 2, 1910, p. 11.

2. John O. Holzhueter, "Ezekiel Gillespie, Lost and Found," *Wisconsin Magazine of History* 60 (Spring 1977): 179, 180,183; *Minneapolis Journal*, January 1924, Bobby Marshall Scrapbook, in possession of Bette Marshall Session, Bobby Marshall's daughter, Southfield, Mich.; *Minneapolis City Directory for 1890–91* (Minneapolis: Harrison & Smith, 1890), 842; *Davison's Minneapolis City Directory 1900* (Minneapolis: Minneapolis Directory Co., 1900), 926; U.S., *Census, 1900,* Minneapolis, Ward 5, Vol. 20, p. 13B.

3. U.S., *Census, 1900,* Minneapolis, Ward 5, Vol. 20, p. 13B. "Marshall Testimonial Dinner, March 31, 1950," transcript, p. 10; Walter C. Robb to W. K. Jennings, March 1950; J. M. Howe to Bobby Marshall, Mar. 29, 1950, p. 1; *Minneapolis Daily News*, April 1920—all Marshall Scrapbook.

4. *Minneapolis Times*, Nov. 2, 1901, p. 13; *Minneapolis Tribune*, Nov. 2, 1901, p. 3; *Minneapolis Journal*, Oct. 19, 1901, p. 8, Nov. 2, 1901, p. 4; *Minneapolis Daily News*, April 1920, and *Minneapolis Star Journal*, Aug. 21, 1971, Marshall Scrapbook.

5. *The Appeal* [St. Paul], Mar. 3, 1900, p. 3; *Minneapolis City Directory for 1890–91*, 842; *Davison's Minneapolis City Directory 1900*, 926; *Davison's Minneapolis City Directory 1905* (Minneapolis: Minneapolis Directory Co., 1905), 1178, 1179.

6. *Minnesota Daily* [University of Minnesota], Sept. 18, 1906, p. 1, Nov. 27, 1906, p. 1, April 20, 1907, p. 1, Apr. 25, 1906, p. 1, Dec. 20, 1905, p. 9; *Minneapolis Tribune*, Nov. 25, 1906, p. 38, Sports sec., Oct. 23, 1904, p. 33, 36, Nov. 11, 1906, p. 1.; obituary and news clipping from a Minneapolis black newspaper and *Minneapolis Daily News*, April

1920, Marshall Scrapbook; interview with Harry Davis, Minneapolis, Aug. 2, 1999, notes in possession of author; *The History of Minnesota Football* (Minneapolis: General Alumni Association of the University of Minnesota, 1928), 92–98; *Minneapolis Journal*, May 25, 1907, p. 3, May 31, 1907, p. 14, June 1, 1907.

7. Harry Davis interview; *Minneapolis Tribune*, Nov.18, 1906, p. 2, Sports sec.

8. *St. Paul Appeal*, Jan. 19, 1907, p. 3; Steven R. Hoffbeck, "Victories Yet To Win: Charles W. Scrutchin, Bemidji's Black Activist Attorney," *Minnesota History* 55 (Summer 1996): 61; *Davison's Minneapolis Directory, 1908* (Minneapolis: Minneapolis Directory Co., 1908), 573, 1045; *Davison's Minneapolis Directory, 1910* (Minneapolis: Minneapolis Directory Co., 1910), 1158, 1994; *The Appeal* [St. Paul], Oct. 25, 1913; *Twin City Star* [Minneapolis], Sept. 16, 1910, p. 1; interview with Bette Marshall Session, Southfield, Mich., Aug. 10, 1999, notes in possession of author. At some time after 1910, perhaps early in 1911, he did some legal work with the "office of Nash and Armstrong, a firm of well known attorneys."

9. *The Appeal,* Oct. 25, 1913, p. 10; *Minneapolis Journal*, May 25, 1907, p. 3, May 20, 1907, p. 13; *St. Paul Pioneer Press*, May 20, 1907, p. 3.

10. *Twin City Star*, July 21, 1910, p. 1; *Minneapolis Tribune*, July 11, 1911, p. 3, Sports sec.

11. *Minneapolis Daily News*, April 1920, Marshall Scrapbook; *Minneapolis Tribune*, July 19, 1908, p. 4, Sports sec.

12. *Oelwein Register*, July 15, 1908; *Minneapolis Tribune*, July 19, 1908, p. 4, Sports sec; "Joe Hovlick Statistics," BaseballReference.com (accessed Feb. 14, 2003); "Joe Hovlick Statistics," Baseball-Almanac.com (accessed Feb. 14, 2003).

13. *Twin City Star*, July 21, 1910, p. 1, 4; *Minneapolis Tribune*, July 18, 1909, p. 3, Sports sec.

14. *St. Paul Pioneer Press*, July 25, 1909, p. 1, sec. 3; *Minneapolis Tribune*, July 25, 1909, p. 26, July 26, 1909, p. 3.

15. *St. Paul Pioneer Press*, Sept. 21, 1909, p. 8.

16. *Minneapolis Tribune*, July 11, 1909, p. 22.

17. *The Appeal,* June 19, 1909, p. 3; *St. Paul Pioneer Press*, July 27, 1909, p. 7. See Clark and Lester, eds., *Negro Leagues Book,* for George Walter Ball (Georgia Rabbit), career 1902–23, p. 169, Andrew (Rube) Foster, career 1902–26, p. 188,

Bill Gatewood, career 1905–28, p. 189, Charles (Pat) Dougherty, career 1909–15, p. 184.

18. See Clark and Lester, eds., *Negro Leagues Book,* for Johnny Davis, career 1903–10 (actually longer), p. 182, Jonathan Boyce (Steel Arm Johnny) Taylor, career 1903–21, p. 227, Robert "Buster" Garrison, career unknown except for 1909, p. 189, Julius London (listed as "Londo"), career unknown except for 1909, p. 203; *St. Paul Pioneer Press,* July 17, 1909, p. 8; *Minneapolis Tribune,* June 27, 1909, p. 4, Sports sec.

19. *Chicago Tribune,* Oct. 22, 1909, p. 12; *Minneapolis Tribune,* July 27, 1909, p. 8, says the home run was over the center-field fence; a better account is in *St. Paul Pioneer Press,* July 27, 1909, p. 7. For Gophers-Leland Giants, see "Baseball Pioneers," *Twins Magazine,* June/July 1997, MinnesotaTwinsbaseball.com.

20. *St. Paul Pioneer Press,* July 27, 1909, p. 7.

21. *St. Paul Pioneer Press,* July 28, 1909, p. 7.

22. *St. Paul Pioneer Press,* July 29, 1909, p. 9.

23. *Long Prairie Leader,* July 30, 1909, p. 1; *St. Paul Pioneer Press,* July 29, 1909, p. 9.

24. *St. Paul Pioneer Press,* July 30, 1909, p. 7.

25. *St. Paul Pioneer Press,* July 31, 1909, p. 7.

26. *St. Paul Pioneer Press,* July 31, 1909, p. 7.

27. *Minneapolis Tribune,* Aug. 30, 1908, p. 4, Sports sec., Apr. 4, 1909, p. 3, Sports sec., June 27, 1909, p. 4, Sports sec., July 18, 1909, p. 3, Sports sec.; *St. Paul Pioneer Press,* July 17, 1909, p. 8; *The Appeal,* June 19, 1909, p. 3, Sept. 18, 1909, p. 3.

28. *Minneapolis Tribune,* June 27, 1909, p. 4, Sports sec.

29. Dual role explained in Michael E. Lomax, "Black Baseball's First Rivalry: The Cuban Giants Versus the Gorhams of New York and the Birth of the Colored Championship," *Sport History Review* 28 (Nov. 1997): 138. *Bemidji Daily Pioneer,* June 28, 1909, p. 1.

30. *Minneapolis Tribune,* Mar. 31, 1950, Marshall Scrapbook.

31. *Chicago Tribune,* Oct. 18, 1909, p. 11, Oct. 19, 1909, p. 8; *Minneapolis Tribune,* Mar. 31, 1950, Marshall Scrapbook; *Bemidji Daily Pioneer,* Apr. 23, 1909, p. 1. One source noted that the pitcher's throw to Marshall was an error on the pitcher; *Chicago American,* Oct. 18, 1909, p. 1. Joe Tinker played in the series against the Leland Giants, but Johnny Evers and Frank Chance did not.

32. *Chicago Tribune,* Oct. 18, p. 11, Oct. 19, p. 8, Oct. 22, p. 12, Oct. 23, p. 14—all 1909.

33. *St. Paul Pioneer Press,* Apr. 10, 1910, p. 2, sec. 4; *Minneapolis Tribune,* Mar. 31, 1950, Marshall Scrapbook; *Chicago Tribune,* May 13, 1910, p. 8, May 12, 1910, p. 8.

34. "Marshall Testimonial Dinner," transcript, p. 28, *Minneapolis Tribune,* Mar. 31, 1950, *Minneapolis Daily News,* April 1920, Marshall Scrapbook; *St. Paul Dispatch,* Apr. 8, 1910, p. 18; *St. Paul Pioneer Press,* Sept. 4, 1910, p. 2, sec. 4. Rube Foster's Chicago American Giants of 1913–16 made a tour of Washington state and the Northwest; see "The Chicago American Giants in the Northwest: Mr. Foster Comes to Washington," sabr.org.

35. *St. Paul Pioneer Press,* June 4, 1910, p. 8, 9; Jerry Malloy, "Rube Foster and Black Baseball in Chicago," in *Baseball in Chicago* (Cooperstown, N.Y.: Society for American Baseball Research, 1986), 25; *St. Paul Dispatch,* June 2, 1910, p. 11.

36. *St. Paul Pioneer Press,* July 25, p. 6, July 26, p. 7, July 27, p. 7, July 28, p. 7, July 29, p. 8—all 1910.

37. *Hibbing Daily Tribune,* Aug. 26, 1910, p. 3; *Chisholm Tribune Herald,* Aug. 26, 1910, p. 5.

38. *The Appeal,* Oct. 25, 1913, p. 10; *Davison's Minneapolis Directory, 1908,* 573, 1045; *Davison's Minneapolis Directory, 1910,* 1158, 1994; *Twin City Star,* Sept. 16, 1910, p. 1. Franklin may have been a difficult man for Marshall to deal with, for he was reported to be suffering from depression and later blinded himself in an unsuccessful suicide attempt; see *St. Paul Appeal,* Aug. 15, 1917, p. 5.

39. *Davison's Minneapolis City Directory, 1910,* 1574, 1416; *Twin City Star,* May 20, 1911, p. 1, Apr. 29, 1911, p. 1; *Minneapolis Tribune,* Apr. 23, 1911, p. 3, Sports sec., Apr. 16, 1911, p. 3, Sports sec., April 19, 1911, p. 12, July 2, 1911, p. 3.

40. *Alexandria Post-News,* June 29, 1911, p. 1.

41. *The Appeal,* Oct. 25, 1913, p. 10; *Minneapolis Journal,* January 1924, magazine sec., Marshall Scrapbook; *Twin City Star,* Sept. 9, 1911, p. 1, Sept. 16, 1910, p. 1; interview with James Griffin, St. Paul, July 30, 1999, notes in possession of author.

42. *Minneapolis Tribune,* June 2, 1912, p. 2, Sports sec., Apr. 21, 1912, p. 3, Sports sec., Apr. 7, 1912, Sports sec.; *Davison's Minneapolis City Directory, 1910,* 1574, 1416; *Twin City Star,* May 20, 1911, p. 1, Apr. 29, 1911, p. 1; *Minneapolis Tribune,* Apr. 19, 1911, p. 12 (Selden), Apr. 13, 1911, p. 14 (Foster),

Apr. 23, 1911, p. 3, Sports sec. (Marshall as recruiter), Apr. 16, 1911, p. 3, Sports sec.

43. *Northwestern Bulletin*, May 26, 1923, p. 4 (Uptown Sanitary team), May 23, 1925, p. 3 (Potts Motor Co. team); *Twin City Herald*, July 23, 1932, p. 4 (St. Paul Monarchs); *St. Cloud Daily Times*, June 23, 1913, p. 4.

44. *St. Cloud Daily Times and Daily Journal-Press*, Apr. 22, 1937, p. 25; *St. Cloud Daily Times*, Aug. 25, 1913, p. 4, Sept. 15, 1913, p. 4.

45. *St. Cloud Daily Times*, July 27, 1914, p. 8, Aug. 17, 1914, p. 8. The Plutos played two games against Sauk Rapids on July 4 & 5, 1914, winning both; *St. Cloud Daily Times*, July 6, 1914, p. 8.

46. *Cokato Enterprise*, Mar. 16, 1950, Marshall Scrapbook; *Cokato Enterprise*, May 27, 1915, p. 1, Aug. 12, 1915, p. 1; *Minneapolis Tribune*, May 14, 1911, p. 3, Sports sec.

47. Obituary from a Twin Cities newspaper, 1958, Marshall Scrapbook; interview with Donald and Helen Marshall, Guerneville, Calif., Aug. 22, 2000, notes in possession of author; U.S., *Census, 1920*, Hennepin County, Minn., p. 102.

48. David V. Taylor, "Pilgrim's Progress: Black St. Paul and the Making of an Urban Ghetto, 1870–1930" (Ph.D. diss., University of Minnesota, 1977), 258.

49. *Minneapolis Daily News*, April 1920, and *Minneapolis Journal*, January 1924, magazine sec., Marshall Scrapbook; *Minneapolis Messenger*, July 2, 1921, p. 2, July 16, 1921, p. 2; Oct. 1, 1921, p. 2; *Minnesota Messenger* [Minneapolis], Sept. 30, 1922, p. 1, Mar. 10, 1923, p. 1.

50. *Minnesota Messenger*, Mar. 10, 1923, p. 1 (Lee Davis was also on the team; they got around in a Pierce Arrow); *Northwestern Bulletin,* May 26, 1923, p. 4, May 19, 1923, p. 4; Harry Davis interview. Harry Davis was the son of Lee Davis; Harry Davis later served on the Minneapolis school board and was the director of the Golden Gloves boxing program in Minnesota.

51. *Long Prairie Leader*, Apr. 30, 1925, p. 2; Bette Marshall Session interview.

52. Bette Marshall Session interview; Bette Marshall Session to the author, Sept. 3, 1999.

53. *Minnesota Messenger*, Sept. 30, 1922, p. 1, Mar. 10, 1923, p. 1. Little is known about the attempt to bring a Negro League franchise to Minneapolis in 1925; see *Northwestern Bulletin*, Jan. 17, 1925, p. 1.

54. *Northwestern Bulletin*, May 23, 1925, p. 3;

Twin City Herald, July 23, 1932, p. 4; interview with Lee Davis, Minneapolis, Aug. 2, 1999, notes in possession of author.

55. *St. Paul Pioneer Press*, July 27, 1942, p. 12; *Minneapolis Tribune*, Aug. 5, 1942, p. 13.

56. *Minneapolis Spokesman*, Aug. 7, 1942, p. 1, 2. For racism in baseball and Jackie Robinson, see John C. Chalberg, *Rickey & Robinson: The Preacher, the Player, and America's Game* (Wheeling, Ill.: Harlan Davidson, Inc., 2000), 96–97, 122–23.

57. Bette Marshall Session interview.

58. *Minnesota Public Employee*, April 1950, Marshall Scrapbook; "Robert Wells Marshall," *Dictionary of American Negro Biography* (New York: Norton, 1982), 427.

59. Walter C. Robb, Minneapolis, to W. K. Jennings, St. Paul, March 1950 (?), Sig Harris to Marshall, March 1950 (?), Marshall Scrapbook.

60. James Griffin interview; *Minneapolis Star Journal*, Aug. 21, 1971, Marshall Scrapbook; Bette Marshall Session to author, Sept. 3, 1999; *Gopher Goalpost*, Oct. 30, 1971, p. 22; Harry Davis interview; *Minneapolis Spokesman*, Nov. 20, 1936, p. 1, Dec. 6, 1935, p. 1, Dec. 25, 1936, p. 1; *St. Paul Echo*, June 26, 1926, p. 3; *Twin City Herald*, Dec. 30, 1933, p. 1; Donald and Helen Marshall interview.

61. Bette Marshall Session interview; Harry Davis interview; Marshall interview; *Minneapolis Spokesman*, Aug. 29, 1958, p. 1; *Minneapolis Star*, Aug. 28, 1958, p. 1 D, Aug. 29, 1958, p. 11 B.

62. *St. Paul Pioneer Press*, July 24, 1910, p. 5, sec. 4; George A. Barton to W. K. Jennings, Mar. 14, 1950, and unidentified article from a Twin Cities sportswriter, Marshall Scrapbook.

63. *Minneapolis Tribune*, June 14, 1936, Marshall Scrapbook. Leland Giants' record in Jerry Malloy, "Rube Foster and Black Baseball in Chicago," 25.

64. *Minneapolis Star-Tribune*, Dec. 25, 1999, p. S7, S12; *Minnesota Daily*, Nov. 8, 1991.

65. *Hibbing Daily Tribune*, July 16, 1910, p. 3.

66. Bette Marshall Session to author, Sept. 3, 1999.

67. *Minneapolis Tribune*, Mar. 31, 1950, Marshall Scrapbook.

Barnstorming Teams, 1909–1920

1. *St. Paul Pioneer Press*, Apr. 10, 1910, p. 2, sec. 4.

2. *Minneapolis Tribune*, Apr. 18, 1909, p. 4, Apr. 26, 1908, p. 4, Apr. 12, 1908, p. 3, May 3, 1908, p. 4, June 7, 1908, p. 4, July 19, 1908, p. 4, July 12, 1908,

p. 4, July 28, 1908, p. 8, May 2, 1909, p. 3, Oct. 4, 1908, p. 4, (one loss added for the last game of the season), Oct. 5, 1909, p. 3—all Sports sec.; *Davison's Minneapolis City Directory 1908*, 1093; Clark and Lester, eds., *Negro Leagues Book*, 57, 183, 62, 198 (Charles Jessup listed with the Chicago Union Giants as a pitcher in 1911); *Red Wing Daily Republican*, Aug. 24, 1908, p. 8.

3. *Waukon* [Iowa] *Republican*, July 21, 1909, p. 1; *Alexandria Citizen*, Aug. 5, 1909, p. 1; *Duluth News Tribune*, Aug. 14, 1909, p. 7, Aug. 15, 1909, p. 1, Sports sec.; *Minneapolis Tribune*, Apr. 18, 1909, p. 4, Sports sec., May 2, 1909, p. 3, Sports sec.

4. *Twin City Star*, June 2, 1910, p. 4; *Minneapolis Tribune*, Mar. 13, 1910, p. 3, Sports sec., Apr. 16, 1911, p. 3, Sports sec.; *Alexandria Post News*, July 6, 1911, p. 1; Holway, *Complete Book of Baseball's Negro Leagues*, 141, 223.

5. *Granite Falls Tribune*, July 28, 1908, p. 4, Aug. 4, 1908, p. 4; *Arlington Enterprise*, Aug. 27, 1908, p. 1; *Zumbrota News*, Sept. 25, 1908, p. 2.

6. *New Prague Times*, Aug. 13, 1908, p. 1; *Merrill* [Wisc.] *Daily Herald*, Aug. 10, 1908, p. 4; *Osage* [Iowa] *News*, July 9, 1908 (the Osage team won the first game 5–2, but the Gophers took the second game 4–0. See also, *Bismarck Tribune*, July 14, 1911, p. 2, July 15, 1911, p. 5.

7. *Duluth Herald*, July 31, 1909, p. 8, Aug. 2, 1909, p. 9; *Duluth News Tribune*, July 31, 1909, p. 11.

8. *Minneapolis Journal*, June 5, 1910, p. 4, Sports sec.; Janice A. Beran, "Diamonds in Iowa: Blacks, Buxton, and Baseball," *Journal of Negro History* 75 (Summer–Fall 1990): 89–91; *Minneapolis Tribune*, Sept. 6, 1908, p. 2, Sports sec.; *Oskaloosa* [Iowa] *Daily Herald*, Aug. 26, 1909, p. 3; *Monroe County News* [Albia, Iowa], Aug. 26, 1909, p. 10.

9. *Decorah Journal*, Aug. 17, 1909, p. 1; *Calumet* [Iowa] *Courier*, July 15, 1910, p. 1; *Decorah Public Opinion*, Aug. 31, 1910, p. 2.

10. *Twice-A-Week Plain Dealer* [Cresco, Iowa], Aug. 18, 1908, p. 1 (advertisement), Aug. 25, 1908, p. 1; Haskell Institute in http:// history.lawrence.com/project/community/ haskell/haskell.html (accessed July 16, 2002).

John Wesley Donaldson, a Great Mound Artist

1. Warren I. Susman, *Culture as History: The Transformation of American Society in the Twentieth Century* (New York: Pantheon Books, 1984), 138–43.

2. *Little Falls Herald*, Aug. 26, 1927, p. 1.

3. *Minneapolis Tribune*, Sept. 21, 1924, Sports sec., p. 4.

4. *New York Age*, May 2, 1925, p. 1.

5. *Long Prairie Leader*, Sept. 1, 1927, p. 7.

6. Here and below, *Wells Forum Advocate*, Sept. 10, 1914, p. 1.

7. *Wells Forum Advocate*, Sept. 10, 1914, p. 1; Riley, *Biographical Encyclopedia of the Negro Baseball Leagues*, 242, 243.

8. *Wells Forum Advocate*, Oct. 6, 1911, p. 10.

9. *Little Falls Daily Transcript*, Aug. 8, 1912.

10. *Barnesville Record Review*, July 16, 1914, p. 1; *Wells Forum Advocate*, Sept. 10, 1914, p. 1.

11. *Long Prairie Leader*, June 6, 1912, p. 7, June 13, 1912, p. 7; *Marshall News Messenger*, May 31, 1912, p. 7; *Mesaba Ore* [Hibbing], June 8, 1912, p. 1.

12. Janet Bruce, *The Kansas City Monarchs: Champions of Black Baseball* (Lawrence: University Press of Kansas, 1985), 14–17; Riley, *Biographical Encyclopedia of the Negro Baseball Leagues*, 544, 545; *Mesaba Ore*, June 8, 1912, p. 1; *Little Falls Daily Transcript*, July 25, 1914, p. 3. Means pitched for the St. Paul Colored Gophers in 1907, see *Jerauld County Review* [Wessington Springs, S.Dak.], July 18, 1907, p. 1; *Aberdeen* [S.Dak.] *Weekly American*, July 25, 1907, p. 5; *Minneapolis Journal*, Sept. 15, 1907, p. 3, Sports sec.

13. *Marshall News Messenger*, Aug. 29, 1913, p. 1; Riley, *Biographical Encyclopedia of the Negro Baseball Leagues*, 242; *Little Falls Daily Transcript*, Aug. 8, 1912, p. 3.

14. *Marshall News Messenger*, May 31, 1912, p. 7; *Melrose Beacon*, June 7, 1912, p. 4; *Faribault Journal*, Aug. 6, 1913, p. 1.

15. *New Ulm Review*, July 29, 1914, p. 1, Sports sec.

16. *Good Thunder Herald*, Aug. 14, 1913, p. 1; *McIntosh Times Herald*, Aug. 14, 1913, p. 1; *McIntosh Times*, July 16, 1914, p. 6.

17. *Melrose Beacon*, June 14, 1912, p. 1; *Long Prairie Leader*, June 13, 1912, p. 7.

18. Clark and Lester, eds., *Negro Leagues Book*, 68; Holway, *Complete Book of Baseball's Negro Leagues*, 110, 111, 115.

19. Riley, *Biographical Encyclopedia of the Negro Baseball Leagues*, 242; Bruce, *Kansas City Monarchs*, 16–17; Holway, *Complete Book of Baseball's Negro Leagues*, 129.

20. Bruce, *Kansas City Monarchs*, 15, 16, 17, 21; Riley, *Biographical Encyclopedia of the Negro Baseball Leagues*, 242–43.

21. Clark and Lester, *Negro Leagues Book*, 76, 80, 82; Holway, *Complete Book of Baseball's Negro Leagues*, 141, 155, 167, 173.

22. *Long Prairie Leader*, Apr. 13, 1922, p. 2; *Bertha Herald*, Mar. 20, 1924, p. 1; Society for American Baseball Research, *Minor League History Journal* 2 (1993): 22.

23. U.S., *Census, 1920*, Bertha, Todd County, Minn.

24. *Long Prairie Leader*, Mar. 13, 1924, p. 7, June 13, 1912, p. 7, *Little Falls Daily Transcript*, Aug. 8, 9, 1912; *Melrose Beacon*, June 14, 1912, p. 1.

25. *Long Prairie Leader*, May 1, 1924, p. 7, Aug. 6, 1925, p. 7.

26. *Long Prairie Leader*, May 8, 1924, p. 2.

27. *Albany Enterprise*, July 14, 1927, p. 1.

28. *Long Prairie Leader*, May 15, 1924, p. 5.

29. *Long Prairie Leader*, June 5, 1924, p. 8.

30. Michael Fedo, *The Lynchings in Duluth* (1979; St. Paul: Minnesota Historical Society Press, 2000); Hoffbeck, "Charles Scrutchin, Bemidji's Black Activist Attorney," 71–73; *Staples World*, Sept. 4, 1924, p. 1; *Bemidji Pioneer*, Aug. 21, 1924, p. 1; *St. Paul Pioneer Press*, Oct. 29, 2002.

31. *Fairmont Daily Sentinel*, July 15, 1932, p. 6; Riley, *Biographical Encyclopedia of the Negro Baseball Leagues*, 243; *Melrose Beacon*, May 17, 1928, p. 8.

32. *Long Prairie Leader*, June 5, 1924, p. 8; *Northwestern Bulletin* [Minneapolis], June 14, 1924, p. 3.

33. *Long Prairie Leader*, July 17, 1924, p. 2.

34. *Fairmont Daily Sentinel*, May 13, 1932, p. 6; *Long Prairie Leader*, Aug. 24, 1924, p. 2.

35. *Long Prairie Leader*, Sept. 25, 1924, p. 7.

36. Statistics for 1924 season compiled by Peter Gorton; *Minneapolis Tribune*, Sept. 21, 1924, Sports sec., p. 4; *Long Prairie Leader*, Sept. 25, 1924, p. 7.

37. *Long Prairie Leader*, Mar. 26, 1925, p. 7.

38. *Long Prairie Leader*, Apr. 28, 1925, p. 2.

39. *Long Prairie Leader*, May 7, 1925, p. 5.

40. *Long Prairie Leader*, Apr. 30, 1925, p. 2.

41. *Long Prairie Leader*, May 21, 1925, p. 11.

42. *Long Prairie Leader*, July 30, 1925, p. 5.

43. *Long Prairie Leader*, July 14, 1927, p. 7.

44. *Wadena Pioneer Journal*, July 9, 1925, p. 1; *Long Prairie Leader*, July 16, p. 7, July 30, p. 5, 1925; *Park Region Echo*, July 30, 1925, p. 1.

45. *Minneota Mascot*, Aug. 21, 1925 p. 1; *Clarkfield Advocate*, Oct. 15, 1925, p.1; *Murray County Herald* [Slayton], Sept. 17, 1925, p. 2.

46. *Long Prairie Leader*, Sept. 3, 1925, p. 11; *Lismore Free Press*, Sept. 11, 1925, p. 1.

47. *Clarkfield Advocate*, Oct. 15, 1925, p. 1.

48. *Murray County Herald*, Aug. 20, 1925, p. 1, Sept. 17, 1925, p. 2.

49. *Long Prairie Leader*, Apr. 1, 1926, p. 5.

50. *Long Prairie Leader*, Apr. 1, 1926, p. 5.

51. *Bertha Herald*, Mar. 25, 1926, p.1.

52. *Long Prairie Leader*, Apr. 1, 1926, p. 5.

53. *Lismore Free Press*, Oct. 22, p. 1, July 23, p. 1, July 30, p. 1, Aug. 13, p. 1, Aug. 20, p. 1—all 1926.

54. *Staples World*, Apr. 28, 1927, p. 1; Clark and Lester, *Negro Leagues Book,* 188; *Sauk Centre Herald*, Apr. 28, 1927, p. 2.

55. *Sauk Centre Herald*, Apr. 28, 1927, p. 2; *St. Paul Pioneer Press,* Sept. 21, 1926, p. 10; *Long Prairie Leader*, May 5, 1927, p. 4.

56. *Long Prairie Leader*, May 5, 1927, p. 4, July 7, 1927, p. 4.

57. *Long Prairie Leader*, Oct. 20, 1927, p. 2.

58. *Long Prairie Leader*, Aug. 25, 1927, p. 7.

59. *Long Prairie Leader*, Sept. 1, 1927, p. 7, Sept. 8, 1927, p. 1.

60. *Long Prairie Leader*, Sept. 29, 1927, p. 7.

61. *Long Prairie Leader*, Feb. 2, 1928, p. 5.

62. *Melrose Beacon*, May 10, 1928, p. 1.

63. *Melrose Beacon*, May 17, 1928, p. 1.

64. *Arlington Enterprise*, June 18, 1903, e-mail message, Dwight D. Grabitske to Steve Hoffbeck, April 29, 2002.

65. *Little Falls Daily Transcript*, Apr. 18, 1928, p. 5.

66. Bruce Mellor notes, February 1991, Morrison County Historical Society, Little Falls, Minn.

67. *Marshall News Messenger*, May 31, 1929, p. 1; *Granite Falls News*, Sept. 6, 1929, p. 1.

68. *St. Cloud Daily Times*, May 24, 1930, p. 14.

69. *St. Cloud Daily Times*, Sept. 30, 1930, p. 15.

70. *Crookston Daily Times*, July 20, 1931, p. 7.

71. *Fairmont Daily Sentinel,* Apr. 19, 1932, p. 6.

72. *Fairmont Daily Sentinel,* May 18, 1932, p. 6; *Little Falls Daily Transcript,* May 21, 1928.

73. *Fairmont Daily Sentinel,* May 16, 1932, p. 6.

74. *Fairmont Daily Sentinel,* May 16, 1932, p. 6.

75. *Fairmont Daily Sentinel,* May 20, 1932, p. 6.

76. *Fairmont Daily Sentinel,* May 23, 1932, p. 6.

77. *Fairmont Daily Sentinel,* Aug. 31, p. 6, Sept. 17, p. 6, Oct. 10, p. 6—all 1932.

78. *Chicago Daily Defender,* Apr. 18, 1970, p. 33; Jeremy Krock to author, e-mail, May 4, 2004.

The Mystery of Lefty Wilson

1. Riley, *Biographical Encyclopedia of the Negro Baseball Leagues,* 117; Holway, *Complete Book of Baseball's Negro Leagues,* 140–42.

2. Echevarria, *Pride of Havana,* 171, 176. Here and below, Riley, *Biographical Encyclopedia of the Negro Baseball Leagues,* 117.

3. *New York Age,* May 2, 1925, p. 1, 6; Riley, *Biographical Encyclopedia of the Negro Baseball Leagues,* 511, 840.

4. *Lismore Free Press,* July 2, 1926, p. 1, July 9, 1926, p. 1.

5. *Pipestone County Star,* May 7, 1926, p. 1; *Spencer* [Iowa] *Reporter,* Aug. 18, 1926, p. 6; U.S., *Census, 1920,* Minnehaha County, S. Dak., p. 24. For the Pipestone Black Sox, see Alan Muchlinski and David Muchlinski, "Pipestone Black Sox," http://instructional1.calstatela.edu/amuchli/Pipestone.html.

6. *Pipestone Leader,* July 22, 1926, p. 1; *Pipestone County Star,* July 27, 1926, p. 8.

7. *Minneota Mascot,* Aug. 27, 1926, p. 1; *Lismore Free Press,* Aug. 27, 1926, p. 1.

8. *Murray County Herald,* Sept. 2, 1926, p. 1; *Comfrey Times,* Sept. 9, 1926, p. 1.

9. *St. Paul Pioneer Press,* Sept. 21, 1926, p. 10.

10. *The Northern Light–Lamberton,* July 21, 1927, p.1; *Long Prairie Leader,* Sept. 1, 1927, p. 7.

11. *Comfrey Times,* Sept. 15, 1927, p. 4, Sept. 22, 1927, p. 1.

12. *St. Paul Daily News,* Sept. 23, 1927, p. 29.

13. *Wabasso Standard,* Apr. 5, 1928, p. 1; *Bertha Herald,* Feb. 16, 1928, p.1.

14. Bruce Mellor notes, February 1991; *Long Prairie Leader,* Sept. 27, 1928, p. 7.

15. *Long Prairie Leader,* May 2, 1929, p. 1.

16. *Little Falls Herald,* July 19, 1929, p.1; *Marshall News Messenger,* Sept. 20, 1929, p. 9, Sports sec.

Maceo Breedlove: Big Fish in a Small Pond

1. Phone interview with Harry Davis, Minneapolis, April 25, 2002, notes in possession of author.

2. Here and below, phone interview with Larry Brown, St. Paul, April 25, 2002, notes in possession of author.

3. Here and below, Davis interview.

4. *Jamestown Sun,* May 25, 1934, p. 6.

5. *Jamestown Sun,* May 25, 1934, p. 6.

A Negro League Team in Minnesota, 1942

1. *Minneapolis Spokesman,* Apr. 17, 1942, p. 1.

2. *Minneapolis Spokesman,* July 10, 1942, p. 1; Riley, *Biographical Encyclopedia of the Negro Baseball Leagues,* 120–21.

3. *St. Paul Pioneer Press,* June 21, 1942, p. 4, sec. 3; *Minneapolis Tribune,* June 22, 1942, p. 9.

4. *Minneapolis Spokesman,* July 10, 1942, p. 1; *St. Paul Pioneer Press,* June 22, 1942, p. 13.

5. *St. Paul Pioneer Press,* June 24, 1942, p. 11, June 25, 1942, p. 18, June 29, 1942, p. 14, June 28, 1942, p. 2, sec. 3; *Minneapolis Tribune,* June 29, 1942, p. 9.

6. *Minneapolis Tribune,* June 29, 1942, p. 9, July 13, 1942, p. 8; *St. Paul Pioneer Press,* July 12, 1942, p. 2, sec. 3, July 13, 1942, p. 12; *Minneapolis Spokesman,* July 17, 1942, p. 4.

7. *Minneapolis Spokesman,* July 17, 1942, p. 4, July 24, 1942, p. 4.

8. *Minneapolis Tribune,* Aug. 6, 1942, p. 14, Aug. 7, 1942, p. 13–14.

9. Clark and Lester, eds., *Negro Leagues Book,* 133; "Reece 'Goose' Tatum, Harlem Globetrotters Legend," http:// harlemglobetrotters.com/history/leg-tatum.php (accessed July 17, 2002).

Roy Campanella and the Breaking of the Color Barrier

1. Roy Campanella, *It's Good to Be Alive* (Boston: Little, Brown, 1959), 141–42.

2. Campanella, *It's Good to Be Alive,* 141.

3. *St. Paul Pioneer Press,* May 18, 1948, p. 15.

4. *St. Paul Pioneer Press,* May 18, 1948, p. 15.

5. Campanella, *It's Good to Be Alive,* 135–36.

6. Campanella, *It's Good to Be Alive,* 140.

7. Donn Rogosin, *Invisible Men: Life in Baseball's Negro Leagues* (New York: Kodansha International, 1995), 203.

8. *St. Paul Pioneer Press,* May 18, 1948, p. 15.

9. Dan W. Dodson, "The Integration of Negroes in Baseball," *Journal of Educational Sociology* 28 (Oct. 1954): 73–82.

10. William Marshall, *Baseball's Pivotal Era, 1945–1951* (Lexington: University Press of Kentucky, 1999), 126, 128.

11. Murray Polner, *Branch Rickey: A Biography* (New York: New American Library, 1983), 206.

12. Larry Moffi and Jonathan Kronstadt, *Crossing the Line: Black Major Leaguers, 1947–1959* (Jefferson, N.C.: McFarland, 1994), 11–25.

13. *Minneapolis Tribune,* June 3, 1948, p. 19.

14. Campanella, *It's Good to Be Alive,* 142.

15. *St. Paul Pioneer Press,* June 1, 1948, p. 26.

16. *Minneapolis Tribune,* June 3, 1948, p. 19.

17. Campanella, *It's Good to Be Alive,* 142.

18. *St. Paul Pioneer Press,* July 1, 1948, p. 24.

19. *St. Paul Pioneer Press,* July 1, 1948, p. 24.

20. Campanella, *It's Good to Be Alive,* 143.

21. Campanella, *It's Good to Be Alive,* 144.

22. Jules Tygiel, *Baseball's Great Experiment: Jackie Robinson and His Legacy,* expanded ed. (New York: Oxford University Press, 1997), 241.

23. *St. Paul Pioneer Press,* Aug. 26, 1948, p. 18.

24. John LaFarge, S.J., "The Development of Cooperative Acceptance of Racial Integration," *Journal of Negro Education* 21 (Summer 1952): 430–44.

Willie Mays with the Minneapolis Millers, 1951

1. *Minneapolis Tribune,* May 1, 1951, p. 18, May 27, 1951, p. F1; *Minneapolis Star,* May 2, 1951, p. 41, May 8, 1951, p. 29; Willie Mays, *Say Hey: The Autobiography of Willie Mays* (New York: Simon and Schuster, 1988), 49.

2. *Minneapolis Tribune,* May 27, 1951, p. F1, F3; Mays, *Say Hey: The Autobiography of Willie Mays,* 16, 17, 20; *Minneapolis Star,* May 25, 1951, p. 35; Riley, *Biographical Encyclopedia of the Negro Baseball Leagues,* 523–24; Clark and Lester, eds., *Negro Leagues Book,* 144, 146, 148.

3. Mays, *Say Hey: The Autobiography of Willie Mays,* 47, 49; *Minneapolis Tribune,* May 27, 1951, p. F3.

4. Mays, *Say Hey: The Autobiography of Willie Mays,* 54–55.

5. Mays, *Say Hey: The Autobiography of Willie Mays,* 53–54.

6. *Minneapolis Tribune,* Apr. 10, 1951, p. 7.

7. *Minneapolis Tribune,* Apr. 23, 1951, p. 21.

8. *Minneapolis Star,* May 8, 1971, p. 29; Mays, *Say Hey: The Autobiography of Willie Mays,* 58–59.

9. Mays, *Say Hey: The Autobiography of Willie Mays,* 59.

10. *Minneapolis Star,* May 21, 1951, p. 26, May 10, 1951, p. 42, May 8, 1951, p. 29.

11. *Minneapolis Star,* May 22, 1951, p. 36, Apr. 24, 1951, p. 33, Apr. 30, 1951, p. 25, May 10, 1951, p. 42.

12. *Minneapolis Tribune,* May 27, 1951, p. F3.

13. Mays, *Say Hey: The Autobiography of Willie Mays,* 60–61.

14. Nancy Caldwell Sorel, "Willie Mays and Leo Durocher," *The Atlantic,* July 1993, p. 63.

15. "National Baseball Hall of Fame: Willie Mays," www.BaseballHallofFame.org (accessed Jan. 14, 2003).

16. Johnson and Wolff, eds., *Encyclopedia of Minor League Baseball,* 400; *Minneapolis Star,* May 25, 1951, p. 35.

17. "1965 All-Star Game," Baseball-Almanac.com/asgbox/yr1965as.shtml (accessed Jan. 13, 2003).

18. "Baseball's 100 Greatest Players, the Sporting News," Legendary Lists, Baseball-Almanac.com (accessed July 15, 2002); *Minneapolis Star-Tribune,* July 23, 2002, p. C5; "National Baseball Hall of Fame: Willie Mays's Plaque," www.BaseballHallofFame.org (accessed Jan. 14, 2003).

Satchel Paige: Barnstorming in Minnesota

1. Riley, *Biographical Encyclopedia of the Negro Baseball Leagues,* 600.

2. "Satchelfoots," *Time,* June 3, 1940, p. 44; Leroy (Satchel) Paige, *Maybe I'll Pitch Forever* (1962; Lincoln: University of Nebraska Press, 1993), vii, 18–19.

3. Richard Donovan, "The Fabulous Satchel Paige," *Collier's,* May 30, 1953, p. 68; John Holway, *Voices from the Great Black Baseball Leagues* (New York: Da Capo Press, 1992), 97; *New York Times,* July 8, 1948, p. 26; Paige, *Maybe I'll Pitch Forever,* vii.

4. Paige, *Maybe I'll Pitch Forever,* vii, 29; Ted Shane, "Chocolate Rube Waddell," *Saturday Evening Post,* July 27, 1940, p. 20, with a variation of the story, where Taylor asked: "Does you do that constantly?" "No suh," said Satchel, "Ah does it all the time!"

Paige was on the roster of the Birmingham Black Barons in 1928, playing under the direction of manager Bill Gatewood, who was with the St. Paul Colored Gophers in 1908; see Peterson, *Only the Ball Was White,* 133; *Stillwater Daily Journal,* Aug. 24, 1908, p. 2.

5. Riley, *Biographical Encyclopedia of the Negro Baseball Leagues,* 309–10 (Gatewood), 598 (Paige).

6. Donovan, "Fabulous Satchel Paige,"68; Paige, *Maybe I'll Pitch Forever*, 16; "Satchelfoots," 44; "Satch Makes the Majors," *Life*, July 26, 1948, p. 49, 52; Peterson, *Only the Ball Was White*, 132; "Satchel Paige, Negro Ballplayer, Is One of Best Pitchers in Game," *Life*, June 2, 1941, p. 90; Richard Donovan, "Satch Beards the House of David," *Collier's*, June 6, 1953, p. 22; Riley, *Biographical Encyclopedia of the Negro Baseball Leagues*, 598; Michael Bamberger, "Double Duty Radcliffe," *Sports Illustrated*, July 15, 2001, p. 131.

7. *Washington Post*, Feb. 10, 1971, p. D1.

8. Donovan, "Fabulous Satchel Paige,"65. There are a number of variations on legends of how fast Paige could pitch, see Paige, *Maybe I'll Pitch Forever*, 58.

9. Bamberger, "Double Duty Radcliffe," 132; e-mail from Kyle McNary to the author, Sept. 27, 2002; Richard Donovan, "Time Ain't Gonna Mess With Me," *Collier's*, June 13, 1953, p. 54.

10. Donovan, "The Fabulous Satchel Paige," 68, and "Satch Beards the House of David," 22.

11. Marc Conrad, "A Paige in Bismarck's History," in *Bismarck by the River* (Bismarck: Bismarck Tribune, 1997), 91–92.

12. *St. Paul Pioneer Press*, June 28, 1941, p. 9, June 27, 1941, p. 15; *Twin-City Leader* [Minneapolis], June 21, 1941, p. 1; *St. Paul Dispatch*, June 27, 1941, p. 24; *Minneapolis Tribune*, June 27, 1941, p. 21.

13. Donovan, "Time Ain't Gonna Mess With Me," 58; *Moorhead Daily News*, June 2, 1950, p. 5; *Fargo Forum*, June 3, 1950, p. 6; *Minot Daily News*, June 3, 1950, p. 13; interview with Edwin "Sonny" Gulsvig, Moorhead, Sept. 10, 2002, notes in possession of author.

14. *Moorhead Daily News*, June 1, 1950, p. 5, June 5, 1950, p. 8; *Fergus Falls Daily Journal*, June 6, 1950.

15. *Moorhead Daily News*, May 31, 1950, p. 5.

16. Interview with Boyd Christenson, Fargo, Sept. 24, 2002, notes in possession of author; *Minot Daily News*, July 2, 1959, p. 10.

17. *Austin Daily Herald*, June 8, 1950, p. 10, June 6, 1950, p. 8.

18. *Moorhead Daily News*, June 6, 1950, p. 5; *Detroit Lakes Tribune*, June 8, 1950.

19. Christenson interview; "When Batters Wobble," *Newsweek*, July 14, 1958, p. 58.

20. Donovan, "Time Ain't Gonna Mess With Me," 58; *Moorhead Daily News*, May 26, 1950, p. 5; *Minot Daily News*, May 27, 1950, p. 13; Paige, *Maybe I'll Pitch Forever*, xiii. Bankhead in Riley, *Biographical Encyclopedia of the Negro Baseball Leagues*, 51; Arnold Rampersad, *Jackie Robinson: A Biography* (New York: Ballantine Books, 1997), 184; stats in Clark and Lester, eds., *Negro Leagues Book*, 313.

21. *New York Times*, Sept. 1, 1948, p. 28; *Moorhead Daily News*, May 26, 1950, p. 5; *Fargo Forum*, May 27, 1950, p. 7.

22. Donovan, "Time Ain't Gonna Mess With Me," 58; Riley, *Negro Leagues Book*, 600.

23. *Minot Daily News*, July 1, 1959, p. 18; *Ward County* [N.Dak.] *Independent*, June 25, 1959, p. 1; Conrad, "A Paige in Bismarck's History," 92.

24. Interview with Robert Orr Baab, Wooster, Ohio, Sept. 19, 2002, notes in possession of author.

25. Baab interview.

26. "Philosopher's Consolation," *Sports Illustrated*, Jan. 27, 1964, p. 17; Peterson, *Only the Ball Was White*, 139.

27. *New York Times*, Feb. 10, 1971, p. 52; *Washington Post*, Aug.10, 1971, p. 1D, 2D.

28. "Slow," *New Yorker*, Sept. 13, 1952, p. 32; Donovan, "The Fabulous Satchel Paige," 65, 66; *New York Times*, Feb. 10, 1971, p. 52; Donovan, "Time Ain't Gonna Mess With Me," 54, 55.

29. Shane, "Chocolate Rube Waddell," 80; Donovan, "Satch Beards the House of David," 24.

30. P. Mills, "Satchel Paige: The Great Integrator of the Game," NegroLeagueBaseball.com (accessed Oct. 6, 1999), p. 1, 2, 3, 4, reprinted from *Black Ball News;* Peterson, *Only the Ball Was White*, 129.

31. Paige, *Maybe I'll Pitch Forever*, vii, 28, 29, 30, 22–26, 15; Donovan, "Time Ain't Gonna Mess With Me," 56.

32. James, *New Bill James Historical Baseball Abstract*, 359, 360; "Baseball's 100 Greatest Players, *Sporting News*, Baseball-Almanac.com (accessed July 15, 2002), p. 1, 2; "SABR, 100 Greatest Baseball Players," and "SABR, 40 Greatest Negro League Figures," Baseball-Almanac.com (accessed July 15, 2002), p. 1.

33. *Washington Post*, Feb.10, 1971, p. D1; Donovan, "The Fabulous Satchel Paige," 68, 64; *Minot Daily News*, July 2, 1959, p. 10; the story appeared earlier in Donovan, "The Fabulous Satchel Paige," 62.

34. "Anniversary Special-Editions/Heritage Boxes," in Wheaties History, WheatiesPackages.doc, GeneralMills.com (accessed Sept. 9, 2002).

35. Poem listed in www.wvu.edu/~lawfac/jelkins/lp-2001/allen.html (accessed Sept. 25, 2002).

Jackie Robinson Visits Minnesota, 1955

1. *Minneapolis Spokesman,* Jan. 28, 1955, p. 1.

2. *Minneapolis Tribune,* Jan. 26, 1955, p. 17.

3. Here and below, *Minneapolis Spokesman,* Jan. 28, 1955, p. 1.

4. *Minneapolis Tribune,* Jan. 26, 1955, p. 17.

Toni Stone: A Tomboy to Remember

1. "The Girls of Summer," *Exploratorium's Science of Baseball: Toni Stone* (1998), www.exploratorium.org/baseball/stone_2.html.

2. *Pioneer Planet,* Feb. 1, 1997, p. 1A, 10A.

3. *Minneapolis Star Tribune,* Mar. 6, 1990, p. 1A

4. Barbara Gregorich, *Women at Play: The Story of Women in Baseball* (New York: Harcourt, 1993), 169–70; "Stone, Toni," *Women in American History* (Encyclopaedia Britannica, 1999), http://women.eb.com/women/articles/Stone_Toni.html.

5. *St. Paul Pioneer Press,* Feb. 1, 1997, p. 1A, 10A.

6. *Minneapolis Spokesman,* June 5, 1936, p. 1.

7. Phone interview with St. Paul School District, Mar. 11, 2002, notes in possession of author; "Toni Stone," *Biography Resource Center* (Gale Group, Inc., 2001), www.africanpubs.com/Apps/bios/0564StoneToni.asp?pic-none; *Minneapolis Spokesman,* July 30, 1937, p. 6.

8. "Toni Stone," *Biography Resource Center.*

9. *Minneapolis Star Tribune,* Mar. 6, 1990, p. 1A; *Twin City Leader,* July 19, 1941, p. 1; phone interviews with colleges, Mar. 11, 2002, notes in possession of author.

10. Gregorich, *Women at Play,* 170–71.

11. *San Francisco Gate,* Nov. 6, 1996.

12. Gregorich, *Women at Play,* 171.

13. Larry Lester and Sammy Miller, *Black Baseball in Kansas City* (Chicago: Arcadia, 2000), 32.

14. *San Francisco Gate,* Nov. 6, 1996.

15. Alberga, Aurelious P., Golden Gate National Cemetery, www.interment.net/data/us/ca/sanmateo/ggate/a/golden-ao3.htm; "Aurelious Alberga," www.fortdesmoines.org/

graduates_a_g_shtml.

16. Gregorich, *Women at Play,* 175.

17. *New York Times,* Nov. 10, 1996, p. 47.

18. Gregorich, *Women at Play,* 171, 173; Riley, *Biographical Encyclopedia of the Negro Baseball Leagues,* 746.

19. *New York Times,* Nov. 10, 1996, p. 47; Bruce, *Kansas City Monarchs,* 116–19.

20. Bruce Johnson, "The Indianapolis Clowns: Clowns of Baseball," reprinted from *The Clown In Times* Vol. 6, no. 23 (2000), www.charliethejugglingclown.com/baseball.htm (accessed Feb. 8, 2002)

21. *Minneapolis Star Tribune,* Mar. 6, 1990, p. 1A.

22. *St. Paul Pioneer Press,* Feb. 1, 1997, p. 1A, 10A.

23. "The Girls of Summer," *Exploratorium's Science of Baseball: Toni Stone.*

24. *St. Paul Pioneer Press,* Nov. 5, 1996, p.1.

25. Gregorich, *Women at Play,* 173–74.

26. *Minneapolis Star Tribune,* Mar. 6, 1990, p. 1A.

27. Lester and Miller, *Black Baseball in Kansas City,* 78–79; *San Francisco Gate,* Nov. 6, 1996.

28. Lester and Miller, *Black Baseball in Kansas City,* 78–79.

29. *San Francisco Gate,* Nov. 6, 1996.

30. Amy Nutt, "Sport Short Takes," *Sports Illustrated Women* (1997), http://cgi.cnnsi.com/features/1997/womenmag/stleagucofown.html.

31. *Minneapolis Star Tribune,* Mar. 6, 1990, p. 1A.

32. Golden Gate National Cemetery, www.interment.net/data/us/ca/sanmateo/ggate/a/golden-a03.htm (accessed Feb. 10, 2002).

33. *St. Paul Pioneer Press,* Dec. 19, 1996.

Barnstorming Black Teams: The End of an Era

1. *Bagley Farmers Independent,* June 25, 1959, p. 1, July 2, 1959, p. 1.

2. *Bagley Farmers Independent,* June 25, 1959, p. 1.

3. *Bagley Farmers Independent,* July 9, 1959, p. 1.

4. Letter from Jerry Riewer, Staples, to the author, July 16, 2002; letter from Tom Wolhowe, Staples, to the author, July 16, 2002. Riewer and Wolhowe were long-time, championship coaches in Staples, now retired, and on the teaching staff there with the author in the 1980s.

Earl Battey and the Integration of Spring Training

1. *Boston Globe,* Nov. 18, 2003, boston.com (accessed June 9, 2004).

2. *New York Times*, Feb. 19, 1961, p. 181 (ProQuest Historical Newspapers); "End of an Era for Negroes in Baseball," *Ebony*, June 1961, p. 36; interview with Sid Hartman, Minneapolis, June 24, 2004, notes in the possession of Hoffbeck.

3. "End of an Era for Negroes in Baseball," 36; *New York Times*, Feb. 19, 1961, p. 179, Feb. 1, 1961, p. 44 (ProQuest Historical Newspapers).

4. *New York Times*, Feb. 19, 1961, p. 181.

5. The collaborative work of the chapter's authors included a formal interview. Kwame McDonald's participation in these events is recounted in the third person for ease in understanding. Interview with Kwame J. C. McDonald, St. Paul, by Steve Hoffbeck, June 5, 2004, notes in possession of Hoffbeck; *New York Times*, Feb. 19, 1961, p. 181; State of Minnesota, *Legislative Manual, 1963–1964* (St. Paul: State of Minnesota, 1964), 232–33; State of Minnesota, State Commission Against Discrimination, "Memorandum For Commission Members," Feb. 7, 1964, MHS.

6. Interview with Rabbi Max Shapiro, Minnetonka, Minn., by Steve Hoffbeck, June 15, 2004, notes in possession of Hoffbeck; Hartman interview; State of Minnesota, State Commission against Discrimination, Memorandum, Attorney General Walter Mondale to Governor Karl Rolvaag, Feb. 5, 1964, MHS.

7. McDonald interview.

8. McDonald interview; Brad Snyder, *Beyond the Shadow of the Senators* (Chicago: Contemporary Books, 2003), 283–84.

9. "Joe Black" and "Lenny Green," BaseballReference.com (accessed on June 28, 2004); Riley, *Biographical Encyclopedia of the Negro Baseball Leagues*, 86; Snyder, *Beyond the Shadow of the Senators*, 282–87.

10. State of Minnesota, State Commission against Discrimination, Memorandum, Mondale to Rolvaag, Feb. 5, 1964; Jack E. Davis, "Baseball's Reluctant Challenge: Desegregating Major League Spring Training Sites, 1961–1964," *Journal of Sport History* 19 (Summer 1992): 161.

11. *Minneapolis Spokesman*, Feb. 20, 1964, p. 1; Davis, "Baseball's Reluctant Challenge," 161.

12. Here and below, McDonald interview; *Minneapolis Star*, Feb. 24, 1964, p. 6A; *Minneapolis Spokesman*, Mar. 5, 1964, p. 1, Feb. 20, 1964, p. 1; *New York Times*, Feb. 19, 1961, p. 179. The reversal

by Griffith "was quietly made" according to Andersen, *Minneapolis Star-Tribune*, Nov. 21, 2003, p. A20. It should be noted that Andersen was elected in 1960 and served until March 25, 1963, when Karl Rolvaag was sworn in after a close and disputed election in November 1962.

13. State of Minnesota, Commission against Discrimination, Memo from [Kwame] J. C. McDonald for Commission Members, Feb. 7, 1964, MHS.

14. Kwame McDonald interview with Earl Battey, St. Paul, 2002, notes in possession of McDonald.

15. *Washington Post*, Apr. 5, 1960, p. D1 (ProQuest Historical Newspapers).

16. Jim "Mudcat" Grant, comments at Twins Hall of Fame induction for Earl Battey, Minneapolis, June 5, 2004, and Kwame J. C. McDonald interview with Jim "Mudcat" Grant, Minneapolis, June 5, 2004, notes in the possession of McDonald.

17. Here and below, Herb Carneal comments at Twins Hall of Fame induction for Earl Battey, Minneapolis, June 5, 2004, notes in the possession of Hoffbeck.

18. Sonia Battey, comments at Twins Hall of Fame induction for Earl Battey, Minneapolis, June 5, 2004, notes in the possession of Hoffbeck.

Bobby Darwin: Escape from Watts

1. "The 1965 Watts Riots," University of Southern California Library Sources for the Study of the 1965 Watts Riots, www.usc.edu/isd/archives/la/watts.html (accessed June 15, 2004).

2. Here and below, Arthur Bobby Lee Darwin, phone interview with Joel Rippel, April 7, 2004, notes in possession of author.

3. *Minneapolis Star*, Mar. 7, 1972, p. D3.

4. *Minneapolis Star*, Mar. 7, 1972, p. D3.

Dave Winfield: Making a Name for Himself

1. Tim Kurkjian, "Mr. Longevity," *Sports Illustrated*, Sept. 27, 1993, p. 55; Dave Winfield, *Ask Dave: Dave Winfield Answers Kids' Questions about Baseball and Life* (Kansas City: Andrews and McMeel, 1994), 22; "Bobby Thomson," BaseballLibrary.com (accessed Sept. 10, 2002).

2. Dave Winfield with Tom Parker, *Winfield: A Player's Life* (New York: W.W. Norton & Co., 1988), 45.

3. Winfield and Parker, *Winfield*, 39, 40–41; David Shaw, "Dave Winfield: The Prince of the Padres," *Sport*, January 1980, p. 83.

4. *Grand Forks Herald*, Aug. 4, 2002, p. 3D.

5. *Minneapolis Tribune*, Dec. 24, 1980, p. 3C; Winfield, *Ask Dave*, 68 (quote); Phil Berger, "The $20 Million Gamble," *New York Times Magazine*, Mar. 29, 1981, p. 34; Charles Moritz, ed., *Current Biography Yearbook* (New York: H. W. Wilson Co., 1984), 457; Shaw, "Dave Winfield," 83.

6. *Star Tribune*, Aug. 5, 2001, p. S10; "Induction Speech: Dave Winfield," transcript in BaseballHallofFame.org (accessed Sept. 23, 2002); *Minneapolis Tribune*, Dec. 24, 1980, p. 3C.

7. Winfield, *Ask Dave*, 68.

8. *St. Paul Pioneer Press*, Aug. 5, 2001, p. 1A, 8A; *Minneapolis Star and Tribune*, July 16, 1985, p. 2D; Winfield, *Ask Dave*, 68.

9. Winfield, *Ask Dave*, 73, 38; *Minneapolis Star Tribune*, Aug. 5, 2001, p. S10.

10. *Minneapolis Star Tribune*, Jan. 17, 2001, p. S3, S4; Winfield, *Ask Dave*, 63, 71; *Minneapolis Tribune*, Sept. 1, 1981, p. C1.

11. *Minneapolis Star Tribune*, Aug. 5, 2001, p. S10, Jan. 17, 2001, p. S3, S4; Winfield, *Ask Dave*, 63.

12. *Minneapolis Star and Tribune*, July 16, 1985, p. 2D; Berger, "$20 Million Gamble," 34; Winfield, *Ask Dave*, 38, 65; *St. Paul Pioneer Press*, Aug. 5, 2001, p. 8A.

13. Winfield and Parker, *Winfield*, 54; *Minneapolis Star Tribune*, Aug. 5, 2001, p. S10; "Most Outstanding State Tournament Players, Minnesota American Legion Baseball," TricityLegion.org (accessed July 6, 2002).

14. Winfield and Parker, *Winfield*, 54; *Minneapolis Star Tribune*, Aug. 5, 2001, p. S10.

15. *St. Paul Pioneer Press*, Aug. 5, 2001, p. 7N; Winfield and Parker, *Winfield*, 56; *Minneapolis Star and Tribune*, July 16, 1985, p. 2D.

16. Winfield and Parker, *Winfield*, 68, 69; "Connie Mack," BaseballHallofFame.org (accessed Sept. 24, 2002); "Dick Siebert," BaseballReference.com (accessed Sept. 23, 2002).

17. Berger, "$20 Million Gamble," 33; Winfield and Parker, *Winfield*, 62–66.

18. *Minneapolis Tribune*, Jan. 14, 1973, p. 7C; Winfield and Parker, *Winfield*, 62–66; *St. Paul Pioneer Press*, Aug. 5, 2001, p. 8A.

19. Winfield and Parker, *Winfield*, 73.

20. *Minneapolis Tribune*, Jan. 14, 1973, p. 7C; Winfield and Parker, *Winfield*, 74.

21. *Minneapolis Tribune*, Jan.14, 1973, p. 7C; *New York Times*, Feb. 6, 1972, sec. V, p. 6; *Minneapolis Star Tribune*, Sept. 17, 1993, p. 3S; Winfield and Parker, *Winfield*, 79, 80, 81.

22. Winfield and Parker, *Winfield*, 83.

23. Winfield and Parker, *Winfield*, 83–85; Moritz, ed., *Current Biography Yearbook*, 458.

24. *Minneapolis Tribune*, June 8, 1973, p. 1C, June 5, 1973, p. 1C.

25. *Minneapolis Tribune*, June 9, 1973, p. 1B.

26. *Minneapolis Tribune*, June 12, 1973, p. 1C, June 10, 1973, p. 4C.

27. *Minneapolis Tribune*, June 13, 1973, p. 1C; Alan Schwarz, "Greatest College World Series Moments," ESPN.com/Baseball (accessed Sept. 12, 2002).

28. *Minneapolis Tribune*, June 9, 1973, p. 2B, June 13, 1973, p. 1C.

29. *Minneapolis Star Tribune*, Sept. 17, 1993, p. 7C; *Minneapolis Tribune*, June 14, 1973, p. 3C; *St. Paul Pioneer Press*, Aug. 5, 2001, p. 7N.

30. Berger, "$20 Million Gamble," 30.

31. *Minneapolis Tribune*, Apr. 25, 1973, p. 1C, Apr. 26, 1973, p. 1C, June 6, 1973, p. 1C.

32. *Minneapolis Tribune*, June 19, 1973, p. 2C; "Dave Winfield, Inductee Information," BaseballHallofFame.org (accessed July 24, 2001); Winfield and Parker, *Winfield*, 94.

33. "Dave Winfield," BaseballReference.com (accessed Sept. 13, 2002); *Minneapolis Star Tribune*, Aug. 5, 2001, p. S11, Sept. 17, 1993, p. 4S; Ron Fimrite, "Good Hit, Better Man," *Sports Illustrated*, July 9, 1979, p. 34.

34. "San Diego Padres," MLB.com (accessed Sept. 17, 2002); Moritz, ed., *Current Biography Yearbook*, 459.

35. Winfield and Parker, *Winfield*, 107; "Willie McCovey," BaseballHallofFame.org (accessed Sept. 17, 2002); "Willie McCovey," TheBaseballPage.com (accessed Sept. 17, 2002); "Induction Speech: Dave Winfield," BaseballHallofFame.org (accessed Sept. 12, 2002).

36. Winfield and Parker, *Winfield*, 149; Fimrite, "Good Hit, Better Man," 33; William Oscar Johnson, "Al Gave It His All," *Sports Illustrated*, July 9, 1979, p. 28.

37. Winfield and Parker, *Winfield*, 148.

38. Craig Thomas Wolff, "The $24-Million Man Tells Why," *Sport*, March 1981, p. 18; *Minneapolis Tribune*, Feb. 10, 1977, p. 3D, Aug. 17, 1977, p. 2C.

39. Winfield and Parker, *Winfield*, 94, 208, 209, 210; Wolff, "$24-Million Man Tells Why," 18.

40. Berger, "$20 Million Gamble," 28.

41. *Minneapolis Tribune*, Dec. 16, 1980, p. 1A, Dec. 18, 1980, p. 10A.

42. *Minneapolis Tribune*, Dec.16, 1980, p. 2C.

43. *Minneapolis Tribune*, Sept. 1, 1981, p. 1C; Moritz, ed., *Current Biography Yearbook*, 459; "Dave Winfield," BaseballReference.com (accessed Sept. 18, 2002).

44. *New York Times*, Oct. 26, 1992, p. 1A.

45. "1980s statistics," Baseball-Almanac.com (accessed Sept. 18, 2002).

46. Tim Kurkjian, "This Old Man, He Plays Well," *Sports Illustrated*, Nov. 2, 1992, p. 27; "The Steinbrenner Probe," *Sports Illustrated*, July 23, 1990, p. 17; E. M. Swift, "Yanked About by the Boss," *Sports Illustrated*, Apr. 11, 1988, p. 38.

47. Swift, "Yanked About by the Boss," 36.

48. Winfield and Parker, *Winfield*, 24; Ralph Wiley, "The Reviews Are Raves for Big Dave," *Sports Illustrated*, May 30, 1988, p. 62; William Ladson, "Dave Winfield," *Sport*, Aug. 1991, p. 86; Swift, "Yanked About by the Boss," 37.

49. Ladson, "Dave Winfield," 86; *Minneapolis Tribune*, Dec. 16, 1980, p. 4C.

50. Tim Kurkjian, "Fallen Angels," *Sports Illustrated*, May 21, 1990, p. 90; *St. Paul Pioneer Press*, Aug. 5, 2001, p. 6N.

51. *St. Paul Pioneer Press*, Aug. 5, 2001, p. 6N; *Minneapolis Star Tribune*, Sept. 18, 1993, p. 9C; *New York Times*, Oct. 26, 1992, p. 5C.

52. *New York Times*, Oct. 26, 1992, p. 4C, 5C.

53. *New York Times*, Oct. 26, 1992, p. 1A, 4C.

54. Winfield, *Ask Dave*, 50–51.

55. *New York Times*, Oct. 26, 1992, p. 4C; Kurkjian, "This Old Man, He Plays Well," 27.

56. *Minneapolis Star Tribune*, Sept. 18, 1993, p. 9C, Sept. 17, 1993, p. 4S; Kurkjian, "Mr. Longevity," 55.

57. *Minneapolis Star Tribune*, Sept. 17, 1993, p. 3S.

58. Ladson, "Dave Winfield," 86. Winfield made $600,000 in salary in his last year; see "Dave Winfield," BaseballReference.com (accessed Sept. 23, 2002).

59. *Minneapolis Star Tribune*, June 18, 1986, p. B1; Winfield and Parker, *Winfield*, 121, 193–94, 306; "An Uncommon Marriage," *People*, Aug. 7, 1989, p. 79.

60. Winfield and Parker, *Winfield*, 235.

61. *New York Times*, Oct. 26, 1992, p. 4C; Berger, "$20 Million Gamble," 30; Winfield and Parker, *Winfield*, 293, 21.

62. *New York Times*, Dec. 9, 2001, reprinted in www.talentdevelop.com/acquired.html (accessed Jan. 3, 2003), and http://familymatters.org/acqnarci.htm (accessed Jan. 22, 2004); "Celebrity Big Head," *Reader's Digest*, April 2002, p. 19.

63. "Winny Ways," *Around the Horn* [Baseball Hall of Fame], vol. 8, no. 8 (August 2001) (accessed Aug. 6, 2002); "Statistics," Baseball-Almanac.com (accessed Sept. 13, 2002); Wiley, "Reviews Are Raves for Big Dave," 65.

64. Shaw, "Dave Winfield," 80; "Winny Ways," *Around the Horn;* "Dave Winfield; Inductee Information," BaseballHallofFame.org; *St. Paul Pioneer Press*, Aug.5, 2001, p. 5N; *Minneapolis Star Tribune*, Sept. 17, 1993, p. 4S, 10C; Kurkjian, "Mr. Longevity," 55.

65. *Minneapolis Star Tribune*, Sept. 18, 1993, p. 2C, 9C.

66. "Induction Speech: Dave Winfield," BaseballHallofFame.org.

Lyman Bostock, Jr.: Death of an Outfielder

1. "Lyman Wesley Bostock, Sr.," Negro League Baseball Players Association website, nlbpa.com/bostock__lyman (accessed Aug. 26, 2004); Clark and Lester, *Negro Leagues Book*, 173; Holway, *Complete Book of Baseball's Negro Leagues*, 376, 383, 394, 405; *Minneapolis Tribune*, Sept. 26, 1978, p. 4C, Sept. 25, 1978, p. 11A; Riley, *Biographical Encyclopedia of Negro Baseball Leagues*, 97–98; *New York Times*, Mar. 7, 1978, p. 28 (ProQuest Historical Newspapers).

2. *Minneapolis Tribune*, Sept. 26, 1978, p. 4C.

3. *Minneapolis Tribune*, Sept. 25, 1978, p. 11A.

4. *Minneapolis Tribune*, Sept. 25, 1978, p. 11A; *Washington Post*, Sept. 26, 1978, p. E1 (ProQuest Historical Newspapers).

5. *Washington Post*, Nov. 5, 1977, p. D3, July 25, 1976, p. 36; *Minneapolis Tribune*, July 25, 1976, p. 1C; *New York Times*, Nov. 22, 1977, p. 43–44, Mar. 7, 1978, p. 28.

6. *Minneapolis Star Tribune,* Sept. 25, 1988, p. 1CC; *New York Times,* Mar. 7, 1978, p. 28.

7. *Minneapolis Tribune,* Sept. 25, 1978, p. 11A; *Washington Post,* Nov. 5, 1977, p. D3; *New York Times,* Nov. 6, 1977, p. S1, Nov. 4, 1977, p. 31; "For the Record," *Sports Illustrated,* Oct. 2, 1978, p. 103.

8. *New York Times,* Mar. 7, 1978, p. 28.

9. *Washington Post,* Sept. 25, 1978, p. D1, Sept. 26, 1978, p. E1; *Minneapolis Tribune,* Sept. 25, 1978, p. 1A; *Minneapolis Star Tribune,* Sept. 25, 1988, p. 1CC.

10. *Washington Post,* Sept. 25, 1978, p. D1; *Minneapolis Tribune,* Sept. 25, 1978, p. 1A.

11. *Washington Post,* Sept. 29, 1978, p. E2.

12. *Washington Post,* Sept. 25, 1978, p. D1, Sept. 26, 1978, p. E1.

13. *Minneapolis Star Tribune,* Sept. 25, 1988, p. 1CC.

Kirby Puckett: All Player All the Time

1. Kirby Puckett interview with author, Apr. 26, 2002, notes and audio tape in possession of author.

2. *Minneapolis Star Tribune,* Dec. 25, 1999, p. 12S.

3. Frank Deford, "The Rise and Fall of Kirby Puckett," *Sports Illustrated,* Mar. 17, 2003, p. 58–69.

4. Deford, "Kirby Puckett," 58–69.

5. "Salaries Soared, According to Annual Survey," Associated Press, Dec. 21, 2000, nexis.com.

6. "Will Baseball Strike Out?" CNNfn.com, Apr. 12, 2001.

7. Minnesota State Planning Agency, Demographer's Office, 1998 report, mnplan.state.mn.us.

8. U.S. Census General Population Characteristics for Minnesota, 2000.

9. Puckett interview with author.

10. Puckett interview with author.

11. "Bob Costas Calls It as He Regretfully Sees It," *New York Times,* Oct. 8, 1995, Sec. 2, p. 36.

12. "Kirby Puckett's Tarnished Image," *Minneapolis Star Tribune,* Apr. 7, 2002, p. 1A.

13. James, *New Bill James Historical Baseball Abstract,* 727.

14. "Kirby Puckett," HistoricBaseball.com.

15. "New Twin Ends Up Playing For Time," *Minneapolis Star Tribune,* May 8, 1984.

16. U.S. Census General Population Characteristics for Minnesota, 1970.

17. Alexander von Hoffman, "High-Rise Hellholes," *American Prospect,* Apr. 9, 2001, p. 40.

18. *Minneapolis Tribune,* Oct. 1, 1978, p. A1.

19. "The Last of the Pure Baseball Men," *Atlantic Monthly,* August 1981.

20. *Minneapolis Star Tribune,* Apr. 28, 1986, p. 1D.

21. Puckett interview with author.

22. Kirby Puckett interview with Jim Bickal, Minnesota Public Radio, "Voices of Minnesota" series, Sept. 29, 1998, news.minnesota.publicradio.org.

23. Kirby Puckett, *I Love This Game! My Life and Baseball* (New York: HarperCollins, 1993).

24. Puckett, *I Love This Game!,* 31.

25. *Houston Chronicle,* Sept. 1, 1996, Sports sec., p. 11.

26. *Houston Chronicle,* Sept. 1, 1996, Sports sec., p. 11.

27. Puckett interview with Bickal.

28. *Minneapolis Star Tribune,* May 8, 1994, p. 1C.

29. James, *New Bill James Historical Baseball Abstract,* 868.

30. Puckett interview with author.

31. Puckett interview with author.

32. Puckett, *I Love This Game!,* 217.

33. Puckett, *I Love This Game!,* 229.

34. Puckett interview with Bickal.

35. *Minneapolis Star Tribune,* unsigned editorial, July 14, 1996, p. 20A.

36. Puckett interview with author.

37. *Minneapolis Star Tribune,* Apr. 7, 2002, p. 1A.

38. *Minneapolis Star Tribune,* Feb. 24, 1993, p. 1C.

39. Kirby Puckett, Baseball Hall of Fame induction speech, Aug. 5, 2001, BaseballHallofFame.org.

40. Puckett interview with author.

41. *Minneapolis Star Tribune,* June 1, 2003, p. 12C.

42. Highlights compiled from various sources, including Twins media guides and *Minneapolis Star Tribune,* July 13, 1996.

Quotation Sources

Page 23: *Grand Forks Herald,* Aug. 22, 1888, p. 2.

Page 37: Fredrick L. McGhee, attorney and black activist, St. Paul, Emancipation Day speech, Jan. 1, 1891, *St. Paul Appeal,* Jan. 3, 1891, p. 3.

Page 70: "A Base Ball Fan," *Leeds* [N.Dak.] *News,* Aug. 8, 1907, p. 8.

Page 83: *Fargo Forum,* July 15, 1911, p. 1.

Page 101: George Edward "Rube" Waddell, pitcher, St. Louis Browns, 1910, "How I Win," *Valley City Morning Patriot,* July 2, 1910, p. 3.

Page 115: Ernest Burke, pitcher, Baltimore Elite Giants, in Jeff Kolpack, "Tour of Duty," *Fargo Forum,* July 28, 2002, p. F3.

Page 141: Jim "Mudcat" Grant, pitcher, Fargo-Moorhead Twins, 1954, *Fargo Forum,* June 24, 2003, p. D1–D2; Grant grew up in Lacoochee, Fla.

List of Contributors

Daniel Cagley is the collections manager at the Minnesota Historical Society and is on the board of directors of the Halsey Hall Chapter of SABR (Society for American Baseball Research). Formerly an intern at the Baseball Hall of Fame in Cooperstown, Cagley is a member of the Quicksteps vintage baseball team and is a director of the Minnesota 19th Century Baseball Research Project team.

Ted Genoways is editor of the *Virginia Quarterly Review*. He is the author of *Bullroarer* (2001), winner of the Samuel French Morse Poetry Prize, the Natalie Ornish Poetry Award, and the Nebraska Book Award. His other awards include a Pushcart Prize, a 2003 NEA Fellowship in Poetry, and two Guy Owen Poetry Prizes from *Southern Poetry Review*. He is the editor of numerous books, including *Hard Time: Life in a State Prison, 1849–1914* (2002), *The Selected Poems of Miguel Hernández* (2001), and *The Collected Writings of Walt Whitman: The Correspondence,* volume 7 (2004).

Teri Ann Finneman, a native of Hazen, North Dakota, is a journalist who has worked for fourteen newspapers in Minnesota and North Dakota, including her most recent position at the *Dickinson Press*.

Peter W. Gorton, a native Minnesotan and a graduate of the St. Cloud State University broadcast journalism program, has fifteen years of experience in television journalism. Currently he is working in freelance television production. Peter lives in Northeast Minneapolis with his wife, Kelly.

William D. Green is a history professor at Augsburg College in Minneapolis and is writing a multi-volume history of the civil rights movement in Minnesota. He has written several articles on African American history for *Minnesota History* magazine and for other publications.

Steven R. Hoffbeck, a history professor at Minnesota State University Moorhead, is author of *The Haymakers* (2000), winner of a Minnesota Book Award. He is a member of SABR.

Jim Karn is a lifelong baseball aficionado and an inductee of the Minnesota Amateur Baseball Hall of Fame. A SABR researcher and long-time manager of the Crookston Red amateur baseball team, Karn has coached baseball at the University of Minnesota-Crookston and assisted with the St. Cloud Cathedral High School championship teams. He is a retired State of Minnesota employee.

Kwame McDonald is currently the assistant director of the School Reform Project of the Center for School Change, Hubert H. Humphrey Public Policy Institute of the University of Minnesota. The Central State (Ohio) graduate has been at the HHH Institute for four years following a lengthy career as a youth and sports advocate, high school and college educator, community activist, state government administrator, and photojournalist.

He has served on several local, state, and federal government commissions, committees, and task forces. Kwame hosts

SPNN-TV Sports Rap and writes for the *Minnesota Spokesman-Recorder*. He also served as a community columnist for the *St. Paul Pioneer Press*. He is the author of *Jim Griffin: Son of Rondo* (2001).

Kyle McNary is the author of *Black Baseball: A History of African-Americans and the American Game* (2003) and *Ted "Double-Duty" Radcliffe* (1995). He is the webmaster of the Pitch Black Baseball website that celebrates the history of Negro League baseball.

Joel A. Rippel is a news assistant in the sports department at the Minneapolis *Star Tribune* and the author of *75 Memorable Moments in Minnesota Sports* (2003). He has been a sports reporter for more than twenty years and has contributed articles to *Minnesota Magazine.*

Jay Weiner, a sports reporter for the Minneapolis *Star Tribune* since 1980, is the author of *Stadium Games* (2000). He has been the main reporter for the Minnesota Twins and for the Metrodome Stadium controversies. His reporting and analysis on the business and political aspects of professional sports have appeared in the *New York Times* and *Business Week.* He has delivered sports commentary on Minnesota Public Radio.

Acknowledgments

As general editor, I want to acknowledge the people who have contributed to this history of black baseball in Minnesota. My deepest debt of gratitude goes to my team of writers: Jay Weiner, Peter Gorton, Kwame McDonald, William Green, Ted Genoways, Dan Cagley, Jim Karn, Kyle McNary, Teri Finneman, and Joel Rippel. They researched the stories and placed the tales in a format that is pleasing to the reader and faithful to the history of America's game.

Special thanks go to Peter Gorton, who found information for me, uncovering stories that were buried deep in archives in Texas, Missouri, Wisconsin, and Minnesota. I also pay tribute to Brendan Henehan for indexing the black newspapers of Minnesota. My gratitude goes to Leah Hoffbeck and Katie Hoffbeck for organizing box-score data into my computer files. I am grateful to Joel Rippel and Jay Weiner of the Minneapolis *Star-Tribune* for their help in gaining access to interviews and photographs for the book.

At the Minnesota Historical Society, my gratitude flows to seven people who have been particularly important to me in this work. Greg Britton and Ann Regan authorized the project; Kevin Morrissey promoted it. Anne Kaplan refined the Bobby Marshall biography, and Debbie Miller provided the major research grant. I will always be grateful to editor Sally Rubinstein, who trimmed and sharpened the text, searched out rare photographs, and put all the pieces together so smoothly.

I appreciate the help provided by the Minnesota Twins organization, especially Molly Gallatin and Communications Director Brad Ruiter for access to Twins photographs. Thanks are due to Sid Hartman and Dave Lee of WCCO Radio for historic baseball insights.

The writing team wishes to thank the staff at several museums and archives, especially Jim Gates, librarian at the National Baseball Hall of Fame; Glenn Johnson and John Blashack at the Bertha Historical Museum; Brent Peterson of the Washington County Historical Society in Stillwater; John Decker at the Stearns County Museum; Chris Scheulke and Kathy Evavold in Otter Tail County; Bob Karn at the Minnesota Amateur Baseball Hall of Fame; and Ron Kurpiers at the Minnesota Historical Society.

I thank Dr. Roland Barden of Minnesota State University Moorhead (MSUM) for providing a faculty research grant. I am grateful for the support of MSUM's Dr. Roland Dille, Larry Schwartz, Glenn Tornell, Dr. Paul Harris, and Dr. Margaret Sankey for this project and for the work of Brian Krause, Mark Moss, Matt Kouba, Hannah Vanorny, Dana Schouten, Andrea Paulson, Jason Mattheis, Susan Kudelka, all of MSUM. I acknowledge with gratitude the help of Jane Cunningham and Mark Gleason of the Minnesota Humanities Commission for a Works-In-Progress Grant.

Many thanks go to Bette Marshall Session and Donald Marshall, children of Bobby Marshall, for sharing Marshall's personal scrapbook with me. Thanks also to Harry Davis of Minneapolis for passing on his recollections of early baseball days and to Odis "Oats" LeGrand and Edwin "Sonny" Gulsvig for Satchel Paige stories.

Special thanks go to a number of baseball researchers, especially Larry Lester and Dick Clark of the SABR Negro Leagues Committee; to Stew Thornley, David Grabitske, Dean Thilgen, Rich Arpi, and Fred P. Buckland of the Halsey Hall SABR Chapter; and to Rick Morris, Chuck Chalberg, Brian Larson, and Kathleen Ebert.

I give my personal thanks to friends who supported this project: Jim Koenig, Jim Musburger, Dan and Theresa Carlson; Rich Iverson, Carlton Moe, Jay Nord, and Gene Prim of Barnesville; Pat Miller, Don Droubie, Jerry Riewer, Tom Wolhowe, Corinne Adamietz, and Dr. John and Sally Gorton of Staples. Thanks, too, to Alvina Hoffbeck for research work and to John and Annette Hoffbeck of Woodbury for hosting me in the Twin Cities. And I express my deepest appreciation to my lovely wife, Dianne, for contributing to this work in so many ways, through her love and devotion. And I happily thank my children, Leah, Katie, Mary, and Johnny, for traveling with me to history places in Minnesota. I thank God for the grace and good health to carry out this project with the abilities He has given me.

And lastly, I thank the black baseball players who took a place on the ball diamonds of Minnesota, willing to play for little money or glory, in order to advance social equality in sports. They endured abuse and pain within themselves in order to help integrate baseball in the state. These athletes would have understood a great thought that St. Augustine wrote so long ago: "Anger is a weed, hate is the tree." Ballplayers like Bobby Marshall, Walter Ball, and John Donaldson withstood discrimination and verbal taunts and thus were able to pull out the weeds of their own anger and that of others. They would not allow a tree of hatred to grow— a tree that could not be easily uprooted. Because of their faith and because of their vision, it was possible for a fellow Minnesotan, Dave Winfield, to play in the major leagues and to gain entry into the National Baseball Hall of Fame.

Index

Page numbers in italic refer to pictures and captions.

Choosing sides by going fist-over-fist to see who gets first pick of players.

Picture Credits

Names of photographers, when known, are in parentheses.

Frontispiece, 4 (Charles Alfred Zimmerman), 15, 53 (*Minneapolis Tribune,* June 15, 1908), 61, 68 (*Renville Star Farmer,* June 4, 1909), 76 (A. P. Rhodes), 83, 89 (*Paynesville Press,* June 7, 1923), 105 (*Fairmont Daily Sentinel,* June 10, 1932), 109 (*Pipestone County Star,* June 21, 1927), 121 (*Minneapolis Spokesman,* July 10, 1942), 128, 129 (*St. Paul Dispatch and Pioneer Press,* June 13, 1948), 132 (*Minneapolis Star Tribune*), 133 (*Minneapolis Tribune,* May 27, 1951), 135 (*Minneapolis Star Tribune*), 147 (*Minneapolis Tribune,* Jan. 26, 1955), 152 (Ernest C. Withers), 153, 159 (General Mills Photography), 244—Minnesota Historical Society

Page x, 65, 66, 82 (all *Chicago Daily News*)—Chicago Historical Society

Page 11—Otter Tail County Historical Society, Fergus Falls, Minn.

Page 25, 28, 63—National Baseball Hall of Fame Library, Cooperstown, N.Y.

Page 39—Grand Forks County Historical Society, Grand Forks, N.Dak.

Page 45—Waseca County Historical Society, Waseca, Minn.

Page 56—courtesy of Ronald Ebert in memory of John Davis

Page 75—collection of Brian Larson, Eden Prairie, Minn.

Page 92, 93, 97 (both)—Bertha Historical Society, Bertha, Minn.

Page 113—courtesy of Maceo Breedlove family

Page 139—collection of Charles Martin, Pelican Rapids, Minn.

Page 143—collection of Odis LeGrand, Fergus Falls, Minn.

Page 157—Leroy and Jerry Riewer

Page 163, 164, 168, 183, 184, 189, 191, 198, 207, 209—Minnesota Twins

Page 171, 172—courtesy of Dave Winfield family

Swinging for the Fences was designed and set in type by Dennis Anderson, Duluth, Minnesota, and was printed by Thomson-Shore, Dexter, Michigan.